# Between Two Revolutions

# Between Two Revolutions
*Stolypin and the Politics of Renewal in Russia*

Peter Waldron

Northern Illinois University Press
DeKalb

Published by Northern Illinois University Press
in conjunction with UCL Press.
Direct questions regarding permissions
to NIU Press, DeKalb, IL 60115.

Library of Congress Cataloging-in-Publication Data are available

ISBN: 0-87580-235-4

Typeset in Sabon by Acorn Bookwork, Salisbury, UK
Printed and bound by Arrowhead Books Ltd, Reading, UK

# Contents

v

# Preface

I am very grateful to the many people who have helped in the writing of this book. My initial work on this period was supervised by Olga Crisp, and her deep knowledge of imperial Russia, together with her generosity of spirit, have been of enduring value. The annual meetings of the Study Group on the Russian Revolution have provided an ideal forum for debating issues in a comradely atmosphere, and members of the Study Group have both provided specific advice and contributed to my overall thinking on Russia before 1917. Simon Dixon and Bob McKean very generously took the time to read the entire text and make many comments that have much improved the book. I am also grateful to Jeremy Black, John Burnett, Peter Durrans and Don MacRaild who have been of particular assistance during the writing of the book.

Librarians and archivists in Europe and America have assisted in locating and providing material. In Russia, the staff of the Russian State Historical Archive in St Petersburg have been exceptionally helpful on successive visits. I am also grateful to the staffs of the State Archive of the Russian Federation in Moscow and of the Russian National Library in St Petersburg. In Finland, the Slavonic Department of Helsinki University Library has provided an ideal environment for summertime research. The staffs of the British Library and the library of the School of Slavonic and East European Studies in London have always been of the greatest assistance. The interlibrary loan staff of the University of Sunderland have helped locate a multitude of obscure materials with efficiency and good humour. In

America, the staff of the libraries of Harvard University were of great assistance.

Clare Crowley has commented on the text in detail. Her contribution to the book's completion has been, in this and many other ways, inestimable.

# *Note on conventions and transliteration*

Russian names have, with few exceptions, been transliterated directly into English. Dates are given according to the old-style, Julian calendar used in Russia until 1918; between 1900 and 1918 Russia was 13 days behind western Europe.

# Introduction

The period between the two Russian revolutions of 1905 and
1917 was of critical importance in setting the course of Russia's
future development. The tsarist regime made one last attempt to
reform itself in the aftermath of its near-downfall in 1905 and,
under the leadership of Peter Stolypin, prime minister from 1906
until his assassination in 1911, plans were laid for reforms that
would have changed the face of Russian politics and Russian
society. These came to naught, however, and the unreformed
Russian autocracy was left to face the onslaught of the First
World War and its attendant social and economic strains. Stolypin therefore occupies a pivotal role in the history of modern
Russia.

His reputation since his death has been very mixed. By the time
he was assassinated, Stolypin was disliked by much of the political establishment of the tsarist state and, during the few remaining years of tsarism, he was largely forgotten. His popular
reputation became connected not with his programme of reform,
but with the coercive measures that he took to pacify Russia after
the rebellions of 1905, symbolized by the "Stolypin necktie" – the
hangman's noose. Even during the 1930s, at the height of Stalin's
terror, the railway trucks that transported prisoners to labour
camps in Siberia were colloquially referred to as "Stolypin
wagons". Soviet historians painted Stolypin in uniformly negative

1

terms. Taking their cue from Lenin, they depicted Stolypin as an unprincipled "bonapartist" politician who tried to be all things to all men and indulged in slippery manoeuvring in an attempt to maintain the authority of tsarism.[1] Russian émigré commentators took a very different view of the assassinated premier. Stolypin's daughter, Maria, published near-hagiographical memoirs of her father,[2] and others of his acquaintances portrayed him as the lost saviour of the Russian Empire, the man who could have prevented the collapse of the tsarist regime.[3]

Mikhail Gorbachev's rise to power in the Soviet Union during the mid-1980s provoked a renewed interest in Stolypin. Comparisons between the two men appeared striking: both attempted fundamental reform of societies that were in a state of crisis. Both had emerged from elites whose power they then proceeded to attack. Both engaged in the most difficult of political tasks – reforming a despotism while trying to maintain intact the state itself. Stolypin's belief that agrarian reform was the key to restructuring the Russian Empire was mirrored by Gorbachev's deep concern with the moribund state of Soviet agriculture. Gorbachev appeared to be the heir to the reforming tradition in Russia that had lain dormant since Stolypin's death 70 years earlier. In Russia, Stolypin's reputation underwent a transformation after 1985: his career was reassessed and his reforming zeal emphasized.[4] The collapse of the Soviet Union hastened this process. Russians became able to debate openly the course of their own history and to examine the causes of the revolution of 1917, freed from the ideological framework imposed upon them by the Soviet state. Discussion of the last years of the tsarist empire has been an essential part of this process. Stolypin's efforts to reform the imperial Russian state and thereby to avert revolution have been analyzed in detail in post-Soviet Russia.[5]

This book examines the programme of reform that Stolypin attempted to implement and seeks to explain the reasons for his failure. Reform has been a perennial difficulty for the rulers of Russia, both before and after 1917, and Stolypin's experience can help to illuminate the reasons for the problems faced by Russia's rulers in trying to accomplish peaceful change. The relationship between state and society in imperial Russia was never easy and attempts to bridge the gulf between ruler and ruled were treated with suspicion by both sides. Stolypin had to cope with an inheritance that rendered reform problematical; he bequeathed a legacy of failure that brought revolution closer.

## CHAPTER ONE

# Reform or repression? The dilemma of tsarism

## Autocracy and reform: the 1860s

In 1905 imperial Russia experienced a series of crises that brought the very survival of the tsarist regime into question. Russia's defeat in war with Japan in the Far East was accompanied by large-scale and widespread disturbances in the cities and country-side of the empire. At the same time, sections of the educated elite of the country mounted articulate and repeated attacks on the policies of the autocracy that they believed had brought Russia to the point of collapse. The regime was thus assailed from all sides by demands for change, demands that had been long in maturing. The disturbances and clamour of 1905 had been fuelled over nearly half a century by the failure of the tsarist government to deal with the social and political consequences of economic modernization in Russia. Since the 1860s the regime had pursued policies that were often contradictory and at best had provided only incomplete solutions to the problems of back-wardness and undergovernment that bedevilled Russia; by 1905 the pressure from below for change had become too widespread to be resisted.

During the 1860s and early 1870s attempts had been made by

Tsar Alexander II to move away from the stultifying atmosphere and static society that his predecessor, Nicholas I, had tried to impose upon Russia. The severe shock that defeat in the Crimean War between 1854 and 1856 administered to Russia's self-esteem and to her prestige abroad provided the initial impetus for internal reform, while the accession of Alexander II to the throne in early 1855 gave additional encouragement to those Russians who had a firm commitment to reform. Senior bureaucrats and ministers clearly perceived that action needed to be taken if Russia was to be able to shake off the backwardness that so obviously differentiated her from western Europe. Military defeat was only a symptom of Russia's inferiority, but it provided the most potent stimulus for what was a conscious effort to modernize Russia and her institutions during the 1860s and 1870s.

Russia's leaders believed that it was vital for their country to regain its status as a great European power after the débâcle in the Crimea, but they recognized that this could not be accomplished by military reform alone. The differences between Russia and her western neighbours and rivals ran much deeper and reached into fundamental questions of social and political structure. To the outside observer, the most obvious difference was that of serfdom. Contemporaries saw the system by which some 40 per cent of Russia's rural population existed as the personal property of their masters, deprived of all rights and eking out what was very often a poor existence on the land, as a major component of Russia's backwardness. It was argued that the offence to human dignity that serfdom entailed was not something that a modern state should tolerate. It was also believed that the system of serfdom had an adverse effect on agricultural production. The serf had no incentive to introduce new techniques nor to work harder to improve crop yields, since it would be the landlord, rather than the serf, who would reap the benefit from any such innovation. As well as retarding agricultural progress, serfdom was also perceived as preventing Russia's industrial development by restricting the mobility of the serf population and thereby creating an inflexible labour market. If Russia was to compete effectively with the more industrialized countries of western Europe, these constraints on the growth of her own industrial sector had to be removed. The motivation for the abolition of serfdom was clear, and the process was accelerated by fears among the Russian government and noble elite that unless action was taken by the regime to deal with the problem, the peasants themselves would prove more and more troublesome and pose an even greater threat to the stability of the state.[1]

On 19 February 1861, therefore, serfs belonging to private landowners were emancipated and provided with allotments of land for which they were to have to make redemption payments over a period of nearly half a century. Pressure on the state's finances meant that the government refused to subsidize the process and the redemption process had to be self-financing. This fundamental reform, which had an immediate effect on over 25 million peasants, and on a further 25 million in 1866 when it was extended to cover those peasants who were the property of the state, was accompanied by high expectations on the part of all sections of the population. The government believed it would remove a brake on economic growth and open the way to the modernization of the Russian economy. The peasantry expected that emancipation would result in their acquisition of land, and were bitterly disillusioned when they learnt that they would have to pay for what they believed belonged to them anyway. Emancipation was viewed as the solution to all of Russia's ills: by bringing about a profound transformation in the status of the majority of the Russian population, it would provide the means by which the country could advance both economically and socially. However, it proved to be only the starting point for a series of other reforms designed to reflect the position of the emancipated peasantry.

Local government needed reform in order to allow the peasantry some say in their own administration. In 1864 a system of local self-government was introduced in the majority of the provinces of European Russia. This established a two-tier system of elected local councils, the *zemstvo*, at district and provincial levels. The district council was to be directly elected by the population of the area, but the franchise was arranged so that the landowning gentry gained a disproportionate 40 per cent share of the seats, while other groups – and especially the peasantry – were grossly underrepresented. This situation was exaggerated in the provincial councils since they were elected by and from the members of the lower-tier council. Consequently, the first sets of elections produced a situation where almost 75 per cent of the members of the provincial councils came from the nobility. The duties of the new local councils were very varied and gave them substantial local responsibilities: on the one hand, they acted as agents of central government in such matters as road building and conscription, but they also had great independence in the provision of services such as education, health care and agricultural advice.[2] The councils were allowed to levy their own taxation and this gave them the opportunity to employ their own professional staff, a group that became collectively known as the "third element". The introduction of local elected councils did much to improve conditions of life for the provincial population of Russia, and especially for the newly emancipated peasantry, but the councils also proved to be a thorn in the flesh of central government.

The local government reform established a source of authority in the Russian Empire that did not derive all its influence from the institution of the autocrat and his government. The power of the new councils to raise their own revenue and thus to gain some degree of financial independence from the central authorities was of crucial importance, since it allowed the new bodies to operate free of outside interference in many important areas and to establish their own policies that often proved to be at odds with the wishes of central government. Conflict between local and central authorities became increasingly common during the 1860s and 1870s. Many local councils believed that social matters were a vital part of their responsibilities and as a consequence employed more and more of their own staff. These professional people, in frequent and close contact with the rural population, in time became a source of irritation for the government through their pressure for social reform and improvements in living conditions in the countryside. By the mid-1870s the "third element" was perceived as one of the chief sources of opposition to the tsarist state. Some of the local councils also provoked antipathy in St Petersburg bureaucratic circles by calls for an even greater say in the affairs of the country.[3] The more liberal of the new councils argued that if the principle of popular participation had been accepted at a local level, there was no reason why the same principle should not play a part in the national administration of the state. Such an idea was unwelcome to successive tsars as it represented a direct assault on their autocratic powers and calls from below for a national representative assembly – a national *zemstvo* – were invariably rejected and their proponents often punished.

A further source of trouble for the autocratic regime was provided by a major judicial reform. Russian courts had been notorious for their corruption, delay and inefficiency. The change in the status of the peasant population, and the consequent need to recognize the former serfs as individual legal entities and provide them with access to a system of justice, provided an opportunity to overhaul completely the Russian legal structure. A system of civil and criminal courts based on Western models was introduced. These had clear lines of appeal and were staffed by a judiciary whose independence was assured by their being paid good salaries, thus obviating the need for them to take bribes, and by their irremovability from office. Judges whose verdicts displeased the government could no longer be dismissed. Furthermore, jury trials in criminal cases were instituted for the first time, thus introducing another element into the administration of justice that was outside the control of the government.[4] During the 1860s and 1870s an independent and articulate legal profession came into existence, encouraged by the new freedoms that lawyers had under the legal reform. The courtroom became a scene of substantial challenges to the authority and style of the autocratic government. Lawyers came to be viewed by the regime as being in the same category as the *zemstvo* professionals – a major source of direct opposition to the government – and the government made attempts to restrict their freedom. This proved more difficult than in the case of the local councils, however, since court proceedings could be openly reported in the press and speeches made by both defendants and their lawyers in the course of a trial could not be the basis for further prosecution.

These legal reforms had most effect on the populations of the large cities and especially on the atmosphere and situation in St Petersburg and Moscow, the scenes of the most significant and controversial trials. For the majority of the population, the peasantry, access to justice was very different: offences concerning solely peasants were dealt with by a village court that was made up of judges elected by and from the peasantry themselves, and which continued to administer customary law. Minor disputes that involved both peasants and other members of society were to be tried by Justices of the Peace (JPs): these magistrates were elected by the district *zemstvo* and appeals against their decisions could be made to a higher court. The JPs proved to be of significant benefit in making justice more accessible to the population at large, since their courts worked quickly, cost nothing to those appearing in them and came to be perceived as equitable. While the regime's aims of improving the judicial system and providing the peasantry with access to proper courts were largely satisfied, the 1864 legal reform also laid the basis for a substantial challenge to the autocrat's power. The regime could no longer expect to go wholly unchecked if it acted in an arbitrary manner and, perhaps most importantly, the empire's population perceived that this was now the case. What Wortman has called the "development of a Russian legal consciousness" helped to undermine the strength of the tsarist regime: instead of providing a buttress for the state, it gradually came to undermine the foundations of the autocracy.[5]

The tens of millions of newly freed peasants had the potential to cause many problems for the Russian government; one means by which this might be averted was by improving the range and quality of education available. Education was also seen as vital by the tsarist regime because of its impact on the elite of the empire's population. Russian universities, overwhelmingly attended by the sons of the nobility, were viewed as being the seed-bed for discontent with the regime. The state wanted to take action to deal with this situation. The 1860s was, therefore, a period of wide-ranging educational reform. Measures were taken to increase the numbers of primary schools in the empire, but this stopped far short of providing universal primary education. The Orthodox Church continued to play a very large part in basic education but, despite the combined efforts of church and state, primary education during the 1860s and 1870s remained available to only a small minority of Russian children. Secondary education was also reformed and the curriculum revised to place more emphasis on "modern" subjects.[6] It was in the field of university education, however, that the greatest changes took place and this reflected the importance that was attached to higher education by the government during the 1860s. A new university statute was issued in 1863, removing many of the restrictions that had been placed on Russian universities during the reign of Nicholas I. They were granted a large degree of autonomy from the ministry of education in their own administration and teaching, as well as in the vital area of student discipline. The universities continued, however, to be centres of discontent and demonstration and the government found it necessary to intervene on many occasions, especially at St Petersburg University, in order to restore order. Educational reform, therefore, served not so much to inculcate the virtues prized by the autocracy as to stimulate dissatisfaction and encourage debate among Russia's social elite. The universities continued to be a constant irritation to the autocracy and acted as an important breeding ground for ideas inimical to tsarism right up to the beginning of the twentieth century.

Censorship was also relaxed during the 1860s in order to shift responsibility for the publication of a work from the censor on to the publisher and writers themselves. Legislation in 1865 abolished the system of prepublication censorship for the majority of items, introducing instead examination by the censor after works had been printed. It would thus be the authors themselves who would be responsible for any contraventions of the censorship code and would face proceedings in the courts, should they produce a work that offended the government. Censorship after 1865 worked with less effectiveness since works could reach the public before they were declared to be seditious by the censor. Authors also became increasingly adept at concealing their real meaning behind a façade of Aesopian language or metaphor.[7] In this area, too, the regime's attempts to use reform as a means of strengthening its own position failed: the 1865 reform was intended to make authors and publishers more responsible in the way in which they worked, but instead it served to relax the hold of the authorities on what was published inside the empire.

The army was the last major area in which change took place during the 1860s and 1870s. The defeat in the Crimea had made military reform imperative, and the emancipation of the serfs made this even more urgent. The Russian army was made up traditionally of serfs forcibly conscripted to serve for life. The change in peasant status with emancipation meant that such a practice could no longer continue and that new methods had to be found to recruit ordinary soldiers. For the minister of war, D. A. Miliutin, it was clear that the burden of military service had to be spread more equally across the population and that a properly defined term of military service was needed. Prussian success in the Franco-Prussian War helped to accelerate the process of military reform, and in 1874 he instituted a system of conscription that would fall upon the entire population: each year a cohort of conscripts would be selected by lot from among a particular age group. Service in the army was to be limited to six years on active service and nine years in the reserves. Measures were also instituted during Miliutin's tenure of office to improve military education for officers and to establish a proper general staff in order to give more attention to military strategy.[8] While the new structures introduced by Miliutin did improve the quality of the army, a generation later, in 1904–5, the Russian army still suffered a severe defeat at the hands of the Japanese.

The major series of reforms during the 1860s and 1870s produced results that were far different from those anticipated by their authors. The "Great Reforms" had been intended to modernize Russia and enhance the authority of the regime, but instead served to stimulate discontent and to weaken the structure of the Russian state. Alexander II's reforms were incomplete and inconsistent, since the regime itself had not fully considered their consequences. In the political sphere, the implications of giving local councils and the judicial institutions a large degree of independence were not clearly perceived. The regime was surprised when calls were heard for the restructuring of national government to allow the population some say in its workings. It was the institution of the autocracy itself that lay at the core of the problem: reform had been conceived by the tsar and his advisers as a means of reinforcing the authority of the autocratic system and preserving intact the status and powers of the autocrat himself. The regime believed that reform would put an end to disquiet and would enable society to coalesce around the government and thus provide added impetus to the drive for modernization. Instead, reform served to stimulate the appetite of the Russian population for further changes and for greater responsibility and authority independent of the autocrat. The problems engendered by political reform ran deeper than this, however, since the reforms themselves acted to lessen the authority of the tsar. Accustomed to governing without any constraints on his authority, the autocrat now found himself impeded by the activities of institutions that he had established to strengthen his regime. While the Russian regime was prepared to implement reform at the lower levels, it was not ready to make changes to government at the highest levels and continued to believe that a modern economy and society could be directed by an autocratic political system that was outdated in comparison to the structures of western Europe. The autocracy was prepared to make many demands of the population of Russia in terms of changes to its economic and social structure, but the regime itself was not ready to respond to calls for it to reform itself.

This contradiction between the economic and social and the political aspects of the policies pursued by the autocracy after 1855 was heightened by the regime's attitude to the consequences of its efforts to modernize Russia. While the state actively promoted economic change in both countryside and city, it was reluctant to follow this up by making any great improvement to living conditions for its subjects and continued to deal with expressions of discontent through the traditional coercive means employed by the Russian autocracy. The government refused to countenance any positive response to the growing number of demands for further reform from widely disparate groups and individuals during the late 1860s and 1870s. The most widespread and frequent of these were for further action to improve the lot of the peasantry, but the government was determined not to yield to outside pressures and continued to reject such calls. It dealt severely with those whom it perceived as opponents of the regime, exiling, imprisoning and executing such people, often trying to avoid the judicial processes by utilizing "administrative" means. This approach served to alienate important sections of the Russian social elite from the government. The increasingly violent opposition that was displayed towards the autocratic regime during the 1870s was a direct result of the refusal of the state to take substantive notice of the opinions being voiced by highly educated and politically aware people. As reform during the 1860s had not gone far enough to satisfy their demands, terrorism and direct action became their chief method of expressing discontent.

By the end of the 1870s, however, the government could no longer ignore the fact that its reforms had failed to satisfy the aspirations of society. There was a series of assassinations of leading public officials and a number of attempts on the life of the tsar himself. Student unrest grew apace and even inside the government itself there was a feeling that new moves were needed to reconcile government and society. At the end of the 1870s, therefore, plans were prepared under the direction of M. T. Loris-Melikov, the minister of internal affairs, for a form of limited consultative assembly to be introduced. This was to include representatives from local councils on a number of levels and was designed to ensure that the needs and requirements of the provinces were properly heard at the highest levels of government.[9] The proposed three-tier system was to have no legislative power and the government would be under no obligation to listen to the advice that was proffered, but the regime hoped that its willingness to take the views of its social elites into account would serve to reduce the level of discontent from this group. The state was well aware that many of its opponents sprang from the most privileged sections of Russian society, and it hoped that by drawing the nobility more directly into the governing process, it could bring about their return to the position of support for the regime that they had traditionally occupied.

By the beginning of 1881, government and tsar were agreed on the need for the introduction of such a system and Alexander II was preparing to sign the proposals into law when he was assassinated by a terrorist bomb on 1 March 1881. Overnight, this dramatically changed the political outlook of Russian government, for the tsar's son and successor, Alexander III, was not a man who shared any of his father's inclinations for reform.[10] The power wielded by a Russian autocratic monarch was immense and a change in ruler could therefore materially alter the policies pursued by the state. By temperament Alexander III was sympathetic to the traditional view of the autocracy and unwilling to see his powers limited in any way; he believed that the regime should reassert its authority not by making concessions to society, but by using the coercive forces at its disposal. Alexander

III's outlook certainly did not include allowing any form of consultative assembly to be set up and Loris-Melikov's plans were quickly abandoned. The new tsar was also surrounded by a set of advisers whose sympathies were firmly set against reform. Prime among these was Konstantin Pobedonostsev, who had been the tsar's tutor as a child. For the first part of Alexander's reign he exerted a strong influence upon the ruler: Pobedonostsev was devoted to the principles of autocracy and had no intention of seeing his former pupil deflected from what he saw as the only reliable way to regenerate Russia – a strong and unlimited autocracy.

## Autocracy and reaction: the 1880s and 1890s

During the 1880s and 1890s, therefore, the government strove to regain some of the authority that it had lost as a result of the reforms of the 1860s and 1870s. A two-pronged approach was adopted: first, the government tried as far as possible to limit the scope of the reforms through administrative measures and secondly, where this first approach was unsuccessful, it prepared new laws to claw back some of the concessions that had been made to public opinion and to society in general under Alexander II. These measures were accompanied by vigorous steps to deal with the upsurge in terrorism that had killed the tsar, as well as by attempts to curb the spread and growth of the opposition movement to the regime. In August 1881 temporary legislation was introduced to give provincial governors special powers to deal with situations that they perceived as dangerous: this allowed the local authorities very great discretion since it provided them with the power to suspend many of the ordinary laws of the empire and was a potent weapon against all forms of opposition, real or imaginary.[11] Although intended to be temporary, the provisions of this legislation were regularly renewed and it continued in force until 1917. By 1912 it was estimated that the majority of the empire's population lived under the provisions of this legislation; measures intended to be temporary had become a permanent and major part of the government's efforts to counter opposition.

Local self-government and the judicial system were the major areas of the reforms of the 1860s that Alexander III and his ministers viewed as harmful to central government's attempts to impose its own authority across all areas of Russian society. It was difficult for the government during the 1880s and 1890s to interfere directly with the new legal structures; the guarantees of judicial independence and the watchful eye of the legal profession proved too strong for such direct action by the regime. Instead, the government moved to limit the damage it felt it was suffering through the system of open courts and jury trials by reducing the scope of the offences that were subject to the full rigours of the system. A major problem for the government had been that defendants accused of terrorist or political offences had used the new courts as a platform from which to make political speeches from the dock – speeches that were eagerly reported by sympathetic newspapers. Furthermore, the new juries had shown, in the government's eyes, a disturbing tendency to acquit people whom the regime would have preferred to see given severe sentences. The most celebrated such case was that of Vera Zasulich, accused of murdering the St Petersburg police chief – an act that she did not deny – but who was acquitted by a jury because she pleaded that the act was politically justified. Such verdicts prompted the government to have as many cases as possible of this type tried by courts-martial. This avoided the publicity that the civil courts generated and it also made it very much less likely that verdicts would be out of line with the government's own judgments.

In the area of the administration of justice at the lower levels, the government also moved to bring matters more tightly under its control. This reinforced the aim of keeping a more general watch on the activities of the peasantry and of trying to counter to some extent the influence of the *zemstva* and their employees. In 1889, therefore, the post of land captain (*zemskii nachal'nik*) was instituted so that peasant affairs could be more effectively monitored by the regime.[12] The land captain was given charge of a relatively small number of peasant communities and was provided with wide powers to supervise and discipline local inhabitants. There was no real appeal possible against the decisions of the land captain and he was able to impose his authority more or less arbitrarily on the peasantry, generating enormous dislike as he did so.

Measures were also taken to deal with the *zemstva* themselves. The government was well aware that one of the keys to their power lay in their financial independence and it therefore took steps to limit the amount of money that the councils could raise through taxation. From 1889 the annual increase in local taxation was limited to 3 per cent and it was hoped that this would prevent the further expansion of the *zemstva*'s role in Russian society by restricting their activities. Furthermore, the government wanted to try to limit the councils' scope for independent action by altering the franchise so that more weight would be given to those elements of the population whom the regime regarded as reliable. The government placed its hopes on the rural gentry, whom it regarded as being conservative and uncontaminated by the liberal ideas and attitudes that it felt permeated the elites in St Petersburg and the other large cities of the empire. To balance an increase in representation from this stratum of society, the government wanted to further reduce the already meagre place that the peasantry occupied in the local councils. The peasants were seen as the least reliable sector of society, easily swayed by views that were opposed to those of the regime and all too influenced by the "third element". In 1890, therefore, the *zemstvo* electoral system was reorganized in order to achieve these results and thus to try to bring the activities of local government more into line with the ethos that St Petersburg itself propounded.[13] During the 1880s and 1890s, therefore, the tsarist regime pursued traditional conservative policies aimed at reasserting the power of the autocrat. There was a total rejection of all measures of "reform" in the sense in which the changes of the previous two decades had been introduced. In the political sphere, therefore, the thrust of policy was to reverse the work of Alexander II.

In the economic sphere, however, the tsarist government pursued a set of policies that were diametrically at odds with its political and social ends. Emancipation had not, by itself, succeeded in modernizing Russia's economy to any great extent and by the end of the 1880s Russia was slipping even further behind her Western competitors. Once again there was a clear perception inside the regime that vigorous steps needed to be taken to push

Russia forward in economic terms, and it was only the state that could mobilize the resources necessary to do so. The important role that the Russian government had traditionally played in the promotion of commerce and industry inside the empire had resulted in the very slow emergence of an entrepreneurial middle class. By the end of the nineteenth century there was still no great tradition of private entrepreneurship and the chief source of capital investment in industrial development was the state itself, closely followed by foreign investors. In planning for future industrial development, therefore, the state needed to continue to play the key role. This was clearly recognized by Sergei Witte, minister of finance from 1893 until 1903, who put in place a series of measures to promote domestic industrial development. He continued the policies of his predecessors by imposing increasingly heavy tariffs on imported manufactured goods entering Russia, thus providing an incentive for domestic industry to increase its production. To make distribution easier and encourage the flow of goods around the empire, the railway network was enormously expanded: as a former railway director, Witte was uniquely suited to such a role, and during his tenure as minister of finance the Russian railway network expanded by 40 per cent. There were two further and interlinked steps that the state had to take in order to promote the development of industry. First, it could not by itself provide finance for the necessary investment and as sources of domestic capital were very limited, the only other option was to look abroad. Russia, therefore, had to be made attractive to foreign investors as a destination for their capital and the tsarist regime had to demonstrate that investment in Russia presented little risk. Secondly, an important marker of stability was the currency, and Witte took steps to ensure that the stability of the ruble was recognized: in 1897 Russia adopted the gold standard. Foreign investment in Russian industry continued to increase, so that by 1905 some 45 per cent of investment came from abroad.

The effect of the regime's economic policies during the 1880s and 1890s was to produce an annual rate of growth of eight per cent during the last decade of the nineteenth century. Heavy industry – iron, coal and oil – expanded rapidly and this laid the foundations for the further growth of industry during the first part of the twentieth century. However, it was the social consequences of industrialization that proved of most concern to the tsarist regime. Industry, and especially heavy industry, required the concentration of large numbers of workers in a relatively small number of places, and consequently the urban centres of Russia grew very quickly indeed around the turn of the century. While the proportion of the empire's population that lived in cities remained fairly static, the rapid increase in the population as a whole meant that the urban population grew from 6 million in 1860 to more than 18 million by 1914. However, the two largest cities of the empire, St Petersburg and Moscow, grew far more rapidly, so that by 1900 the population of Petersburg was 1.4 million. Living conditions for the inhabitants of these new metropolises were harsh: the rapid expansion in population had not been matched by any comparable increase in the facilities available to house people and to provide the essentials of life. Housing was cramped and usually lacked sanitation, and disease was rife among the cities' inhabitants. Working conditions for the new workers were hard: hours were very long, wages low and penalties for indiscipline severe.

The government did very little to deal with the large new urban communities. For the regime, questions of factory conditions were chiefly a matter for the owners of individual enterprises and although a factory inspectorate had been created in 1881, it remained a small and largely powerless organization. The government did little to improve living conditions in the cities, partly as a result of disagreements inside the regime about the priorities it should adopt. On the one hand, the ministry of finance was very keen to improve Russia's economic position and it therefore acted to encourage the growth of industry and thereby the growth of cities. On the other hand, however, the more traditional forces inside the regime, headed by the ministry of internal affairs, saw their main task as being to maintain order and preserve intact the authority of the autocrat. They had no great desire to see the cities of the empire expand since this would result in the concentration of large numbers of people in a small space and could pose grave problems for law and order. Certainly the need to maintain political authority did not incline the ministry of internal affairs to make conditions in the cities too pleasant:

such an approach would only serve to further encourage migration into urban areas and accentuate the already difficult problems of keeping control of the population.

This lack of co-ordination between different elements of the government had serious consequences, as the appalling living conditions for the new working classes stimulated the growth of discontent among them. This was qualitatively different from the earlier discontent of a small number of educated Russians during the 1870s and 1880s when, even though small numbers of dedicated revolutionaries had been able to assassinate some of the highest officials of the empire, they had proved incapable of attracting popular support. Instead, during the 1890s and the first years of the twentieth century, movements began to emerge that were dedicated to improving the conditions of life for the Russian worker by whatever means were necessary. Discontent was not, however, confined to the cities. The rural population of the empire also had grounds to feel dissatisfied with its lot, for the decades after emancipation had not witnessed any great improvement in the prosperity of the peasantry. Although emancipation marked a break in the formal status of the peasants, it did little by itself to deal with the real problem of Russian agriculture — low yields. Agricultural techniques remained unchanged by emancipation and, with the sharp increase in population, the peasantry were placed under great pressure. This was accentuated by the financial burdens they had to bear: the redemption payments for their allotments were substantial and they also had to pay increased taxation. Industrialization also placed strains on the peasant because the increased urban population meant that the quantity of food produced by the peasantry needed to increase proportionately. The state, desperate to increase its own revenues in order to stimulate industrial growth, also raised the levels of taxation very substantially during the later part of the nineteenth century, especially on items such as sugar and kerosene, which were vital to the peasant economy. By 1900 the peasant population had tangible reasons to feel discontented. Even so, the rural economy was just holding its own: the net per capita production of grain showed a small increase over this period, even though Russia's grain exports were increasing. Between 1883 and 1914, even though the population expanded at an annual rate of 1.5 per cent, grain production grew by 2.1 per cent annually.[14]

The second half of the nineteenth century in Russia produced a crisis inside the empire. Although at the accession of Alexander II in 1855 there had been a conscious desire on the part of the government to modernize the country, the tsar and his ministers embarked on their programme of reform without any clear comprehension of the effects that it would have. The absence of any central government policy-making body meant that measures could be implemented on an *ad hoc* basis, without any consideration of their impact on each other. The fundamental misapprehension about the effects of emancipation, which was widespread throughout Russian government, meant that when economic progress failed to materialize, the other reforms that had been introduced during the 1860s provided a method for society to demonstrate its dissatisfaction with the regime's policies. While Alexander II was on the throne, there was some inclination on the part of the government to take note of the reaction of Russian society to its actions, as witnessed by Loris-Melikov's desire to bring about some reconciliation between state and educated society, but this disappeared under Alexander III and during the first part of the reign of Nicholas II. Reform had been seen during the 1860s and 1870s as a means of strengthening the autocracy, as a way by which the power of the state could be preserved and increased by meeting some of the most pressing needs of the regime's critics and thereby reasserting that autocracy was the most suitable and beneficial form of government for the Russian Empire. For the assassinated tsar's successors, however, the reforms of the previous two decades appeared to have been the cause of the terrorism and discontent that had ended in Alexander II's death. For Alexander III and his advisers, the way to strengthen the regime and keep Russia strong was to abandon the reformist ideas of his father and revert to the traditional autocratic policies of repression and conservatism. While such a solution might have been workable during a period of economic and social stability when it would have been possible to reassert control over a quiescent and stable population, the tsarist regime failed to realize that the rapid economic change that it was itself promoting, doomed such a policy to failure. Industrialization and all that it brought with it made the demands for political and social change all the more urgent, but this only served to stiffen the regime's resolve not to weaken its position.

The refusal of the tsarist regime to contemplate reform, and its insistence on relying on repression to deal with any sign of discontent did nothing to reconcile the educated elite of Russian society to the government. The alienation and discontent that had been evident during the 1860s and 1870s deepened as the century progressed: there was an increase both in the numbers of Russians advocating revolution and violent change and in the quantity of moderate men who wanted to see Russia evolve into a form of constitutional monarchy. From the government's point of view, it was the latter group that presented the most insidious threat, for the lawyers, doctors and other professional and educated men who made up a large segment of these groups were articulate and well able to voice their concerns in ways that attracted much attention.[15] While the formation of political parties was illegal in Russia before 1905, liberal groups were formed in the years before this, calling not for revolution in Russia, but for gradual and non-violent change.


## Revolution: tsarism in crisis

By 1905, therefore, Russia was a divided society. A rapidly developing economy and society was still controlled by a political structure that was out of touch with the population and which did not respond to the wishes of the people under its control. Economic change was not producing the benefits for the ordinary people of Russia that might have persuaded them that the form of government under which they lived was worth tolerating. The inhabitants of both town and countryside were suffering under the strains of economic modernization; tsarism offered them no compensation. Reform had been discredited in the eyes of the government because it had led to the growth of discontent and the weakening of the regime's powers, but it was clear by the end of the nineteenth century that the failure to implement reform during the 1880s and 1890s had produced exactly the same effect. The situation that had been produced by 1905 was, however, far more serious than that which had resulted in Alexander II's assassination in 1881: at the beginning of the twentieth century the isolated discontent of two decades earlier had been transformed into a nationwide phenomenon.

It was in this situation that the tsarist government was drawn into war with Japan in 1904.[16] The idea of a short, successful war that would serve to unite the country around the tsar and his government had aroused some support among ministers conscious of the divisions in Russian society and they believed that the Japanese offered an easy target. Japan was viewed as a backward, Asian country, infinitely inferior to any European power and the Russians expected that they would have little trouble in defeating her. The shock that the state received when it became clear that the Japanese were proving superior to the Russian forces was, therefore, severe. On land the Russian armies were beaten back and Port Arthur, their chief base in the region, captured. At sea the fleet was sent to the bottom by the Japanese navy at the battle of Tsushima. The defeat of Russia, recognized both at home and abroad as one of the great powers of Europe, destroyed her aspirations to be accepted as a modern industrial country; the Japanese had called her bluff. At home, the defeat intensified the crisis of the autocracy: the population of the empire came increasingly to realize that not only had the autocracy failed to provide an adequate standard of living for them, neither could it successfully defend the state against outsiders. Defeat in war served to highlight the latent disillusion, and the number and seriousness of disturbances in both town and country increased during 1904, turning into bloody and threatening revolt at the start of 1905.

Urban discontent was the most immediate threat to the tsarist regime. The events of Bloody Sunday in January 1905, when several hundred workers taking part in peaceful demonstrations in St Petersburg were killed or wounded by troops firing on them, acted as the spark for movements to emerge in other cities of the empire. The original demands that the demonstrators made were largely economic and related to their working and living conditions: better pay, shorter hours, the recognition of trade unions and the like.[17] Such demands appeared wholly reasonable to a large proportion of the Russian elite, including a section of the government, but the view that prevailed inside the regime was that making any form of material concession to these demands would only demonstrate that the regime was powerless and open to further pressure. The response that the government adopted was, therefore, the traditional one of the Russian autocracy. It attempted to assert that it held absolute power and could maintain itself by force. A half-hearted effort was made to set up a commission to look into the grievances being displayed by the workers, but it foundered over its terms of reference. The refusal of the regime to meet what appeared to be legitimate demands with anything other than bullets did not persuade the urban population that they should return to their previous quiescence and most of the large cities were plagued by strikes and demonstrations during 1905.

Trouble was not confined to the cities: the links between city and village in Russia were very strong, as most of the new working class maintained their ties with their home villages. News travelled quickly back to the countryside and the peasantry were well aware of the difficulties being endured by their counterparts in the factories. The war with Japan also affected the peasant as soldiers were sent off to fight in the Far East, and the catalogue of defeats and deaths put doubts into the peasant mind as to the competence of the regime to take care of its population. These pressures came on top of the economic hardship that was already being felt in the countryside and they combined to produce outbreaks of revolt and disturbances in many parts of European Russia. Peasants refused to accept decisions of the land captains, landowners' houses were sacked and their crops destroyed, but although there were over 3,000 separate incidents reported during the year, they did not develop into any kind of mass uprising against the government on the lines of the great peasant revolts of earlier centuries.[18] Nevertheless, these disturbances presented great problems for the government as they were concentrated into short periods of the year: most of the trouble took place in the spring, before sowing, and especially in the autumn, after the harvest was completed, so that the regime's military and police resources were stretched to the limits. This situation was exacerbated by the fact that many of Russia's crack troops were in the Far East. Even though the war with Japan was over by mid-1905, it was difficult to transport troops back to European Russia with any speed along the still incomplete Trans-Siberian Railway.

The demands of the Russian population during 1905 varied from region to region and group to group, but as the regime showed itself completely unwilling to meet the early demands for economic change, calls for political reform became louder. It was clear that, under the existing tsarist regime, the urban masses were not going to achieve better working conditions, nor would the peasants receive the land that they wanted. As revolt became more widespread, the number of demands for political change as a prerequisite for economic change grew substantially. The articulation of political demands was made most forcibly and coherently by members of Russia's educated elite who were close to the centres of power in St Petersburg and Moscow and were able to voice their aspirations in ways that could not fail to be heard by the government.[19] While on the far left of the political spectrum parties such as the Social Democrats wanted a revolution in Russia and the complete overthrow of the tsarist regime, the majority of political opinion was more moderate and was prepared to see the continuation of the monarchy, albeit in a severely limited form. The main component of the programmes put forward by Russia's embryonic political parties was for a legislative assembly, elected on a very wide franchise, which would ensure that the tsar could never again act in an arbitrary and despotic manner. As 1905 progressed, the consensus became stronger and stronger that the establishment of such an assembly was essential.

During 1905 the tsarist regime found itself assailed from all sides. For the first time it faced a situation in which it was difficult to rely on the support of any section of the community: the countryside was in turmoil; Russia's cities beset by strikes and demonstrations and the defeated military engaging in mutiny. Among the nobility too there was a clear perception that the country needed change, although there remained a very substantial segment of the gentry who wanted to see the autocracy remain unlimited and all-powerful. This great upsurge of feeling against the government was the result of the regime's failure over the previous four decades to implement any sort of coherent policies with clearly defined aims. The aims that the state had pursued – the maintenance of autocracy and the strengthening of Russia as a great power – had led to confusion and contradiction about the best methods of achieving these ends and this had directly resulted in Russian society becoming fragmented and itself confused. By 1905 the tsarist regime was reaping the whirlwind sown by its inaction over the previous 40 years.

The dilemma that presented itself to the government during 1905 was expressed in much sharper terms than the regime had faced for half a century. In 1905 it was obvious that the very survival of tsarist Russia was at stake and crucial decisions about the future of the country had to be taken quickly if the government was to continue to direct the affairs of the country. For the traditional supporters of autocracy, the way ahead was clear. The disturbances of 1905 had come about because of the liberal reforms of previous generations, combined with a lack of firmness on the part of the state in dealing with opposition and discontent. In order to quell these disturbances and restore the authority of the autocracy, extreme conservatives wanted policies of repression to be intensified and for the state to stand absolutely firm against all calls for reform. By the autumn of 1905 the situation inside Russia was so difficult that serious consideration was given to the establishment of a military dictatorship as the only means by which order could be restored.[20] This would have allowed the imposition of martial law and the use of courts-martial to deal with rebels, but the idea foundered because no suitable candidate could be found for the post of military dictator. Nicholas II was temperamentally unsuited to this sort of role and the only possible figure, the tsar's cousin, Grand Duke Nikolai Nikolaevich, refused outright.

Such a policy of increased repression was strongly resisted by other members of the governing elite in Russia, and especially by Sergei Witte. The former minister of finance had been recalled to public service by Nicholas II to handle the delicate negotiations for peace with Japan. His success, resulting in the Treaty of Portsmouth, had greatly enhanced his reputation and provided him with the opportunity to make his views known on internal government policy. The government took some steps during the summer of 1905 to respond to popular pressure for political change by announcing the establishment of a consultative assembly, known as the Bulygin Duma, after the minister who conceived it. This move was designed to quell discontent and to demonstrate that the government was prepared to take some notice of the views of the population. But the idea backfired. Instead of putting an end to the calls for political reform, the concession that the government offered in the form of the Bulygin Duma served to stimulate the public's appetite for further and more far-reaching reforms. The offer of a purely consultative assembly was inadequate and failed to satisfy the pressures that had built up during the first part of 1905. The fact that the regime had shown itself prepared to make some concessions seemed to demonstrate to society that, if further pressure was exerted, more concessions would be forthcoming. By the early autumn of 1905 it was obvious to Witte that unless fundamental reforms were made to the institutional structure of the state, there was a serious possibility that the combined weight of urban and rural revolt would succeed in toppling the tsarist regime. He therefore proposed to the tsar a series of measures designed to satisfy as many of the demands for political change as possible without damaging the essential structure of the autocracy.

Witte hoped that by establishing a legislative assembly and by making promises to observe fundamental civil freedoms, the most vociferous and articulate of the critics of the regime would be appeased and would divert their energies into the new institutions and away from opposing the government. Witte's desire to change the structure of the Russian state did not meet with universal approval among the ruling circles of the country. Nicholas II himself was deeply sceptical about the idea of relinquishing some of his power and his instincts lay in the direction of continuing to govern Russia as a traditional autocracy, using severe measures if necessary.[21] During October 1905, as revolt intensified in both town and country, Witte worked hard to persuade the tsar and his advisers that the only way forward was that of reform. His arguments were accepted by the middle of the month and, on 17 October 1905, resulted in the issuing of the October Manifesto, establishing a legislative Duma to take part in the work of governing Russia. This manifesto clearly signalled that the Russian autocracy had taken an irreversible step in allowing its subjects, for the first time, some say in the way in which the country was governed. The implications of this measure were wide-ranging and far from fully understood by the majority of those inside the regime who were to have to implement the new system. By giving the population of the Russian Empire a permanent say in the way in which the country was governed, the state was ensuring that reform could never again disappear from the political agenda. The October Manifesto, however, showed signs of the tensions within the autocratic regime. It was formally entitled "On the improvement of order in the state" and at the same time as it embraced the language of rights and representation, it stressed that the state would act to deal with outbreaks of disorder. The manifesto maintained an equivocal position, but the presence of elected representatives of the population as an integral part of the governing apparatus of the state meant that the regime could no longer easily impose its will on its subjects, confident that it could ignore their wishes and response. By giving the population a formal place in government, the population of the empire would come to expect that its views would be taken into account and would not expect the government to act in direct opposition to its interests.

## Political reform: parliament and cabinet

Institutional change also brought reform to the top of the political agenda in Russia because alterations to the structure of government did nothing by themselves to improve the conditions in which the population lived. While Witte and those who supported him saw the creation of new institutions as an end in themselves, for most of articulate political opinion in Russia they were only a means to an end. Liberal political activists believed that constitutional change was no more than the foundation on which they could build a new Russia: by itself it would achieve very little and could only be given substance by using it as a tool with which to implement reform. This was a fundamental difference between the perceptions that government and society had of the constitutional reforms of 1905: for Nicholas II they were the maximum that he was prepared to concede, but he failed to realize the logic of the situation that he had allowed to develop.

The establishment of a parliament in Russia could only be the prelude to the intensification of public pressure for further change and the new Duma provided a formal structure through which this could be expressed. By the end of 1905, therefore, the question of reform was firmly established as a pressing need to which the regime's attention was going to be turned, willingly or not. After half a century of indecision, the government's hand was to be forced.

The progress that the reform process made in the years after 1905 depended to a huge extent on the institutional structure of government that had been created by Witte during 1905. The changes that took place during 1905 did not represent a complete overhaul in the methods of governing Russia, but were rather a somewhat confused addition to the methods that had been used for centuries. Before 1905 Russia was an autocracy in which the tsar held complete and unlimited power and, according to the Fundamental Laws of the empire, was free to do as he wished with the state that he headed. The tsar was both head of state and head of government, and in pre-1905 Russia there was no perceived difference between the two functions. The powers that the tsar possessed are clearly seen in the way in which law was made in nineteenth-century Russia. Although the State Council had been created in 1810 to act as an advisory body to the monarch on legislative and other matters, and although it was composed of senior and experienced bureaucrats and functionaries, the tsar was under no compulsion to listen to, or even to ask, its advice.[22] The tsar appointed all the State Council's members and he was quite at liberty to dismiss them, while should they proffer advice that he found unpalatable he could simply ignore it without any fear of reprisal. There was no formal procedure by which law was made before 1905, since as the tsar possessed complete power, anything that he authorized was automatically the law of the land. Legislation could be issued in any number of ways and this was reflected in the variety of terms for a legislative document in tsarist Russia: edict, manifesto, regulation, statute and many others all indicated that the document was law. There was no set channel through which a proposal had to pass before it could become law: the only mandatory requirement was for it to receive the tsar's approval and this could come in very many different ways, even by oral agreement.

A ministerial structure had been introduced into Russian government at the beginning of the nineteenth century, but it was on lines that were very different from those of western Europe. Each Russian minister had very substantial independence in the policies that he pursued, for he was responsible only to the tsar. Although ministries had been created, no system had been established that provided an institutional framework for their work to be co-ordinated. The head of government remained the tsar and this personal link was the only thing that bound the work of government together. A committee of ministers had been set up in the early nineteenth century, ostensibly to act as a forum for the discussion of government policy as a whole. But all its authority derived from the tsar, who acted as chairman and, should the monarch prefer to carry on business with his ministers individually, the committee lost its significance. There was no collective ministerial responsibility and ministers were able to pursue policies that were at odds with those of their colleagues. The only person who could act as co-ordinator of the government's actions was the tsar, and Russian rulers during the nineteenth century did not show themselves to be deeply or consistently interested in the work of government.

The institutional divisiveness (*vedomstvennost'*) at the highest levels of Russian government had substantial implications for the country as a whole.[23] Without agreement in St Petersburg about the aims and methods that the government was to pursue, there was little hope that local officials deep in the Russian countryside would have a clear idea of their duties and priorities. When this was combined with the autocratic powers of a tsar ruling at the centre, a man who could change his mind from day to day and thereby change the law of the land and the aims of the government, it resulted in arbitrary government being the rule for the Russian Empire. As the monarch could operate without a fixed body of law to which he must adhere, so local officials at every level in the empire were able to act in a similar way. It was recognized that even though officials might receive directions from above, contravention of such orders would not necessarily result in punishment or dismissal, since there was no corpus of law against which such instructions could be tested. Russian government, therefore, operated with few fixed limits or guides. As a consequence, corruption and bribery were rife.

The process of decision-making inside the government was also deeply affected by the institutional framework of the administration. Especially where a matter concerned more than one ministry, decisions were taken without full discussion and consideration of all the issues involved. Without any proper forum where the government's policy as a whole could be debated, it was easy for contradictory policies to be pursued, especially since the whole structure of government pivoted around the person of the tsar. Should he lack a sensitivity to the whole range of problems affecting Russia, it was easy for the monarch to fail to appreciate the wider implications of the adoption of a particular policy. Furthermore, the lack of a central decision-making body could weaken the apparatus of Russian government since the energies of ministers and officials were diverted into intragovernment conflict about the course of policy, rather than into policy itself. Witte, a prickly personality and a man who was resented by traditional bureaucrats, found himself at the centre of many such disputes. Since the tsar's word on a subject need not necessarily be the final decision, ministers were at liberty to continue their disputes even after a decision had apparently been taken, in the hope of changing the monarch's mind. When the tsar was as easily influenced a man as Nicholas II, ministers could see much possible profit in continuing to advocate a policy that had apparently been rejected. This added to the already chaotic nature of Russian government.

The autocratic nature of Russian government had also precluded any form of consultation with the state's subjects. Autocracy meant rule by a single individual and one of its chief features was that the tsar possessed power that was unlimited and unrestricted. Attempts had been made during the 1860s and 1870s to persuade Alexander II to set up some form of consultative assembly. This would provide a means of ensuring that policy formation could take into account the views of people outside the government machine who nevertheless felt that they had a part to play in running the country. There had been pressure to establish some sort of assembly both from outside the bureaucracy, and especially from the new *zemstva*, as well as from inside the government itself. During the 1860s there were two attempts by high-ranking officials to persuade the tsar of the benefits of a consultative assembly: P. A. Valuev, minister of internal affairs, and Grand Duke Konstantin Nikolaevich, the tsar's brother, both argued that such an assembly would serve to strengthen the regime by giving it a much broader base of support and by making it more responsive to the opinions of significant members of the community. A decade later, in the mid-1870s, P. A. Shuvalov, the head of the secret police, put forward the view that the establishment of such a body would be a deeply conservative step, as it would not be seen as giving way to popular pressure, but rather it would be a reinforcement of the regime and would ensure that more far-reaching constitutional reforms could be avoided.[24] None of these projects came to anything as the tsar believed that their implementation would represent a diminution of his powers; this was not a step he was prepared to take except in the most extreme circumstances.

These extreme circumstances did present themselves at the end of the 1870s and Alexander II was persuaded by Loris-Melikov that the only way for him to preserve his position as autocrat without losing complete control was to make the limited concession of instituting a system of consultative assemblies. Alexander II's assassination in March 1881 put paid to this idea and his successor viewed the idea of putting any restraints on the power of the monarch with disdain. It was only with the death of Alexander III in 1894 and the accession to the throne of Nicholas II that hopes of major structural change surfaced again. The young tsar showed himself, however, to be as determined as his father not to be seen to be making concessions to public opinion and spoke very early in his reign of the "senseless dreams" of those who wanted to see some form of parliament in Russia. By putting up such a prolonged and vigorous resistance to any form of constitutional change, the Russian autocracy was merely paving the way for much more radical demands to be made and ensuring that the pressure for change continued to build up.

By 1905 Russian government was in considerable disarray. The institutional apparatus of the state made it difficult for it to present a unified response to outside pressure, while the behaviour of officials at the local level provoked severe discontent among the population. The nature of the autocratic system and the continual infighting and disagreements that arose among high officials and ministers meant that the regime was very poor at reacting quickly and effectively to such discontent and, indeed, to any form of attack on its authority. The only method in which the regime had faith during the later part of the nineteenth century was repression. When the resources to implement this were lacking or the scale of the problem was so great that repression could be, at best, only a temporary solution, the government found itself at a loss as to how to proceed. In 1905 it was clear that, if the Russian autocracy was to survive in any recognizable form, it had to reform its decision-making structures to provide for rapid and unambiguous responses to crises, and in order to try to mitigate the pressure being felt from outside, some form of popular involvement in government had to be permitted.

This was the nettle that Witte grasped during the late summer and autumn of 1905 and he tried to reform both of these areas of the Russian government. The first set of proposals to be implemented brought about a fundamental constitutional change to the Russian Empire: the institution of a parliament without whose consent no law could come into effect. The tsar had conceded in August 1905 that a consultative assembly, the so-called Bulygin Duma, could be summoned and it was to be elected on a limited franchise. By October 1905, however, it was obvious that this would no longer satisfy public opinion and that any assembly would have to have far wider powers. Witte therefore proposed the establishment of an elected, legislative Duma and this was reluctantly accepted by the tsar and his advisers, leading to the manifesto of 17 October 1905. The precise details of the electoral system for the new body and many of its exact functions and responsibilities were initially left vague, mainly due to the speed with which the proposals were drawn up. It was clear, however, that at the time of its conception the Duma was envisaged as being the sole legislative body for the empire, and that this meant a limitation on the powers of the monarch. Nicholas II himself was deeply reluctant to accept that he was no longer the absolute ruler of Russia and he insisted that his powers were still described as "unlimited" even though this was clearly not the case. This caused substantial problems over the next years, as there remained a basic difference of interpretation about the authority that the monarch retained.

The October 1905 proposals for a Duma envisaged a revision of the franchise which had been proposed for the Bulygin Duma, to include "those classes of the population that are now completely deprived of electoral rights". The new electoral law that was issued on 11 December 1905 was a complex document that divided the population of the empire into four *curiae* for electoral purposes: nobility, propertied townspeople, peasantry and workers; along with special representation for the largest cities of the empire. Voting was to be indirect: preliminary elections were to take place to elect deputies from each *curia* to provincial electoral assemblies and these assemblies would then choose the Duma deputies. The electoral system ensured that the peasantry were underrepresented in the Duma, but the government was keen to ensure that the rural population did have an important voice in the work of the Duma.[25] The regime believed that the great bulk of the Russian peasantry were conservative by nature and that those peasants who had taken part in the disturbances of 1905 were untypical of the mass of the rural population. By providing the peasants with what was still a substantial voice in the election of Duma deputies, the government intended to ensure that there was a solid conservative bulwark inside the new institution, able to act as a counterweight to what it perceived as the more radical tendencies of sections of the nobility and middle classes. This fundamental miscalculation of the political attitudes of the peasantry was to cause immense difficulties for the government in the first period of operation of the new Duma.

The second area where Witte's hand was obvious was in the institutional reforms made to the government on 19 October 1905. Witte intended to create a proper ministerial structure and establish a head of government who could co-ordinate the work of the ministries and who would then report to the tsar. He was frustrated in this design, however, both by individual ministers who jealously guarded and fought for their independence and right of access to the monarch, and by the tsar himself who was deeply suspicious of any one individual being able to wield such authority that might enable him to challenge the power of the monarch. Opposition from inside the government came from ministers who had no desire to see themselves subordinated to one of their own number and who valued their ability to pursue their own policies without interference from anyone but the tsar. D. F. Trepov, assistant minister of internal affairs, proved especially adept at maintaining the closest links with the tsar. While there was agreement that the activity of the government did need to be better co-ordinated, ministers were unwilling to accept the consequences of this step by suffering a reduction in their own authority. Part of the problem in the reaction of both ministers and tsar to Witte's proposals was a distrust of Witte himself: Nicholas II felt that Witte was pressuring him to make reforms that would benefit Witte himself rather than Russia as a whole and he was determined to resist his adviser becoming too powerful. The Russian establishment believed that Witte wanted to become the first Prime Minister of Russia and this provided a further focus for opposition to institutional change. The reform that emerged on 19 October was, therefore, a much diluted version of Witte's original intentions. A council of ministers was established to co-ordinate the work of the government and it was to have a chairman appointed by the tsar. However, similarities to a Western cabinet ended there. The chairman of the council, although nominally prime minister, had no authority to direct the work of the government or to impose his views upon the other ministers. There was no collective responsibility among ministers, so that they were free to continue to argue their point of view even after the council of ministers had taken a decision, while each minister was to continue to have the right of access to the tsar. The establishment of such a system was viewed by Witte as a clear rebuff and he became increasingly disillusioned by the experience of government.

As Witte's influence declined, Nicholas II felt himself less constrained by any need to make reform and wanted to be able to reassert his own view of his position as an unlimited monarch. At the same time, severe repressive measures had resulted in a substantial reduction in the level and spread of disturbances across the empire. In these circumstances, it appeared to the tsar and his conservative advisers that the concessions that had been made to public opinion in October 1905 had gone too far and were no longer justified by the level of threat that was posed to the regime in the first part of 1906. Accordingly, when the details of the new structures were being worked out, the regime took steps to limit the impact of the introduction of the Duma by hedging the new institution about with mechanisms designed to restrict its field of activity. This was achieved in two ways: first, by instituting a second legislative chamber and second, through drawing up a new set of Fundamental Laws for the empire.

Even though the government had attempted to ensure that the Duma included a substantial conservative representation, it was clear that reliance on the electoral system and public opinion was not guaranteed to produce the results the government wanted. Instead, the regime looked about for some more permanent method of ensuring that the Duma could not dominate policy-making on its own. The solution it hit upon and that became law in February 1906 was to introduce a second chamber into the legislative process as a counterweight to the Duma. The existing State Council, an advisory body composed of senior bureaucrats and officials, was to be reformed for this purpose and was to retain its heavy conservative bias. The Council was to exist alongside the Duma, so that all legislation had to be approved by it before becoming law, but its composition was to be very different. Half of the members of the Council were to continue to be appointed by the tsar and there was to be an annual intake of new appointments, while the second half of the Council's members were to be elected. These elections were to take place on a very restricted franchise. The empire's elite interest groups were each to elect a specified number of the Council's members. The provincial nobility, the Orthodox Church, universities and commercial groups were each to hold elections every three years through their corporate organizations for up to 12 members from each group. This system of membership was designed to provide a cast-iron guarantee that the State Council would be permanently dominated by a conservative majority, and as half of its members were directly beholden to the tsar for their positions, there was little chance that they would do anything that would jeopardize their occupancy of one of the most prestigious positions in the empire. The State Council did indeed prove to be the counterweight to the Duma that the government wanted and its aversion to radical measures and to reform in general served to frustrate many of the plans that the Duma and the government had for the future of Russia.

The Fundamental Laws of the empire were also revised during the early part of 1906 and set out more precisely how the new legislative system of the empire was to work. This document, the closest the Russian Empire came to a formal constitution, made explicit the continuing role of the tsar in the government of Russia.[26] He was to provide the third tier to the legislative process, for all legislation that had been approved by both Duma and State Council had finally to be confirmed by the tsar himself. This was not a mere formality for the fact that both legislative chambers deemed a measure worthy of enactment was no guarantee that the tsar himself would feel it to be so. Nicholas II felt no compunction about rejecting the views of the population as expressed through the Duma and State Council and relying on the dictates of his own conscience. This was to provide a further and important obstacle to the process of reform.

The powers that the Duma possessed were also made clearer by the Fundamental Laws. The regime was keen to limit the influence of the Duma as much as possible and it did this in two main ways: restrictions on the areas of government work that the Duma could debate, and limits to the areas of the state budget that came under the Duma's jurisdiction. Certain areas of government activity were declared to be exclusively the jurisdiction of the tsar and his ministers, including foreign affairs, defence and Church matters. The Duma could only discuss these topics at the invitation of the government and careful watch was to be kept to ensure that the legislative body did not overstep its jurisdiction. Although the Fundamental Laws declared that in principle the state budget was open for discussion and approval by the Duma and State Council, a large proportion of the budget was "ironclad" and closed to debate or amendment by the legislative bodies. This applied to matters such as military spending and internal security: the total proportion of spending over which the Duma had no control amounted to some 40 per cent of the entire budget. The regime hoped that these restrictions on the new legislature would preserve important sections of the government's activity from public scrutiny and ensure that the Duma emerged as a body that was firmly subordinate to the government itself.

The structures of Russian government that came into being during 1905 and 1906 were as much of a hybrid as those that had existed during the nineteenth century, but they did mark a watershed by providing a potential for further change. Although the tsar and his coterie had tried to claw back as many of the concessions that had been made during 1905 as possible, the central plank of the October Manifesto – a legislative assembly elected on a wide franchise – remained intact and all that had been done during the early months of 1906 was to hedge it about with constraints that left its central role largely untouched. The constitutional changes had, however, introduced a major source of friction into the apparatus of government as there were clear disagreements about the powers that each section of the law-making process possessed. By the spring of 1906, Nicholas II had come to believe that the establishment of the Duma had been forced from him at a moment of extreme pressure that had now dissipated and that, despite the October Manifesto, he remained the autocratic ruler of Russia. The tsar was not prepared to accept that the existence of a properly established assembly meant that he had to act differently and he continued to exercise his prerogative as if nothing had changed. The views of the Duma and State Council were, the tsar believed, no more binding on him than had been the opinions of his advisers before the upheavals of 1905. He still wanted to be supreme ruler of Russia and resented suggestions that his authority had been in any way reduced.

Not surprisingly, Nicholas II was one of the very few people in Russia who saw matters in this light. The political parties that had come into existence during 1905 certainly believed that the reforms did mark a watershed in the way in which Russia was developing. For the liberal and moderate men who had built up experience in the *zemstva* and the professions during the latter part of the nineteenth century, 1905 and its constitutional reforms represented, if not everything they had been calling for, at least a very substantial part of their hopes. Even for those men such as Miliukov, the leader of the Constitutional Democrat (Kadet) party, who warned against seeing the 1905 reforms as the realization of all the hopes of the moderate opposition, these constitutional reforms represented something on which a new Russia could be built.[27] The regime's acceptance that the views of the population of the empire were significant meant that moderate opinion could no longer be sidelined and that it could not be deprived of a role in the running of Russia. The establishment of the Duma provided, for the first time, an institutionalized method for people from right across Russia to make their views known to central government without their opinions being dismissed as "senseless dreams" or being threatened with the loss of privileges or rights. The existence of the Duma afforded the potential for people outside the government to provide a persistent and reasoned critique of what the regime was doing and also, and more importantly, for them to put forward their own detailed and constructive plans for Russia's future.

The reaction of the government itself to the October Manifesto and what it promised was more complex and reflected the increasingly sharp division that existed between the proponents of reform and repression. Many of the ministers who held office during 1905 viewed the institution of the Duma as something that offended against their principles and while they recognized that it was there to stay, they intended to have as little to do with it as possible. Much of this opposition to the new constitutional structures was connected with the personal antipathy that senior officials felt towards Witte since they saw the Duma as essentially his creation and a vehicle for his ambition. There was, however, a body of opinion inside the Russian establishment that wanted to see the involvement of "society" in the work of government. As bureaucratic methods had proved ineffective in influencing the tsar to take action, more liberal ministers and their advisers believed that the Duma could provide the spur to action that was necessary to push the regime towards making change. This belief, however, was predicated upon the Duma proving to be a moderate body that would be prepared to work in co-operation with the government, rather than being constantly at odds with it. Such ministers hoped fervently that the Duma would be dominated by men of a reformist, rather than a revolutionary bent, who would not antagonize the more conservative members of the government but could instead persuade them of their moderation and good sense. The new Russian constitution appeared contradictory: it continued to describe the tsar as possessing autocratic power, but also provided for the establishment of legislative institutions. While the post-1906 structures of the regime were, in strict terms, a "constitutional monarchy", the terms of the constitution itself made it clear that the monarch had not formally surrendered his powers.

## Coming to terms with reform: Nicholas II and his ministers

The reforms of 1905 and 1906 therefore aroused very different expectations and hopes among the players on the Russian political stage. As the institutional structure was brand-new and completely untested in Russia, the opinions and actions of the individuals who were to operate the new system were of vital importance in determining its future, and indeed that of Russia itself. The monarch himself was of particular importance in the apparatus of the state, since Nicholas II had been used to wielding supreme power in Russia for over a decade and had strong views about his task as tsar. Nicholas had been brought up very much in his father's mould: he had been tutored by Pobedonostsev, like Alexander III before him, and had accepted the view of autocracy that his father held. Nicholas believed he had a sacred duty to uphold the greatness of Russia and to maintain the empire so that he could pass it on to his successor in the same condition as he had received it. He believed fervently that the autocratic system had been designed to suit the special conditions of the Russian environment and people and that he had to carry out the tasks of ruling Russia without being deflected by outside influences or pressures. For Nicholas II, autocracy was a God-given institution and the tsar believed that the only responsibility he owed for the stewardship of Russia was to God. He saw no need to account for his actions to any of his subjects, since it was not they who had given him the position that he occupied and he believed that they had no right or power to remove him. The tsar's concept of his duties was firmly bound up with his deep Orthodox religious beliefs. He felt that any diminution of his autocratic powers and rights represented a slight not just to his own authority and person, but more importantly it would be an insult to the Almighty who had entrusted him with autocratic authority. Nicholas's reluctance to implement reforms was there-

fore not simply a pragmatic response to discontent, but was motivated by deeply and sincerely held beliefs that had been part of
his make-up since childhood.

Although the tsar did possess strong convictions about his
rights and duties, his personal characteristics did not match up to
the fervour with which he perceived his task. Nicholas found it
very difficult to be consistent in his opinions or to act decisively
in dealing with his advisers and ministers. The tsar was easily
influenced by others and often simply agreed with the last person
whom he spoke to, even if the advice that was proffered was diametrically opposed to the view the tsar had previously held. This
tendency caused substantial problems in the work of governing
the empire, since ministers could never be sure that a course of
action that had seemingly been agreed on by the monarch was
not going to be altered when the tsar next spoke to an adviser.
The atmosphere of mistrust and intrigue which this engendered
meant that members of the government had to spend much time
ensuring that their own view was the one accepted by Nicholas
II, rather than being able to concentrate on the substance of the
policies they were advocating. It also made it very difficult for the
government to maintain coherent or consistent policies since, as
the head of government was liable to change his mind without
considering the impact this was going to have, there was no guarantee that policy would not change rapidly and irrationally.
While this characteristic of the tsar's was seen as irritating and
detrimental to good government by many of his ministers, Nicholas himself believed that it was an essential part of his prerogatives to be able to implement such policies as he desired whenever
he wanted to.

This difference in the perception of the monarch's duties and
position led to difficult relationships between the tsar and some
of his ministers. An atmosphere of mistrust developed, especially
with those ministers who wanted to develop long-term policies
or else to implement major changes. The strains that existed
between Nicholas and Witte in the autumn of 1905 have already
been seen, but the advent of the Duma and the council of ministers made it all the more important for the government to
present a united front to outside opinion. Reform-minded ministers – such as N. N. Kutler, the minister of agriculture, and V. I.

Timiriazev, the minister of trade and industry – believed it was vital for the monarch to maintain consistent opinions. Mistrust was not one-sided, for the tsar was very suspicious of members of the government who, in his eyes, were trying to pressure him into taking particular courses of action. He was not prepared to accept that the constitutional changes of 1905 and 1906 had resulted in any alteration to his powers and tried to act as he had always done, oblivious to the changed public perception of his role and impatient of ministers who appeared to him to be trying to usurp some of the authority that rightly belonged to him.

Nicholas's basic dislike of reform was also important in creating tension between the monarch and his advisers. For the tsar reform was something to be embarked upon only as a last resort, when there was no possibility of saving the situation by any other means. Reform had no positive virtue for Nicholas II since it merely upset the status quo and represented a move into unknown territory; the tsar's basic instincts were to preserve Russia as unchanged as possible, rather than taking the risk of making changes that might bring unforeseen consequences. Witte had been successful in persuading the tsar that the stresses of 1905 could only be removed by fundamental change, largely because the threat to tsarism was acute and the reforms were couched in generalities. Nicholas was ready to accept reforms in this atmosphere of crisis; all the more so because the detailed implications of the changes were not spelled out. When it came to the detail, however, the tsar was much more reluctant to agree and he became increasingly less keen on the need for radical change. Nicholas's view of reform as a pragmatic measure, to be resorted to only when all else had failed, contrasted sharply with the attitudes of many of his ministers after 1905 who regarded reform as a positive step; it also placed the tsar at odds with moderate political opinion in the country, which saw the constitutional changes of 1905 as being the springboard from which further change would emerge. In a system where the power of the monarch remained considerable, even after the upheavals of 1905, Nicholas's views and character could not be ignored. For those inside the government who wanted to bring about further change, the tsar was one of the great obstacles where their plans could falter. Opponents of reform, however, were able to make their views heard at the very highest level and be assured that they would be listened to with sympathy. Being able to handle the tsar and having the ability to persuade him of the merits of one's case was, therefore, one of the prime requisites for a government minister. Nicholas II himself was well aware of the aims of his ministers, and after the unfortunate experience which he had with Witte, he intended to ensure that the experience would not be repeated.

Sergei Witte had succeeded in working his way up from being an employee of a Russian railway employer to emerge as second only to the tsar during 1905. His rise to power had come as he had demonstrated that he was the architect of Russia's enormous economic growth during the 1890s, and his skill at political manoeuvring resulted in his outshining all his fellow ministers during his decade as minister of finance. When it was clear that peace would have to be negotiated between Russia and Japan, the obvious candidate for the job was Witte: unblemished by the war, as he had not been in office during the struggle, he appeared as the only one of Russia's leaders who had the skill and persistence necessary to bring the war to a speedy conclusion and to find terms that would not humiliate Russia more than absolutely necessary. His success in concluding the Treaty of Portsmouth on terms that were much more favourable to Russia than might have been expected from the course of the war gave Witte an unequalled place in Russian political life: he had appeared out of retirement to solve a problem created by others and he therefore appeared to be the only figure capable of dealing with the disturbances that were sweeping Russia during 1905.

Witte's approach to the problems of the tsarist regime was calculating. He was aware that coercion was not a feasible method of dealing with the revolts in both town and country, for the level of discontent was too high for that and the resources available to the regime insufficient to quell the outbreaks of trouble. As well, the regime had already embarked on the process of making concessions to public opinion and Witte believed that this could not now be halted. The promise of some change had raised public expectations – at least among the articulate and politically conscious sections of society – that the government had chosen the path of reform and any attempt to call a halt to the process would only provoke more severe discontent. Witte felt that the government had to take the gamble that a second set of changes would satisfy public demands; such a move, however, required very careful planning to ensure that public opinion really was satisfied, but at the same time care was necessary lest the powers of the government be reduced by making such reforms. The task Witte set himself was to maintain a balance between the vociferous and radical demands coming from the public and the conservative inclinations of the tsar and his close advisers. In trying to implement constitutional and institutional reform during the late autumn of 1905 Witte won himself few friends. Nicholas II mistrusted Witte because he believed that his minister was trying to usurp some of the tsar's authority for himself, while moderate and radical public opinion denounced Witte because the measures that he proposed did not, in their view, go anywhere near far enough to solve Russia's problems. Witte's departure from the political scene early in 1906 was, therefore, lamented by very few people.

Nicholas II was determined that the next chairman of the council of ministers should be somebody much more in tune with the tsar's own beliefs and aspirations. He was also keen that the incumbent of the post should be pliant and unlikely to pressure the tsar as Witte had done; the man whom he selected was Ivan Goremykin, an aged and experienced bureaucrat who had been minister of internal affairs during the 1890s. Goremykin was the antithesis of Witte: he had spent all his life inside the tsarist administrative apparatus and possessed deeply conservative views. Brought out of retirement at the age of 66 to replace Witte, Goremykin had no sympathy with the new constitutional structure of Russia, nor indeed any real comprehension of what the Duma was intended to do. He viewed it as an irritant to the real work of government and took the view that it should be ignored as far as possible. For Goremykin, as for Nicholas II, Russia was still an autocratic state and he had little intention of changing his political behaviour as a result of the introduction of the Duma. As the number of outbreaks of discontent were diminishing during the first part of 1906, Goremykin felt that the reason for the introduction of the Duma was fast disappearing, and that consequently the Duma itself could safely be sidelined and the regime could revert to its traditional methods of ruling.

Elections to the Duma took place for the first time during the winter of 1906 and it was Goremykin who had to deal with the assembly of the first elected parliament that Russia had ever known. His attitude to the First Duma was made plain in the speech that he delivered shortly after its official opening by the tsar: the chairman of the council of ministers addressed the assembly much as a headmaster might deal with a potentially troublesome pupil. He warned the Duma that certain courses of policy, especially the compulsory expropriation of noble-owned land, had already been rejected by the government and that there was therefore no point in the Duma entertaining false hopes as to its ability to influence matters. Goremykin laid out the limits of the Duma's competence and made it plain that the government would not tolerate any overstepping of these limits.[28] Not surprisingly, his speech was greeted with much antagonism by the bulk of the Duma's members. They had come to St Petersburg expecting to be able to take a real part in the work of government, but Goremykin was delivering a sharp rebuff to their aspirations. For Goremykin and similar-minded ministers, the convocation of the Duma did not mark the beginning of a new era in Russian government. Coping with the Duma was, for the government, an exercise in damage limitation: Goremykin believed that the way to approach this was to treat the Duma simply as a body that could be dictated to by the government. He intended to reassert the authority of the regime by demonstrating to the Duma that it was the government that was in charge, and by stressing immediately that the Duma was in a subordinate position.

The majority of the Duma's members were not, however, prepared to accept this situation and the session of the First Duma witnessed a complete impasse in relations between government and legislature. The Duma insisted on pressing forward and debating policies that had already been rejected by the government, while Goremykin and his colleagues were not prepared to budge from their position and make any form of concession to the Duma. Less than 12 months after their enactment, it thus appeared as if the constitutional reforms of 1905 had done nothing to improve the position of the empire. The only difference was that the opposition to the government had been provided with an institutional framework through which it could express hostility and discontent with the regime. Goremykin himself found the experience of operating in this environment to be extremely unrewarding and difficult. He had been used to the relatively peaceful life of a bureaucrat, well shielded from the political pressures to which politicians in parliamentary states were accustomed. The task that he faced as chairman of the council of ministers was made more difficult by the lack of agreement inside the government on the best way to deal with the new situation.

## The reforming premier

Goremykin's appointment had not been welcomed by all his fellow ministers, some of whom believed that the institution of the Duma provided exactly that opportunity for government and society to work together that they had been seeking for many years. Chief among these was the new minister of internal affairs, Peter Stolypin, appointed from outside the Petersburg bureaucracy to head the single most important ministry in the government. Stolypin, who was to replace Goremykin as head of the government in July 1906, encompassed a range of experience and opinions that was exceptional in a Russian government minister. Born in 1862, he had spent most of his childhood in the countryside, chiefly in the Baltic provinces. The family was wealthy and owned large estates, but this did not indicate a lack of interest in social affairs. Stolypin's uncle, Arkadii, was keenly concerned with the peasant question and had published works on the topic and these must have been available inside the Stolypin household. Stolypin himself went to St Petersburg University, the most prestigious institution of higher education in the Russian Empire, where he studied natural sciences. This set him apart from the majority of future bureaucrats, for the most common field of study for entrants to the civil service was law. Stolypin did not emerge from university in 1884 with a deep knowledge of the principles of government of the empire, but he did go to work inside the state bureaucracy.

He worked initially in the ministry of the interior, and after 18 months he was transferred, at his own request, to the department of agriculture, where he remained as a junior civil servant until 1889. The bureaucratic life evidently did not suit the young Stolypin, now married to Olga Neidgart. She was a member of an extremely wealthy landowning family who brought with her on marriage almost twice as much land as her husband owned. In 1889 Stolypin decided to return to the life of a country gentleman and to take up permanent residence on his estates in the province of Kovno, in present-day Lithuania. He took an active part in the work of local government in his native province, occupying the position first of district marshal of the nobility and then becoming the provincial marshal. This gave him wide experience of the variety and problems of Russian local administration since the marshals of the nobility, although elected by the nobility of the areas in which they lived, performed a wide variety of government functions, especially in the fields of social policy and inspection. By 1902 Stolypin was ready to move back into the mainstream of government work and he was appointed as provincial governor of Grodno, again encompassing his native estates. This was only a short-lived appointment, however, for less than a year later Stolypin took up appointment as the governor of Saratov, a province deep in European Russia, in the Volga region.[29] This was a major change in his career since he was moving away from the area in which he had grown up and had spent the greater part of his life. Saratov was one of the most difficult provinces to administer as peasant unrest was common and the size of the territory exacerbated the difficulties from the governor's point of view. Stolypin dealt firmly and successfully with the growing disturbances during 1905, displaying initiative and drive in his work and earning the special commendation of the tsar for his success in putting down revolt.[30] His obvious success in quelling discontent had drawn Stolypin very much to the attention of the St Petersburg authorities and in April 1906, when the position of minister of internal affairs fell vacant, Stolypin was an obvious candidate for appointment.

But Stolypin was far from being an advocate of ruthless repression on its own. Long years of residence in the countryside had convinced Stolypin that the roots of revolt were to be found in the parlous state of Russian agriculture and he had made it clear, in successive reports to the St Petersburg authorities during his time as a provincial governor, that agrarian reform was vital if further unrest was to be avoided.[31] He insisted that the peasantry needed concessions to divert them away from revolt. He believed that the way to do this was to allow the peasantry to hold their own land, independently of the commune, so that they could use their initiative to the full and thus become a class of well-off and independent landowners. Although proposals for agrarian reform had been on the agenda of the Russian government almost since the emancipation of the serfs in 1861, Stolypin's background made his suggestions rather more valuable and well-founded than most. His personal experience of the peasant economy in two widely differing areas of the empire – the Baltic provinces and the Volga region – gave him practical knowledge of the rural scene and he came into the government ready and willing to push forward schemes for agrarian change.

A further feature of Stolypin's background that distinguished him from the majority of his colleagues was his relatively limited experience of central government. Other than his five years as a civil servant immediately after graduating from university, Stolypin had worked outside the St Petersburg bureaucratic environment and, while the work of a local official involved much contact with the central authorities, he had remained outside the main currents of St Petersburg thinking and attitudes. Talking about his own background in 1907, he argued that, "The fact that I have been a provincial governor for a short time has not made me into a bureaucrat. I am a stranger to the Petersburg official world; I have no past there, no career ties, no links with the court."[32] Stolypin came fresh to the ministry of internal affairs as someone who had been on the receiving end of the ministry's circulars and instructions, but who had never worked at its top level in the capital and had not been involved in national policy-making. He had not been part of the debate over the way in which the disturbances of 1905 should be resolved, although the vigour with which he had dealt with the Saratov revolts had convinced many in the capital that he was a firm politician who would not have much sympathy for notions of reform. As minister of internal affairs he was expected to demonstrate the same qualities he had displayed as a provincial governor in dealing with nationwide discontent. It is difficult to imagine that Nicholas II or Goremykin would have supported his appointment if they had believed that Stolypin was going to press for major reforms to be implemented. The new minister's lack of experience and his evident reluctance to take on the job may have made him an even more attractive candidate for appointment, as his ministerial colleagues no doubt felt that Stolypin could be outmanoeuvred in the St Petersburg bureaucratic environment.

Stolypin's physical appearance made him an imposing figure. He was tall, with a large black beard and penetrating blue eyes. His right hand had been disabled as the result of a childhood illness, but this gave rise to rumours about an involvement in a duel. His physical courage was not in doubt: he had personally led forces to counter the outbreaks of discontent during 1905 in Saratov, and this impression of bravery was reinforced by Stolypin's reaction to a bomb explosion at his St Petersburg house in August 1906. Although his children were seriously injured and much damage was done to the building, Stolypin himself appeared unshaken by the incident and continued working as normal. The man who came to occupy the most significant ministerial chair in St Petersburg in April 1906 and who, three months later, was to add the position of chairman of the council of ministers to his other duties, was not easily frightened and this physical characteristic was enhanced by his intellectual courage. Stolypin did not flinch from taking unpopular decisions or from stating what he believed to be the truth, however unpalatable it might appear to others. He found himself well able to stand up to ministerial colleagues much more experienced than himself in debate and was not prepared to accept unquestioningly all the sacred cows of the Russian establishment. This quality did not endear Stolypin to all his colleagues and the persistence and vigour with which he pursued his goals was to lead to his acquiring many influential enemies who were to act to frustrate his policies.

By the middle of 1906 the worst of the disturbances were over in Russia: a steady decline in the instances of trouble was helped on its way by firm action from the authorities. The sense of emergency that had gripped the Russian ruling elite during the later part of 1905 was gradually subsiding and it was becoming possible for a calmer and more reflective look to be levelled at the problems facing the country. The shock of defeat in war and the great upsurge of discontent during 1905 had clearly revealed that there were severe structural deficiencies in Russian society and that action needed to be taken to remedy these. The extent of the discontent during 1905 showed that almost all sections of society in Russia had strong grievances. They perceived the government to be the cause of these and also the only body able to address them. The economic and social changes that had taken place in Russia during the second half of the nineteenth century had built up pressures that could no longer be resisted and had to find an outlet. If a recurrence of 1905 was to be avoided, some means had to be found to release the pressures that had resulted in 1905. The regime had demonstrated that it did not have sufficient nerve or, indeed, sufficient forces at its disposal to again impose a repressive style of government upon an unwilling population. Simply trying to ignore the causes of discontent, and concentrating merely on its symptoms was no longer viable. Such a course of action could only delay the moment when the problem would have to be faced again, and the government would clearly be unable to continue with this policy in the long term.

If tsarist Russia was to survive, change had to be made to the structures of society that had produced the situation that had burst upon the country in 1905. The regime needed to focus on the causes underlying these problems. There was little disagreement that change had to come, even among those who favoured repression. It was recognized that there were fundamental deficiencies in the way in which Russia was organized, especially in the countryside where most Russians made their living. The real difference was a reluctance to admit that reform needed to be implemented immediately: everybody was aware of the problems that faced Russia, but conservative opinion hoped that the problem would disappear if it was ignored and strong government restored to the country.

Reform was, therefore, long overdue in Russia. But a major difficulty in attempting to implement any change in the quarter century before 1905 had been that the mechanisms of the Russian government were inadequate to take proper account of the needs and views of the population who lived outside St Petersburg. A major deficiency in the reform process of the 1860s and 1870s had been the lack of adequate consultation with the people who were to be most affected by the changes. Their expectations of what reform would bring had been wildly out of kilter with what the regime intended to achieve. In order for change to be managed effectively, the government needed to be sure that the measures that it intended to take would be in tune with the requirements of the great majority of the population who lived in the countryside, and not just the product of the St Petersburg bureaucratic mind. The constitutional changes that Witte pushed through at the end of 1905 provided a means for the expression of the views of the great and hitherto unheeded majority of the population. The introduction of a parliament in Russia for the first time ensured that the regime would find it very difficult to implement reform in the future without being aware of the reaction in the provinces. The existence of the Duma also meant that the government would no longer be able to operate with its accustomed degree of secrecy. Plans for change would now be subject to detailed and expert scrutiny and discussion, so that even if the government rejected the advice of the Duma, it would at any rate be aware of the probable response to its plans.

What the situation still lacked in the spring of 1906 was people at the highest levels of government who were prepared to take the initiative in implementing change. The lukewarm approach of Goremykin was wholly inadequate in attempting to win the support of the Duma and public opinion in general for the government's plans. The prospect of his continuing in office only promised further conflict between government and society. Goremykin's resignation from the post of chairman of the council of ministers, and his replacement by Stolypin, therefore held out the prospect of improved relations between government and parliament. Stolypin's own inclinations were towards introducing fundamental reforms, and with his appearance at the head of the government in the summer of 1906, the last piece had fallen into place for reform to move to the head of the government's agenda.

## CHAPTER 2

# Renewing Russia: Stolypin's programme

## Duma and government

Stolypin was appointed as minister of internal affairs in April 1906, at the same time as the First Duma met in St Petersburg. This coincided with Witte's replacement as chairman of the council of ministers by I. L. Goremykin and a general change in the personnel of the government. The elections to the First Duma had not produced the results that the government had expected since the gamble on the political conservatism of the Russian peasantry had not paid off. The peasants had largely voted for political parties that promised radical change in the countryside, instead of electing representatives who were prepared to support the tsarist regime and the government.[1] The Duma was dominated by parties that had little sympathy either for the aims of the government or for the means that it used to pursue them. Around 40 per cent of the deputies declared their allegiance to the Kadet party, the Constitutional Democrats, who stood for the transformation of Russia into a constitutional monarchy on Western lines and who were determined to point out the deficiencies of an autocratic regime at every possible opportunity. The Kadet party espoused the principles of a Western liberal party and its leaders, especially Pavel Miliukov, prided themselves on their assimilation of Western ideas and saw themselves as the means by which Russia could be transformed into a state that was able to stand as an equal with its Western neighbours. They had no sympathy with the concept or the practice of autocracy and had no intention of offering any support to the government unless it changed its ways substantially.[2]

The Kadets were far from being the Duma party most deeply opposed to the government. To their left sat about 100 Trudoviki, a peasant-based group that comprised nearly 20 per cent of the Duma's membership and aimed at securing radical improvements in the living conditions of the rural poor and of urban workers. They had none of the constitutional pretensions of the Kadets and wanted to use whatever means were possible to achieve their ends. There was also a small representation of Social Democrats in the Duma, although there had been much dispute inside the party about the principle of contesting the elections at all. The Social Democrats wanted to see the complete overthrow of the autocratic regime and intended to have nothing to do with policies that would only serve to prolong the existence of tsarism. The First Duma was, therefore, dominated by members who were completely unwilling to work not just with the tsarist government, but even within the constitutional system that had been established during 1905 and 1906. These groups on the left of the new Russian political spectrum saw their task as being to alter the basis of the Russian political structure and only then to embark on legislating for reform. They did not believe that it was feasible to make real change within the existing institutional framework and therefore saw their task as Duma deputies as being to continue the work of constitutional change that had only just been begun.

The centre parties in the Duma were much less coherent than those to their left. Political parties had only been legalized after the manifesto of 17 October 1905 and while illegal groups had existed on the left for many years before that, centre and right groupings only came into existence at the end of 1905. The principal moderate centre party was the Octobrists, named after the October Manifesto and dedicated to implementing its provisions and working within the structures that it had established. The

Octobrists were the closest supporters that the government had, but their very short history meant that they were disorganized and without proper party structure, so that the support that they could offer the government was very limited in the First Duma.[3] The same was true of conservative groups sitting to the Octobrists' right. Many on the right disagreed with the very idea of the Duma and were unenthusiastic about organizing to ensure effective representation. As a consequence, their formal organization was deficient during the time the First Duma met and they proved no match for the much better organized and vociferous parties on the left.[4]

The predominance of radical parties in the First Duma meant that the proposals that the new parliament made for reform were bound to be at odds with the government's ideas. Agrarian reform was the main topic that was seized upon by all the groups on the left and proposals to redistribute land to the peasantry formed a major part of the Duma's business during the spring of 1906. The most common call was for the compulsory expropriation of land belonging to the gentry and its redistribution among the needy rural poor. The details of the various schemes advanced to achieve this differed according to the party that proposed them, but it was the overwhelming feeling inside the First Duma that rapid and radical action needed to be taken to deal with peasant discontent.[5] Land reform was not the only area where the First Duma's aspirations came into sharp conflict with the government's aims. There was much criticism of the methods that the regime was using to put down revolt and condemnation of the continuation of the supposedly discredited policies that had led to the revolution of 1905 and the introduction of a new system of government. It appeared to the radical majority in the Duma as if the regime had not really abandoned its traditional ways of operating and as if the Duma's existence had made no real difference to Russia's political culture. There was also substantial pressure from the Duma deputies to implement the reforms that had been promised in the October Manifesto and the earlier government decrees of 26 February 1903 and 12 December 1904, which had made wide-ranging commitments to reform local government and peasant life and to provide civil rights for the population.[6] These commitments to introduce legislation to provide full civil liberties for all Russians were particularly valued by Duma members and they repeatedly pressed the government to transform its promises into deeds. In addition, the parties on the left each put forward their own agenda for reform in every area of Russian government and society. The First Duma was very far from being the pliant and conservative body of respectful peasants that the government had hoped for. The demands that the Duma made set it clearly at odds with the regime.

The attitude that the government adopted to the new parliament did nothing to help establish good relations between the two bodies. When Goremykin spoke to the First Duma in mid-May 1906 he made it clear to the assembled deputies that the government intended to impose strict limits on the extent of the Duma's power.[7] The government, Goremykin declared, was prepared to listen to legislative proposals from the Duma, but the Duma must realize that certain policies had already been rejected by the regime and it would therefore be pointless for the Duma to pursue them. In particular, he noted that compulsory expropriation of land and the granting of an amnesty to criminals had already been ruled out as unacceptable. The government was determined to establish limits within which the Duma had to operate and Goremykin stated that the regime needed to have sufficient power to be able to deal with any abuses of the laws that had brought reform to Russia. This was a clear warning to the Duma that any attempt to overstep its powers would not be tolerated by the government and that the regime did not intend to allow the new parliament any sort of free hand in the governing of Russia.

Goremykin's speech was not all threats and warnings, however, for he did give an indication of the legislative proposals that the government itself intended to put before the Duma. The council of ministers had not prepared a comprehensive and coherent programme of reforms, but it did recognize the need for change, especially in the peasant world. The government intended to ensure that the peasantry were granted a status equal to that of the rest of the population in law and in the courts and it also intended to take steps to remove the restrictions on private ownership of land. There would be more help for land acquisition through the Peasant Land Bank and migration to Siberia would also be encouraged. Other than this, however, there was no coherent plan for the development of the rural economy and the very brevity of Goremykin's speech made it plain that he was not prepared to elaborate on the government's plans to the Duma.[8] A number of other proposals for legislation were also listed in Goremykin's address to the Duma, encompassing educational reform and fiscal measures, as well as measures to speed up the administration of justice but they were not fitted into any overarching programme of change and there was no explanation of the government's overall aims in promoting reform.

In these circumstances, it was plain from the very beginning of the Duma's existence that the chances of government and parliament finding a mutually acceptable means of working together were very slim. The Goremykin administration had no sympathy with the idea of a parliamentary system in Russia and simply wanted to shut out the new institution from the decision-making process. The majority of Duma deputies, however, saw their task as being to establish themselves in just such a role. Conflict was inevitable. It came very quickly as the Duma responded to Goremykin's speech by putting forward legislative proposals that he had specifically rejected, and especially by continuing to call for the compulsory expropriation of privately owned land as the solution to the peasant problem.[9] Duma deputies also made full use of their right to interpellate the government by putting down questions to ministers designed to embarrass the government and demonstrate that it was not acting in accordance with the changed structures of Russia after October 1905.[10] It was clear that the First Duma was unable to perform any constructive function in Russian government: it was impossible for it to carry out what was its primary duty, that of legislating, since any Bill that would meet with the approval of the Duma would be rejected almost as a matter of course by the State Council and the tsar. The government found the Duma to be an obstacle to its work and the feeling was reciprocated. Even moderate politicians such as A. I. Guchkov, the leader of the Octobrists, believed that the aged bureaucrats who made up the government, together with the lack of any definite government programme, made conflict inevitable.[11] The two parts of the institutional structure of the empire were incapable of working together. The government did, however, hold the whip hand in this situation, for it was able to exercise the ultimate sanction of dissolving the Duma and calling new elections. This it did at the beginning of July 1906, after the First Duma had sat for little more than two months.

Dissolution was accompanied by far-reaching actions on the part of both government and Duma deputies. Goremykin took the opportunity at the end of the first stage of the Russian constitutional experiment to resign from the position of chairman of the council of ministers. He had evidently found the burden of having to deal with the Duma a heavy one and it was with obvious relief that he announced the tsar's acceptance of his resignation to the remainder of the council of ministers.[12] Simultaneously, he announced that his successor as prime minister was to be P. A. Stolypin, who was to combine this with continuing to hold the portfolio of minister of internal affairs. The reaction of the deputies to the dissolution was overwhelmingly one of anger and frustration. They were furious that the government had simply decided to do away with the Duma after such a short period and they were suspicious of the government's commitment to holding new elections within the prescribed period. However, there was very little that the deputies could do to protest against the action of the regime. The course adopted by the Kadet party was to issue a call for a campaign of civil disobedience by the population as a whole, involving the non-payment of taxes and a refusal to co-operate in the process of military conscription. This declaration, known as the Vyborg Appeal after the small Finnish town where it was made, fell flat: there was no great wave of popular sentiment displayed in support of the dissolved Duma and the summons to civil disobedience found very few takers. For the Kadet party, however, the Vyborg Appeal was a move that permanently soured its relations with the government. The regime was extremely unwilling to put much trust in a party that had issued a summons to the population to disobey the government and this was to create grave difficulties for both the government and the Kadet party in the years to come.

The advent of a new prime minister meant a major shift in the attitudes of the government. The dissolution of the First Duma gave Stolypin a breathing space in which to settle into his new job without having to deal immediately with parliamentary opposition to the government. He was able to use the eight months before the convocation of the Second Duma to become more acquainted with the St Petersburg political scene and to establish his own political style: one quite different from that of his predecessors. When it was clear that the First Duma was to be dissolved, Stolypin had begun tentative discussions with moderate politicians to discover whether there was a basis for inviting them to take ministerial portfolios in the new government.[13] During July and August 1906, with Stolypin now at the head of the government, a variety of encounters took place between Stolypin, Nicholas II and political figures who might be expected to take a positive view of the new government and who had steered clear of illegal activity. These approaches came to nothing: D. N. Shipov and G. E. Lvov would only agree to participate in the government if they could be sure that there would be substantial representation from "society" in the administration and that it would follow a defined and radical programme. Similar conditions came from Guchkov and N. N. Lvov.[14] Even though these attempts came to nothing, the attitude that Stolypin adopted towards the new Russian parliamentary system was much more positive than that of Goremykin. The new prime minister recognized that the Duma was now part of the Russian political system and, whether the government liked it or not, it was there to stay. Legislation that the government wanted to introduce would have to be piloted through the parliamentary system and the government could not afford to treat the Duma as a pariah. When he addressed the Second Duma in March 1907, Stolypin emphasized that he wanted "to find an area where we can cooperate, a language in which we can communicate".[15]

He was well aware that it would not be easy to establish a *modus vivendi* with the Duma, especially after the unhappy experience of the First Duma, and Stolypin noted that:

Many of its [the Duma's] members' main, and sometimes their only, qualification is that they were and are active enemies of the government. It is difficult to imagine that they will approve anything from that source. Personally, therefore, I have few hopes for this Duma. However, if the Duma does work then we will try and work alongside.[16]

This was a more positive attitude than Goremykin had displayed to the First Duma, but Stolypin was not prepared to go overboard in his efforts to find a way for government and Duma to work together. He strongly believed that the relationship between the two bodies was one in which the Duma was subservient and that the government still held the dominant role in the administration of the empire. Although Stolypin declared that he wanted to see co-operation between the two institutions, he was at pains to establish the limits within which the Duma should operate. The Duma, Stolypin believed, did not have the right to express "disapproval, censure or distrust" of the government, and he was at pains to indicate that "if it [the Duma] does not work, then we will dissolve it".[17] The conception that Stolypin had of the functions of the Duma was that it was a useful and indeed vital adjunct to the work of the government itself. He believed that the Duma could act as a positive force in the administration of the country by presenting the views and needs of the provinces to central government and by ensuring that proposals that the government made were in line with the actual conditions of Russia outside the capital. He emphasized the need for the Duma to work constructively and not to spend its time in what he saw as futile and destructive criticism of the government and its actions. The Duma, for Stolypin, was to be tolerated and encouraged if it behaved as a forum for constructive debate and displayed a broad sympathy for the government's objectives and policies. If, however, it acted only as a critic of the regime and showed no inclination to work with the government, Stolypin came to office quite prepared to dissolve the Duma again.

This was a genuine attempt by Stolypin to make the parliament an integral part of Russian government and the attention that he paid to the Duma is clear demonstration that he was keen to win the deputies over to his side. In sharp contrast to the brief and almost contemptuous appearance that Goremykin had made before the First Duma, Stolypin was assiduous in making his policies clear to the deputies and, indeed, to the country as a whole. Within two months of taking office and before the Second Duma met, Stolypin published a comprehensive statement of his government's intentions and policies, an action made all the more surprising since two weeks earlier the prime minister had narrowly survived a bomb attack at his summer residence that had killed 32 people and injured 20 others.[18] The government announced its intention to use the period before the Second Duma was to meet to prepare bills "which would serve as a basis for discussion in the legislative institutions", and it listed a long series of measures that were to be dealt with.[19] When the Second Duma met in March 1907, Stolypin addressed it to present the government's programme in detail. He used the occasion to set out forcefully his view of how Russia should develop and to indicate how the government was going to contribute to this through a major programme of reform. Stolypin was acutely aware of the need to persuade the Duma to support the government's projects and he stayed in the chamber to listen to the debate on his statement, going so far as to make a brief response to the views expressed and stressing the government's desire to work together with the Duma. The actions of both parties, he declared, "should lead not to mutual struggle, but to the good of our motherland".[20]

The government spent a substantial quantity of time preparing bills for introduction to the Duma during the autumn and winter of 1906–7. The council of ministers met on a total of 22 occasions between November 1906 and March 1907 solely to discuss these legislative proposals and individual ministries, especially Stolypin's own ministry of internal affairs, were kept very busy in drawing up the details of measures to be presented to the Duma. Stolypin's own dual responsibility – as prime minister and head of the most powerful and wide-ranging ministry in the government – gave the reform process an important boost. The responsibilities that the ministry of internal affairs possessed ranged from peasant affairs to religious minorities and public order matters, so that its contribution to any package of reform legislation would be of decisive importance. The preparation of bills to bring about reform was not, in most cases, a matter of starting from scratch and hurriedly drafting legislation, but rather a process of bringing to fruition the prolonged and detailed debates about reform that had taken place inside the Russian bureaucratic apparatus over the previous decades. Stolypin's major contribution to the process of change in Russia was to introduce an atmosphere into the government that positively welcomed reform: he provided the opportunity for reforming ideas to find expression in legislative proposals and he made it clear that this was the course that he wanted his government to follow. Stolypin's administration came down firmly and quickly on the side of reform, thus allowing the reform-minded bureaucrats inside the establishment full rein for their long-hoarded plans.

Elections to the Second Duma took place on the same franchise as those for the First and they produced results on much the same lines.[21] Kadet strength was however reduced, partly because those deputies who had signed the Vyborg Appeal were unable to stand for re-election as they were awaiting trial on charges of inciting the population to civil disobedience. The Second Duma met in March 1907 and, despite efforts by the government to influence the outcome of the elections to bring about a result more favourable from its point of view, its political complexion was again firmly slanted towards the left, although the Kadets did suffer a halving of their representation. Soon after his appointment as prime minister, Stolypin had rejected the option of amending the electoral law, but had instead identified steps that the government could take, such as providing scribes to assist illiterate electors, that might have some impact on the pattern of voting.[22] Despite the very much more conciliatory tone that the government adopted in its initial dealings with the Second Duma, relations between the two bodies were no better than they had been between the First Duma and the Goremykin administration. This was evident from the very beginning of the Duma's existence, when the debate that followed Stolypin's address was overwhelmingly negative in character and concentrated on attacking the government, rather than recognizing, as Stolypin had hoped, the new attitude that his government had adopted. Despite the introduction by the government of a large number of bills to bring about reform, the Second Duma showed no inclination to approve them without subjecting them to detailed and prolonged scrutiny intended to result in major amendments to bring the government's proposals into line with the Duma's wishes. Government and Duma therefore continued to be as much at loggerheads as they had been during the First Duma's existence.

As the Duma was now an integral part of the Russian legislative process, the government's plans for reform could be completely frustrated if the Duma showed itself unwilling to approve them. Although the government could and did have recourse to a system of legislating without the immediate approval of the Duma and State Council, through the use of Article 87 of the Fundamental Laws,[23] this was a method that could only be used sparingly if the government was to avoid the accusation that it was trying to operate as if the Duma did not exist. In any case, legislation enacted under this system still had to be submitted for approval by the Duma and State Council within two months of the Duma meeting again and would fall if this approval was not forthcoming. Under these circumstances, there was considerable disquiet inside the government during the spring of 1907 over the political complexion of the Duma and the prospect that the two institutions would continue to be unable to function together.[24] Stolypin himself produced a memorandum for Nicholas II setting out some of the options that the government needed to consider, including a revision of the Fundamental Laws, along with age and literacy qualifications for voters.[25] It was obvious that a second dissolution was by itself no solution, since a further set of elections would in all probability produce a Duma of similar intractability. The postponement of new elections to a Third Duma was not a feasible option, since the Fundamental Laws laid down that the decree dissolving a Duma must stipulate the dates when fresh elections were to take place and when the new session was to begin. The most effective course of action that was available to the government was to introduce a new electoral law and make changes to the franchise that would ensure that those sections of the electorate who had shown themselves prone to voting for radical deputies were given very substantially reduced representation in a new Duma.[26]

Stolypin and his government did not aim to amend the electoral law so that it would create a Duma that was completely under the sway of the government. He wanted particularly to see an increase in the representation of the Octobrist party, since this was the chief group that was interested in working within the new system to bring about reform; but he did not want to exclude more radical groups from participation in the Duma altogether. The proclamation of a new electoral law on 3 June 1907 was timed to coincide with the dissolution of the Second Duma and the new franchise gave greatly increased representation to the provincial and essentially conservative nobility, while reducing the number of seats available to the peasantry. Stolypin expected that a Duma elected on a new electoral system would be in overall moderate opposition to the government.[27] The government's main aim was achieved, as the elections for the Third Duma did produce a tripling of the number of Octobrist deputies, making them the largest single party in the Duma with 153 members. They were still a long way short of an overall majority, since they held only 35 per cent of the seats in the Duma, but this increase in Octobrist strength was matched by a growth in the representation of parties to their right. Between them, more conservative groups held almost the same number of seats as the Octobrists, while parties on the left found their representation severely reduced. The Kadets were only able to muster 54 deputies, half their strength in the Second Duma, while Trudovik representation was reduced by 90 per cent so that the party's 104 Second Duma deputies were reduced to ten in the Third Duma. When the new Duma met in November 1907, therefore, the government entertained hopes that the two bodies would be able to make constructive progress to implement reform.

## Pacifying the empire

Reform was not the only component of the government's policy during 1906 and 1907. Terrorist activity and disturbances were still affecting Russia and the government was intent on putting a stop to them. The pacification of the country therefore formed a vital part of the regime's programme and Stolypin's occupancy of the ministry of internal affairs placed him in a position from which he was able to direct the policy with vigour. Stolypin was directly responsible for the policing of the empire and thus received reports showing that the level of unrest across the country demonstrated little sign of abating during 1906. There were 2,600 recorded disturbances during the year, and over one million industrial workers took part in strikes. There were uprisings at the naval bases of Sveaborg and Kronstadt in July 1906 and a total of 1,126 people died as a result of violence during the year, 288 of whom were employees of the ministry of internal affairs.[28] The council of ministers noted, in August 1906, that terrorist acts were directed at peaceable sections of the population, as well as at the government itself and that this was having an alarming effect on the population, while the workings of government were also being disrupted.[29] Stolypin was determined to face the problem of terrorism on a national scale as resolutely as he had done while a provincial governor, and he was fully supported by Nicholas II. The tsar made a specific request that the government take the most effective anti-terrorist measures,[30] and his prime minister emphasized his commitment to stamping out terrorism by declaring that he saw the survival of the state as being at stake in the struggle with violence. Stolypin was prepared to take extreme action to deal with the problem, and he declared in March 1907 that "the state had as its duty, when it was in danger, to make the most severe, the most exceptional laws to protect itself from disintegration".[31]

The most controversial component of the government's policy to deal with rebellion was the use of field courts-martial to deal with offences committed by civilians. These courts were to be responsible for hearing cases where the commission of a crime by a suspect "is so obvious that there is no point in further investigation, for example where the criminal is caught red-handed at the scene of the crime".[32] Judges in the courts-martial were to be officers from local garrisons and cases were to be transferred to them within 24 hours of an offence taking place. The trial was then to take place within a further 48 hours; there was to be no need for a formal prosecution or defence and there would be no appeal against the sentence. The whole procedure would take place behind closed doors and the sentence was to be carried out within 24 hours of the court reaching its verdict. These courts came into operation in August 1906 and existed until April 1907 when the law implementing them lapsed, as it had not been introduced into the Duma within the requisite period for legislation passed through the extraordinary procedure of Article 87 of the Fundamental Laws. During the eight months they functioned, the courts-martial sentenced 1,102 people to death. Most of these sentences were imposed during the first six months of their existence, since the government urged the courts to curtail their work once the Second Duma met in late February 1907.[33]

The second part of the government's policy of "pacification" was to make considerable use of the extraordinary powers that it possessed through the law of August 1881.[34] This allowed the government to declare an area to be in a state of "strengthened protection" (*usilennaia okhrana*), or, if it considered the situation to be more serious, "exceptional protection" (*chrezvychainaia okhrana*). These gave the local administrative authorities very substantially increased powers to make regulations and impose penalties on those who broke them. Any matter that affected state security or public order – and these terms were left loosely defined – could be the subject of such regulations; fines and terms of imprisonment could be imposed on those who disobeyed them. Individuals who were deemed to have offended could be excluded from any part of the empire, or could suffer the harsher penalty of internal exile to Siberia or other inhospitable regions of the empire. More than 7,500 people suffered this harsher punishment during 1906. The 1881 legislation, originally intended to be temporary, had been periodically extended so that by 1905 it had become a permanent feature of the empire's administrative structures. If the situation in a region became especially disturbed, the government had at its disposal the third option of applying the full weight of martial law: this path was chosen for a large number of areas during 1905 and was not lifted from the Baltic provinces, Poland, the Caucasus and two provinces of southern Russia until 1908. Throughout Stolypin's premiership, the overwhelming majority of the population of the empire lived under some form of extraordinary legislation; it has been calculated that in 1912 only five million out of a total population of 154 million lived in areas that were completely free of any such laws. Sixty-three million lived under "strengthened protection" and 86 million under "exceptional protection".[35]

Alongside taking measures to deal directly with outbreaks of revolt, the government also took steps to restrict anti-government propaganda, which it believed helped to fuel discontent. Newspaper editors were fined for publishing articles that were critical of the government and many papers were closed completely, reaching a peak in 1908, when 73 were ordered to cease publication. The number of books that were prohibited by the censorship also grew substantially: between 1872 and 1904, 172 works had been banned; for 1905–6 there were a total of 46; but between 1907 and 1910, 1,236 were prohibited. These attempts to reduce the flow of information had very limited success, since the quantity of items published in Russia during this period grew enormously and the censorship proved incapable of making comprehensive checks on the flow of books and periodicals that attacked or ridiculed the government.[36]

Stolyin was also concerned to strengthen the position of the government by removing from government service all those whom he saw as unsympathetic to his policies. A circular sent to all provincial governors in late 1906 stated that:

> Officials in government service are prohibited from taking part in political parties, association or unions. This includes not only those that are openly revolutionary, but also those whose programmes or leaders' declarations (for example, the Vyborg Manifesto) or other activities demonstrate that they have as their aim struggle with the government, or else to incite the population to such a struggle.[37]

The main target of this campaign was members of the Kadet party. Between December 1905 and April 1907 the ministry of internal affairs suggested the removal of 248 civil servants because they belonged to the Kadets, while the ministry of education attempted to dismiss university professors who would not give an assurance that they would not belong to an "anti-state" party.

The government's attempts to quell revolts resulted in more than 26,000 people being executed, exiled or imprisoned for political offences between 1907 and 1909, but terrorism still continued at a significant level. More than 2,500 people were killed or wounded as a result of revolutionary activity during 1907, with a further 1,000 suffering in the following year.[38] The government did, however, experience some difficulty in implementing as vigorous a policy of "pacification" as it would have liked. The Duma was implacably opposed to the use of field courts-martial and the government was unable to use them as a permanent part of its policy, while proposals by the ministry of internal affairs to incorporate the 1881 temporary extraordinary legislation permanently into the empire's legal structure were never introduced into the Duma because of the anticipated reaction.[39] Furthermore, the regime faced difficulties in imposing its policy of "pacification" across the entire empire. Particularly problematic was Finland. The Finnish authorities in Helsinki had substantial autonomy in their policing policy and were unwilling to fully assist the imperial government in St Petersburg in pursuing suspected terrorists. The precise constitutional position of Finland was a matter of dispute between the imperial government and the Finnish authorities; the Helsinki administration tried to jealously guard its privileges and was not prepared to see the St Petersburg regime interfere in what it believed were local matters. This attitude made Finland an attractive base for those who wished to disrupt the workings of the imperial capital: the Finnish border was only some 20 miles from St Petersburg and the Finnish administration was in little mood to help the Russians catch people who had committed terrorist acts against a government that it disliked.

The regime therefore faced severe difficulties in trying to implement an effective policy to deal with the aftermath of the 1905 revolution, and these were exacerbated by Stolypin's refusal to allow the "pacification" component of his policy to dictate the shape of the government's activity as a whole. The policy of "pacification" was important if the government was going to be able to implement reforms since Stolypin believed that the two parts of his overall strategy were inextricably linked. Reform would only be possible if Russia was calm and order had been restored, while it would be pointless to embark on a policy of repression alone since this would only deal with the symptoms of discontent and leave the real causes untouched. In a circular sent to provincial governors in July 1906 Stolypin gave expression to the link that he saw as existing between the restoration of law and order and the reforms that he wanted to introduce:

> The struggle is being carried on not against society, but against society's enemies. Therefore indiscriminate repres-

sion cannot be approved. The government firmly intends to enable old and unsatisfactory laws to be repealed or amended in a legal manner. The old order will be renewed.[40]

## The foundations of reform

Stolypin believed that repressive measures should only be used so that the government could get on with its real task – the introduction of reforms. He did not believe that the disturbances that had swept Russia during 1905 and 1906 had been engineered by some revolutionary group, but rather he appreciated that the uprisings had tapped a rich vein of popular discontent. The considerable experience that Stolypin had accumulated as a provincial administrator and landowner who had spent most of his life living on his country estates was valuable in showing him that it was not mindless anarchy that prompted people to revolt against the government. In his 1904 report as governor of Saratov, Stolypin noted that the events of the year "gave sad proof of a basic deficiency in peasant life"[41] and he believed strongly that Russia could only be restored to peace if the causes of popular discontent were addressed. The balance between repression and reform was a delicate one, since too severe a policy of repression would mean that the government had no resources to devote to reform, while complete concentration on reform would be impossible in a country torn by internal strife.

Stolypin and his government put forward a comprehensive programme of reform to "renew" Russia, designed to build upon existing structures, rather than to destroy them. The most fundamental assumption that determined the government's strategy was that tsarism must be preserved and strengthened. Reform was not a means of surreptitiously bringing about a change in the political system or of extending the constitutional changes that had been made during 1905 to reduce or even extinguish the authority of the tsar. Stolypin was convinced that only the tsarist regime could successfully see through a programme of reforms in Russia, and he believed that the tsar's authority was still paramount in the empire. Although Stolypin recognized that the new legislative institutions had an important role to play in the government of the empire, he felt that the tsar had special responsibilities that overrode all other considerations. The tsar still possessed the right to make laws in extreme circumstances, and in this he was answerable only to God. Stolypin did not believe that this power should be used to enact any law that the Duma rejected, but that when the Russian state was in danger, it was the tsar's duty to take action to save it. The June 1907 amendment to the Duma electoral law was technically illegal, since it had not been approved by the new legislative bodies, but the government justified its action by declaring that "only that power which gave the first electoral law, the historic power of the Russian tsar, is able to repeal or change it".[42]

Reform was to be a means to enhance the authority that the monarch and his government possessed, and to ensure that the survival of the tsarist regime would never again be threatened by events like those of 1905. This was a fundamental difference between the aims of the government and the aspirations of many political parties. For the Kadets, reform was a step on the road towards the introduction of full parliamentary democracy in Russia and they saw the reform process as being a way to weaken the existing regime and bring about further fundamental reforms of the Russian political structure. Stolypin, however, had no intention of implementing measures that could lead to a diminution of the tsar's powers, for this would produce the same effect as the disturbances of 1905. The reforms that the government proposed were intended to provide a new bulwark of support for the tsarist regime and to give it new strength to overcome revolt.

Reform was not just to be a palliative designed to cope only with the symptoms of discontent. Stolypin wanted to get to grips with the real causes of the widespread problems, which had reached their most vigorous expression during 1905. He was intent on making structural changes to Russian society so that the population would see no further reason to rebel against the government. The tsarist government intended to utilize more radical measures than it had traditionally employed to buttress a conservative regime; instead of using repression to ensure the survival of tsarism through force, the government now intended to use reform to produce a society that would support and acquiesce in the existence of the regime. This was a major change in the way in which the Russian government tried to keep itself in power: the state was now prepared to accept the value of seeking popular support for the tsarist regime from its subjects; the consent of the population was worth acquiring as a sensible method of keeping Russian society united and providing it with common objectives. While Stolypin's government had no intention of further altering the structure of tsarism, it did aim at changing the basis on which it existed. Stolypin believed that Russia could only survive under the tsarist system, but at the same time the population had to be reconciled to the regime by being persuaded that it did act for the benefit of the people whom it governed.

The second main motivating force for reform was Stolypin's conviction that this was the only way by which a recurrence of the discontent of 1905 could be avoided. It was clear that the regime's coercive powers had only just been adequate to cope with the urban and rural revolts of 1905, and that tsarism could not hope to survive if it could only meet further outbreaks of discontent with repression. For Stolypin, repression only dealt with the symptoms of discontent and did nothing to address the real causes of the problems that were afflicting Russia. He was especially keen to ensure that proper attention was paid to the difficulties that affected the peasantry and to try to ameliorate their living conditions so that they would no longer have any incentive to rebel against the government. "Renewal must begin at the bottom",[43] Stolypin believed, and he aimed at ensuring that the basis of Russian society was such that the peasantry, the vast majority of the population, would have no incentive to rebel.

In 1905 the Russian peasantry had shown that they were ready to revolt, to burn landowners' homes and crops at the slightest opportunity. Stolypin understood that gaining the support of the peasantry was the key to preventing unrest and he aimed at creating a class of independent peasant landowners who would have no reason to attack the government. This was to be achieved through fundamental agrarian reform, but the political and social structures of the Russian Empire were also to be altered to allow the peasantry to take a much greater part in the life of Russian society. By giving the peasant population of the Russian Empire a much greater stake than ever before in the organization of the state, Stolypin's government hoped to create a new bond between the regime and society as a whole. This would help to counter the polarization between the tsarist structures of authority and the mass of the population,which had been so clearly demonstrated during 1905, and would establish a new basis of community of interest between government and governed in Russia.

Reform was not, however, intended to reconstruct Russia on the same principles that existed in her neighbours and competitors in western Europe. Stolypin was at pains to emphasize that change in Russia had to be built on Russian national traditions and history, and he was not prepared to let the necessity for reform become an excuse for Western ideas to infiltrate a part of the fabric of Russian society. He declared that there must be no attempt "to attach a foreign flower to Russian roots" and spoke of:

> Words which express feelings that over the centuries have made the hearts of Russians beat stronger . . . These words are an unbending devotion to the historical foundations of Russia, as opposed to rootless socialism. This desire, this passionate desire to rebuild, enlighten and extol our motherland . . . is in the end a devotion not to life, but a devotion to die for the Tsar, the personification of Russia.[44]

This desire to make reform in ways that would use the traditions of Russia was complemented by Stolypin's reluctance to allow foreign influences to impinge on Russian institutions. In making proposals for religious reform, Stolypin was always prepared to defend the right of the Orthodox Church to be considered as the predominant (*gospodstvuiushchii*) religious institution in the country and there was no question of allowing alien religions to enjoy the full range of privileges that the Orthodox Church did.[45] He was also keen that the interests of Russia and the Russian people should not be subordinated to those of any of the various national minorities that were part of the Russian Empire. Poland and Finland suffered particularly from this attitude,[46] and Stolypin was keen to promote Russian influences in both these areas. In November 1907, replying to a Polish representative in the Duma who had called for local forces to be attracted to participate in local self-government, Stolypin declared that the government could only rely on "a national force" in the *zemstva*. Lest there be any doubt as to which nationality he was referring to, Stolypin followed this by stating that full rights could only be obtained by inhabitants of the empire if they were prepared to call themselves Russian citizens. He declared that,"The highest good is to be a Russian citizen, hold this title with the respect that Roman citizens once held theirs and then you can call yourselves citizens of the first rank."[47]

Stolypin's government did intend to bring about reform, however, and the prime minister was aware that its implementation needed to be handled sensitively. The constitutional changes of 1905 had set Russia on a new path, and this had been emphasized by the commitments to change that had been made by the government in the manifestos of December 1904 and October 1905. These commitments had hardly begun to be implemented by the time Stolypin came to power and he saw himself as presiding over the government of a country that was in a state of transition. His task was to manage this transition to a "new order" successfully and to bring the remainder of Russian society into line with the principles that had been laid down at its head. Stolypin stressed in January 1907 that,"The peculiarities of the present situation mean that there is an acute and urgent necessity to bring the existing order of local administration into line with the new principles and aims which lie at the heart of the recent radical changes."[48]

One of the most difficult and important tasks that the government faced was to ensure that local institutions and officials were aware of the new attitudes that prevailed in St Petersburg and the new legal and constitutional framework within which the regime had to operate. Once the tsar himself had been constrained by laws and institutions that he could not easily override, so his representatives and subordinates throughout the empire were bound to operate within the same set of constraints. The entire apparatus of the Russian government now had to operate within the law and Stolypin was determined to create a state based on law (*pravovoi*) to avoid discrepancies in its interpretation in the various parts of the empire. He noted that "legal norms must be based on precise and clearly expressed law", in order to prevent "arbitrary interpretation of the new by officials and others"[49] and conflict between the old order and the new. Stolypin's conception of law did, however, have its limits. In the spring of 1906, he had specifically rejected the amendment of the electoral law as a means of obtaining a Duma whose composition was more satisfactory to the government, writing that "this, however, [would] require the consent of the Duma and State Council and cannot be done through temporary legislation passed in the period between sessions of these institutions".[50] The enactment of the electoral law of 3 June 1907 represented a complete volte-face for the prime minister, and he defended it by referring to "the right of the sovereign to save the state with which God had entrusted him".[51] There were still occasions on which the state could act outside the law.

Putting an end to arbitrary government demanded not only that the administrative organs of the state operate within a clearly defined set of laws, but also that each individual citizen of the Russian Empire be made aware of his legal position within the state. Stolypin told the Duma in March 1907 that, "While written law does not define the duties and protect the rights of each Russian subject, these rights and duties will depend upon the interpretations put upon them by, and the whims of individuals; that is, they will not be firmly established."[52] Stolypin believed that it was only when the written freedom that he intended to provide through his reforms was transformed into real freedom, understood and appreciated by those people who still lived under a severely limited set of civil rights, that feelings of civic responsibility (*gosudarstvennost'*) and patriotism would be possible for the mass of the population – the peasantry – on whom Stolypin was basing his hopes for the future of Russia.[53]

### Russia transformed

Agrarian change lay at the heart of Stolypin's ideas for a new Russia. Peasant reform had been on the agenda of the Russian government for much of the preceding decade. During Witte's period of office as minister of finance, there had been especially thorough investigations into the condition of the rural population. It was recognized both inside and outside the government that the agrarian structure of the country needed fundamental reshaping. The emancipation of 1861 had not resulted in any great increase in prosperity for the rural population and the growth of the urban population made increased agricultural productivity vital if the workers in the cities were to be fed. The policy of rapid industrialization pursued during the 1890s, together with the agricultural depression in the early part of the decade, did little to improve the situation. Russian agriculture continued to exist on an archaic basis: farming was still largely practised on the strip system while modern machinery and techniques had hardly penetrated the Russian countryside. While the emancipation had freed the serfs from the bondage of their masters, the communal system of agricultural organization continued to dominate the Russian countryside. The commune was perceived by large sections of Russian society as exerting a negative influence on agriculture by restricting individual enterprise, and by 1905 it was the commune that was the focus of proposals for reform. Committees had met both centrally and at the provincial level in 1902 and 1903, and during 1904 Witte expressed the view that the system of communal strip farming should be replaced by one of individual landholding.[54] Committees continued to meet during 1904 and 1905 inside the government to discuss the details of the changes, with V. I. Gurko, head of the land department in the ministry of internal affairs, taking a leading role in the formulation of the reform.[55] The system of collective communal responsibility (krugovaia poruka) for the payment of taxes and redemption dues had been abolished in 1903 and this was followed, in 1905, by the halving of redemption payments from the beginning of 1906 and their complete abolition from January 1907.[56] New officials took up positions in the departments dealing with peasant affairs; especially significant was the appointment of A. V. Krivoshein as acting head of the department of agriculture at the beginning of 1906. A final commission met during the first part of the year and its proposals became the centrepiece of the legislation of 9 November 1906 that was to bear the name of the "Stolypin" land reform.

The agrarian reform was based on two main aims: a desire to improve the economic situation of the peasantry and a belief that the rural population was the key to future political stability. These goals were to be achieved by allowing the peasant a far greater degree of individual freedom than was possible under the commune. A two-stage process was envisaged for the breakup of the communal system: first, individual peasants inside the commune could ask for their pieces of land to be separated from the commune and become their own private property; secondly, they would be able to consolidate all their strips of land into a single plot. The government envisaged that this would lead to substantially increased agricultural production as the removal of communal constraints would provide a much greater incentive for the individual peasant to maximize the output of his own land. The agrarian reform had clearly defined aims, but the means adopted to achieve them were untested and represented a huge gamble by the tsarist regime. Stolypin was aware that his policy was one of high risk: the removal of the "safety-net" of the commune from the peasantry could mean that many would be unable to cope, but the prime minister emphasized that his policy was a "wager on the strong". He expressed faith in the Russian peasant, whom he described as "the able, work-loving peasant, the salt of the Russian earth".[57]

The political element of the Stolypin agrarian reform also carried risks for the government. The regime aimed to put an end to the rural discontent that had beset Russia by creating a class of small, independent landowners who would have no cause to rebel against established authority. Stolypin and his advisers believed that once individual peasants were the owners of their own land, freed of the restrictions placed upon them by the communal system of agriculture, the fundamental demand for land that had been made by the peasantry for generations would have been satisfied. The government envisaged that this transformation in the property status of the peasants would bring about a shift in their political outlook. This was based on the view that peasant revolt had been caused by the poor economic condition of the rural population and their inability to take any positive action themselves to rectify this situation. Radicalism was not, therefore, an inherent characteristic of the peasantry and the government believed that the situation could be transformed by an improvement in the living conditions of the rural population. A class of small independent landowners would provide a conservative base of support for the government in the countryside, since the peasants would jealously preserve their newly acquired land and would support a regime that promised to maintain their new status. The acquisition of land by the peasantry was, therefore, intended to engineer a fundamental shift in the political structure of Russia and to guarantee the survival of the tsarist regime.

This agrarian reform was also intended to provide greater stability for the government in the cities. The close links that existed between the rural population and the new working class in the towns meant that improved conditions in the countryside should work to reduce discontent in the growing urban centres of the empire. Greater prosperity for the Russian peasant would ease the pressure on urban workers to support their families back in the villages. Furthermore, the development of individual enterprise in the agrarian sector and the increased agricultural production that was intended to ensue, should serve to stimulate the flow of affordable food into the cities and thereby relieve some of the shortages that had helped bring about unrest.

The peasantry made up the overwhelming bulk of the population of the empire and had to be the pivot on which the future prosperity of Russia would turn. It was, therefore, important that the legislation to carry out the agrarian reform was enacted as quickly as possible. This was also crucial because agrarian reform was to form the basis for the whole series of other changes that Stolypin intended to implement. Without reform to the economic and social structure of rural Russia, none of the plans that the regime had for its political or social regeneration could bear fruit. The government was well aware that its plans for reform in the countryside were very different from the views of the majority of Duma deputies and that, if it introduced its legislation directly into the Duma, it would be subject to much discussion and consequent delay. The council of ministers therefore debated the advisability of enacting the agrarian reform under Article 87 of the Fundamental Laws that gave the opportunity for legislation to be enacted while the Duma was in recess, as long as it was subsequently introduced into the Duma within two months of the Duma next convening. Although some ministers, especially Kokovtsov, the minister of finance, expressed reservations about the idea of using an emergency provision for this major piece of ordinary legislation, the majority of the council took the view that the need for change in the countryside was so urgent that the government would be shirking its responsibilities if it did not act immediately to try to improve the condition of the peasantry.[58] The agrarian reform was therefore issued as an imperial edict on 9 November 1906.[59]

This was intended to be the foundation for a series of further reforms designed to give the Russian peasantry a social and political status commensurate with their new economic position. The first area to which the government turned its attention was that of local administration, where the situation was as archaic as that of Russian agriculture. The system of local administration that existed at the beginning of the twentieth century had two major defects: it lacked a clear and coherent structure, since the institutions of local government had been built up piecemeal over a long period; and the peasantry were almost completely excluded from the main body of the system. The task that Stolypin's government therefore set itself was to remedy these defects.

The heart of the apparatus of local government was the province (*guberniia*). European Russia had been divided up into provinces under Catherine II and these eighteenth-century divisions had remained intact, despite substantial shifts in the distribution of population inside the empire. At the head of each province – some 50 in European Russia – stood the governor as the main agent of central government; but his loyalties were divided. On one hand, he was the "representative of supreme government power",[60] in other words the tsar's representative, but on the other the governor was the chief agent of the ministry of internal affairs in the province. This situation led to various inconsistencies and difficulties: in his position representing the tsar, the governor had the right to inspect all government institutions in his province, irrespective of the ministry to which they were subordinate, as well as the duty to supervise the work of local self-government. However, his second role as a representative of the ministry of internal affairs meant that other government departments tended to see the governor as attempting to assert the primacy of his own ministry over others. This created resentment and mistrust of the motives of the governor and lessened his effectiveness as an administrator. The governor's workload also contributed to his poor showing as a government official. He was directly responsible for all aspects of the work of the interior ministry in his province, including the police, as well as being chairman of a wide range of provincial committees dealing with matters as varied as military service and statistics. It has been estimated that the gubernatorial chancellery would deal with an average of 100,000 papers annually, with the governor himself seeing some 300–400 daily,[61] and a senior civil servant wrote that, "The Russian governor could be the busiest man in the world, if the quantity of work he performed was measured by the number of official papers which passed through his hands."[62]

While each province was headed by an appointed official responsible to the central government, there was no equivalent figure in the second layer of Russian local government – the district (uezd). Although the population of the average district was approaching 200,000 by the beginning of the twentieth century, there was no unified system of administration for the area and no single individual to co-ordinate the work of the different bodies involved in the governing of the district. District administration revolved around the marshal of the nobility, an official elected by the district assembly of nobility to act as its chairman. The government had progressively imposed more and more administrative tasks upon him, since it was unwilling to establish new institutions, and found the marshal of the nobility a convenient peg on which to hang a very wide range of responsibilities. The marshal played a prominent part in local life. His position meant that he did not need to be paid by the government and, with a shortage of qualified officials, he could be relied upon to bring "a sense of legality and general culture to the administration".[63] By the beginning of the twentieth century, apart from his duties concerned purely with the nobility, the marshal acted as chairman of 11 local bodies and was an ordinary member of 13 more.[64] The marshal had no administrative apparatus with which he could co-ordinate the work of the various agencies in the district and, thus, the only unity in the work of the government at this level was purely personal, dependent on the quality and enthusiasm of the marshal himself. When Stolypin himself was appointed as district marshal of the nobility in Kovno in 1889, he discovered that his predecessor had played "a purely decorative role".[65] As the population of the empire grew and the marshal's administrative responsibilities became ever more onerous, so the number of nobles willing to take on the job declined and with it the quality of district administration.

At a lower level, the government did possess an official who was appointed by and responsible to the provincial governor. This was the land captain (*zemskii nachal'nik*) who, since 1889, had been the main official with responsibility for the peasantry. Each land captain was responsible for a small number of rural areas (*volost'*) and was subordinate to the governor through the district conference of land captains and the provincial board on peasant affairs. Although both a property and educational qualification existed for candidates for appointment as land captains, the educational qualification could be dispensed with if there was a shortage of suitable people, and this helped to accentuate a trend towards the appointment of local gentry who were motivated by the salary offered, rather than by the service tradition of the Russian nobility.[66] The powers of the land captain included judicial authority over the peasantry and police functions in areas where there were no other police officials, together with the supervision of the institutions of peasant self-government in his area. The land captains aroused very great antagonism among the peasantry under their control. It was well-nigh impossible for a peasant to obtain any redress against a land captain who appeared to have exceeded his authority, and the land captains became renowned for the arbitrary way in which they exercised their authority.[67]

Much of the land captain's time was spent in supervising the work of peasant self-government. This existed at both village level and in the rural area. Each village elder dealt with the collection of taxes from his village, could try the most minor judicial offences and acted as a link between the peasantry and the institutions of government. The rural area was a much more significant organization: it had been set up under the terms of the 1861 emancipation edict and had then been intended to contain not more than 2,000 male peasants, but by 1900 it had exceeded this limit in many cases, although the territorial area remained constant with a diameter of about 25 miles. The government of the rural area was made up of the peasant meeting (*skhod*), which consisted of one representative for every ten households, and the area elder, elected by the meeting. He was responsible for the maintenance of law and order and for implementing the decisions of the meeting that had particular responsibility for education and the dispensing of charity. It was difficult to get good candidates to stand for election as area elder. Mackenzie Wallace, a British journalist with wide experience of Russia, noted that, "The more laborious and well-to-do peasants, unless they wish to abuse their position directly or indirectly for their own advantage, try to escape election as office bearers, and leave the administration in the hands of the less respectable members."[68] This resulted in widespread inefficiency and corruption among peasant officials and it was not unknown for areas to have to pay their taxes twice over, as the elder had lost the proceeds of the first collection through speculation. The growth in the population of the rural area had brought a corresponding growth in the size of the area meeting and in many cases it had become an unwieldy body whose size hindered decision-making and discussion. The rural area was essentially an artificial institution, set up by the government as a convenient way of controlling the peasantry, cut off from the remainder of the population administratively and judicially. The majority of the Russian population lived under the control of two officials, the land captain and the local policeman, and had no satisfactory method of redress against actions by these officials.

At a higher level, local self-government existed in the form of the *zemstvo* in the district and the province. Established in 1864, they had been intended to take responsibility for local matters such as health, education and the maintenance of roads and bridges in their area. The *zemstvo* electoral law had been amended in 1890 to reinforce noble dominance of the institutions, so that nobles held over 40 per cent of the seats in the district *zemstva* and over 70 per cent of the seats in the provincial body. Although the elected members of the *zemstva* were overwhelmingly nobles, they had to employ a significant number of professional people to execute their practical responsibilities: doctors, engineers and teachers were especially important. This "third element" of local government – the other two were the elected *zemstvo* members and appointed government officials – tended to act as a counterweight to the more conservative nobles. The activities of this "third element" were an important source of friction between the government and the *zemstvo* for they were seen by the central authorities as inciting opposition to government. The whole relationship between the government and the *zemstvo* was an uneasy one. There was no clear definition of the role that the *zemstva* were to play in the administration of Russia, and the two bodies often found themselves at odds the government unable to impose its authority over the *zemstva*. As Hosking writes, "They [the *zemstva*] did indeed hang rather in mid-air, lacking either a floor or a ceiling."[69]

The problems that Russian local government presented were clear to all. It was unco-ordinated and lacked any consistent structure; government, estate and self-governing bodies all played a part, but without any proper ties between them. There was no coherent framework to local administration and the only connections between the various sets of institutions were provided by the personal links of individual officials. Furthermore, the whole apparatus provided very few means by which checks could be operated on the activities of local government. Corruption and arbitrary administration were rife. The most obvious deficiency from the Stolypin government's point of view, however, was that the peasant population of the empire was isolated from the main sets of local institutions: this situation was out of line with the government's intentions of making the peasants full members of Russian society. Wholesale reform was therefore needed.

This was not a perception that had suddenly arisen in the Russian government. A series of commissions had met under successive tsars during the second half of the nineteenth century to discuss proposals for changes to the entire structure of local government, but none of their recommendations had ever been implemented.[70] Stolypin's ideas for local government reform were based very much upon these earlier deliberations; soon after his appointment as prime minister he assembled a high-level committee to review previous proposals and to put forward new ideas to reform the structure of local government.[71] The committee's conclusions, submitted to the council of ministers in December 1906 and January 1907, were based on three central aims: the creation

of a unified system of local government, to include the elected
*zemstva*; a reduction in the role that "estate" institutions played
in local administration; and finally the establishment of an effective system of supervision over the entire apparatus. Stolypin
intended to establish a coherent system of institutions at each tier
of local government in order to ease the work of co-ordinating
the different branches of government outside St Petersburg. This
would also allow each tier of local government to be linked
firmly to those above and below it, enabling matters to be dealt
with rapidly by the correct institution. Particularly important
from the government's point of view was the integration of the
*zemstva* into the system, since it was "the absence of unity which
. . . served as one of the main obstacles to the ordering of relations between central government and the *zemstva*".[72] Stolypin
wanted to construct more formal links between *zemstva* and government, but he also wanted to bring the *zemstva* into more frequent informal contact with central government and to provide
easily available information about the effect of government policy
on local matters.[73] Stolypin's structural changes to the system of
local government were intended to unify local government both
"horizontally" and "vertically", to make each layer of the system
cohesive in itself, and then to enable the various layers to act
together as a whole.

Institutional reform was only one part of Stolypin's plans for
governing the Russian provinces. He recognized that there was a
pressing need to make changes to the ethos of local administration to bring it into line with "the basis of the great reconstruction – the principle of civil equality",[74] which had been
established through the 1905 reforms. This meant that the estate
basis of much of local government had to be changed, especially
in the case of the peasant institutions that should be abolished
and "local life be renewed with an administrative system in
which the different interests of the local population find complete
and uniform reflection and action, free from estate differences".[75]
The integration of the peasantry into the overall system of local
government was the most significant part of Stolypin's plan to
reduce its "estate" element, but the government also wanted to
replace some of the officials who held administrative office by
virtue of their position in the hierarchy of noble institutions with

people responsible first to the government. The rationale for this was straightforward: the government had come to appreciate that noble officials were unable to carry out effectively the range of duties assigned to them, and at the same time the regime had no means of imposing sanctions on those noble officials who did not fulfil their responsibilities.[76] The government still wanted to retain the services of the gentry in local government but so that they held office, not by virtue of their noble status, but because the government had appointed them to a specific post. It was not only the peasantry who suffered from noble domination of local administration: there was also a need to provide better representation in the *zemstva* for people who paid large amounts of taxation, but did not own substantial quantities of land: in particular, urban merchants and industrialists.

The structure that Stolypin's government proposed for local administration centred on the governor. He was to have the right to supervise the work of all administrative institutions in the province, and would be supported by a provincial council that would include administrative officials as well as representatives of the *zemstva* and gentry. Specialist subcommittees would meet to deal with specific areas of policy. This arrangement would free the governor himself from much routine business and enable him to concentrate on major items of policy and to use his powers of inspection more widely.[77] For the first time, it was proposed that district administration should be structured cohesively: a centrally appointed official would chair a council that was to include both government appointees and *zemstvo* representatives. This official would have more limited powers than the governor; he would have direct control only over institutions subordinate to the ministry of internal affairs and would be without any power of supervision over agencies of other ministries in the district. When Stolypin's bill was debated by the council of ministers, the majority of ministers argued that Stolypin's proposals reduced the importance of the marshal of the nobility too severely and that, "Any belittling of the significance of the marshal of the nobility would be an expression of distrust in the noble estate, not justified by the actual conduct of the gentry."[78]

The council therefore decided that the marshal of the nobility should have first claim on the post of head of district administration. At lower levels, Stolypin proposed the replacement of the land captains by *uchastok* supervisors, officials who were to become the government's closest contacts with the peasantry.[79] He retained the rural area as the centrepiece of local government at the lowest level, but it was to be reformed to become an administrative unit that would have jurisdiction over all the inhabitants of its area, rather than just the peasantry, and it would combine local administration with tasks laid upon it by central government. This would involve the creation of a *zemstvo* at this level, but with less independence than the district and provincial *zemstva*, since the level of taxation that it could impose would be set by the district *zemstvo*.

The existing *zemstva* were also to undergo reform. The government proposed that the areas of jurisdiction of central and local government be more closely defined, while the creation of provincial and district councils would allow *zemstvo* members to play a wider part in local affairs. This process would also be assisted by the revitalization of the council for the local economy (*Sovet po delam mestnogo khoziaistva*), which would act as a forum for the discussion of legislation that had particular local implications before its introduction into the Duma.[80] Although there was internal government debate about the precise extent of the supervisory authority that the government should be able to exercise over the *zemstva*, the government's final proposals allowed the central authorities wide latitude in the control that they could exert.[81] Reform of local government was a vital part of the government's overall objectives of recognizing the social and political consequences of its plans to create a new class of independent small landowners. Reform was intended to provide an opportunity for all sections of Russian society to play some part in the work of local administration, and thus to reduce the dominant position that the nobility held in the local government system. Stolypin's administration wanted to open up local government to a wider range of talents, but it also wanted to ensure that both central and local authorities worked according to the same ethos and pursued the same aims. A greater degree of co-ordination between St Petersburg and the provinces was, therefore, vital and this needed to include provision for central control should the government wish to implement it.

The structure of local government, and the isolation of the peasantry, was echoed in the legal system of the Russian Empire. This too was a target for reform for Stolypin. In the countryside, where the majority of offences occurred and were tried, two sets of courts existed at the beginning of the twentieth century: one exclusively for the peasantry and one for the remainder of the population. Peasant courts had been established in the Emancipation Act of 1861 to deal with the most minor offences, and their judges were elected annually by the *volost'* meeting.[82] In 1889 their structure had been modified as part of Alexander III's attempts to reduce the impact of the reforms of the 1860s, and the newly created land captains were to appoint one-third of the court's judges, while peasant judicial isolation was increased by widening the court's competence to include less minor offences.

Stolypin's government believed that it was important to integrate the two different strands of the judicial system. The peasantry had to be treated on the same basis as the rest of the population in judicial matters, since they were to be regarded as equal to the remainder of the population in other areas. Furthermore, equality before the law for all citizens of the Russian Empire was seen as a vital component of the state based on law (*pravovoi*) that Stolypin wanted to create. This would ensure equal treatment for all the members of the empire and would help to break down the differences that divided them. There had been a number of reviews of local legal arrangements around the turn of the century; recommendations had been made for the reinstatement of JPs, as well as for the abolition of the separate peasant court.[83] The edict of 12 December 1904 had made a specific commitment to the principle of equality before the law for all and the ministry of justice had been instructed in May 1905 to prepare a bill to implement this. The bill that I. G. Shcheglovitov, the minister of justice, presented to the council of ministers at the beginning of 1907 took as its basic premise that "the chaos which reigns in rural life urgently demands the creation of an independent local court, closely linked to the local population".[84] The different statutes that concerned local justice meant that there was a lack of uniformity in its general principles and, while it was inevitable that there would be regional variations in a country the size of Russia, in some places these were so pronounced as to make the courts lose much of their intended simplicity and clarity. Judges were often unsuited to the tasks that they had to perform: in the peasant courts they were often illiterate, and the burden of work and the low pay meant that it was difficult to attract the best peasants to take on the work. The land captains usually had no legal qualifications and the Ministry of Justice was scathing about nobles' reasons for taking the job, seeing them as motivated, "either by the hope of receiving a large salary or else because they wanted to live close to their estates, which they feel could be administered more conveniently by using the prestige of their power and local authority".

The government's proposal for a local court was based on the principles of "jurisdiction over all classes, equality for all before the law, independence of judges from the administration and unity of legal organisation".[85] The peasant court was to be abolished, as were the legal functions of the land captains, and a single judicial institution would have jurisdiction over all sections of the population. The judges for the new court would be elected by the district *zemstvo* and the court would have jurisdiction over an area no larger than three rural areas. It would deal with all the offences previously dealt with by the peasant court and the land captains. The government as a whole decided that it wanted provision to be made for justice for minor offences still to be applied administratively, with the proviso that if the accused individual objected, the matter would be dealt with through the courts. The way in which the new court was to be structured would ensure that those who came under its jurisdiction would have the opportunity, albeit indirectly, to have a say in the selection of judges.

These changes in the way in which justice was to be administered reflected a new attitude on the part of the government to the whole question of civil rights. The series of preliminary declarations made by the government in the two years previous to Stolypin's appointment as prime minister had stressed the commitment of the state to extend and respect the range of civil freedoms available to the Russian citizen. The edict of 12 December 1904 had set out, in very general terms, the reforms that the government intended to introduce. It included a declaration that the legislation dealing with emergency powers would be revised, that the laws governing religious sects would be amended, as would the regulations that limited the rights of foreigners and minorities inside the empire; while there was also to be a relaxation of press censorship. This was followed by the manifesto of 17 October 1905 that, as well as establishing a legislative Duma, also included a declaration that the government would act to establish the basis of civil freedom. This was defined as personal inviolability and the freedoms of conscience, speech, assembly and association. These commitments had been made in the most general terms and the process of drawing up detailed legislation to implement them was already underway when Stolypin took office. As minister of internal affairs, he was responsible for most of the areas relevant to civil rights: the supervision of the press, the holding of public meetings, the rights of religious minorities and the policing of the entire empire came under his control. It was Stolypin's enthusiasm for reform in these areas that resulted in the preparation of legislation being accelerated in the first part of his premiership.

The most extensive set of proposals to increase civil rights concerned the position of religious minorities. In April 1905, a decree had accepted that non-Orthodox Christian religions should not be discriminated against and made special mention of the need to remove the restrictions applied to the Old Believers. This group had split from the Orthodox Church in the seventeenth century and may have numbered some ten million members. It was recognized by the state that the Old Believers were, in essence, deeply conservative and that the only reason for their alienation from the regime was the disabilities that were imposed on them by virtue of their religion. If these were removed, or at least modified, the government believed that it would be able to count on their firm support. These practical political considerations fitted in well with the government's more general commitments, and legislation to set the Old Believers on a more equal footing with other religious groups took priority in the government's plans to extend civil rights. The central part of the proposals was to allow the Old Believers to worship freely and to establish the same sort of parochial organizations as other recognized religions, while the political and social disabilities from which they suffered because of their religion were to be much reduced.[86] Stolypin's government also made a series of proposals to deal with non-Orthodox religions in general: changes of religion were to be facilitated, and religions whose beliefs did not contain anything that was contrary to "the structure of the state, the criminal law or public order"[87] were to be allowed wide latitude in their activities. This was to be the guiding principle of the Stolypin Government's approach to civil rights: individuals and groups were to be allowed to act with minimal restrictions so long as they did not endanger the state or public order.

An exception to this was the Jewish population of the empire. There were severe restrictions on where Jews could live inside the empire, what jobs they could take and the extent of the education they could receive. Stolypin recognized that this policy adversely affected the image of the Russian Empire abroad, while inside the empire Jews were being prompted to resort to revolution as a result of the conditions under which they lived. The government believed that it was, therefore, important to ameliorate the situation of the Jews and Stolypin proposed to allow them greater freedom in commerce and to give them more opportunity to own land. These concessions were deliberately very moderate, as the government was well aware of the suspicion and mistrust that the Jews aroused in Russia, but even this proved to be too extreme for Nicholas II to accept. He wrote that his "inner voice" told him to reject them and "up to now my conscience has never deceived me".[88] The Jews therefore continued to live under considerable restriction and Stolypin accepted that they could not fit into his general scheme of extending civil freedoms.

This scheme was to be firmly buttressed by a new statute on personal inviolability, which was intended "to define, in conformity with the Fundamental Laws, the subjective rights of Russian subjects".[89] The aim of this legislation was, however, severely compromised by the government's determination to deal severely with the threat of terrorism. Although the proposals set out the conditions under which a person could be detained by the police without authorization from a magistrate, it was proposed that detainees need not be brought before a court immediately if they were being held at a place distant from a judicial representative. Private residences were declared inviolable, but this was countered by giving the police the power to make a search if a crime had only just been committed or if a judicial power was too far away for a warrant to be obtained quickly. Secrecy of correspondence was guaranteed, except when a crime was being investigated. The government admitted that:

> In normal times, that is in the absence of disturbance in state and social life, the person of every Russian subject should be protected not only from criminal acts, but also from arbitrary actions by officials. But in exceptional times, personal rights must give way to considerations of state.[90]

It was the interests of the state that had to come first: the interests of the individual would be protected as long as they did not adversely affect those of the empire as a whole.

This was the attitude that governed the administration's approach to implementing the other commitments to civil rights that had been made during 1904 and 1905. Temporary measures had been introduced during late 1905 and early 1906 to deal with the press, the holding of public meetings and the formation of societies and associations,[91] and it was emphasized that they would be replaced with permanent legislation dealing with civil freedoms. When Stolypin's government discussed its priorities for the introduction of legislation into the Duma in January 1907, however, measures to deal with freedom of the press, of assembly and association came at the bottom of the list.[92] The temporary rules gave the government adequate power to regulate civil rights and, in the atmosphere of growing conservatism that prevailed after the increasing success of the regime in quelling revolt, the government was unwilling to introduce measures that would conflict with this mood.

Stolypin's government also intended to act in the field of social policy. Conscious of the part played by the urban working class in the disturbances of 1905, and also of the inaction of previous administrations in dealing with the problem, the government intended to act to alleviate conditions. It declared that "the guiding principle of [the government's] policy is to bring about the maintenance of order in the factories and calm among the workers".[93] The policy had two priorities: to offer positive help to working people and to limit administrative interference in relations between employer and employee. The introduction of a scheme to provide insurance against sickness and accident was the chief positive measure that the state adopted: each worker in factories, mines and transport enterprises who earned less than 1,500 rubles a year would be covered through a workplace-based system. Every enterprise with more than 200 employees could establish its own sickness fund, which was to be independent of the factory administration: it would be run by a committee elected by all the members of the fund, with the employer acting as chairman. While the government was concerned to keep administrative involvement in the affairs of the insurance funds as small as possible, there were pressures, especially from the ministry of internal affairs, for the state to play some role in their conduct. By creating independent insurance funds, the government would be faced with the prospect of powerful workers' organizations coming into being that would have large amounts of money at their disposal and would be outside state control. The government therefore wanted to increase its supervisory powers over the insurance funds and insisted that the provincial governor should act as chairman of each province's insurance board, while the ministry of internal affairs wanted to see its own representation on the national council on workers' insurance much strengthened.[94]

The second area of social policy that concerned the government was education, especially at the primary level. It was important, given Stolypin's determination to improve the lot of the peasantry and his desire to see a new class of small independent landowners develop, that the rural population of the empire should receive at least a rudimentary education. Stolypin's government aimed at establishing a system of universal primary education, available to all children from the age of eight for a period of four years. There were major obstacles to the achievement of this goal, however, because of confusion over where responsibility for the school system should lie. The Orthodox Church already operated a significant number of primary schools, but the government proposed that the zemstva should share responsibility for new schools with the ministry of education. The government agreed that church schools should be included in the new system, but would receive their funds from the Holy Synod – the governing body of the church – rather than the ministry of education, while the zemstva were to deal with the day-to-day running of the lay schools and leave the general management and inspection to the central authorities.[95]

This situation was further complicated by the financial arrangements for the education system. Originally the ministry of education intended that primary schooling should be compulsory for all children aged between 8 and 12, but the financial burden for this provision was to fall on the *zemstva*. It became clear that this would place an enormous strain on the resources of local government, and the government was therefore compelled to greatly reduce the scope of its planned expansion of primary education. The *zemstva* were not to be compelled to provide sufficient schools for all the children in their area, since the provision they made was to be dependent on their financial capabilities. The government was not prepared to make additional resources available to allow for the introduction of compulsory primary education and so the bill remained a half-hearted measure.

Many of the areas in which Stolypin intended to legislate had been the subject of previous investigation by Russian governments and during the 18 months before he became head of government, a considerable amount of government activity had taken place to set out the principles along which policy should proceed. The government declaration of 12 December 1904 and the manifesto of 17 October 1905 had set out, in general terms, the reforms that the tsarist regime intended to introduce: an improvement in the conditions of the peasantry, a greater role for the *zemstva* in local affairs, equality before the law for all, the introduction of workers' insurance and an extension of the civil liberties available to the empire's population. Preparations were already underway before Stolypin came to power to draw up legislation to enact these commitments, so that in some areas of policy his appointment as head of government had only a minor impact. Agrarian change had been long debated inside the imperial government and the reform that was to bear Stolypin's name had been worked out in detail before he was appointed to the St Petersburg government. Other pieces of legislation were also in preparation by the time Stolypin himself was appointed minister of internal affairs: committees had met to discuss the question of workers' insurance and Kokovtsov had put forward a detailed scheme of reform early in 1905,[96] while the problems of religious minorities had occupied the government intermittently for decades.

Stolypin was not, therefore, an innovator in the sense of initiating individual reforms. His contribution to the task of revitalizing the Russian Empire came through his commitment to the concept of reform and his determination to push through change. The appearance at the head of the government of a man who believed that the only way for the empire to survive was for the regime itself to implement peaceful change meant that there was impetus from the top to drive forward the cause of reform. As minister of internal affairs as well as prime minister, Stolypin was able to ensure that the wide-ranging responsibilities of his department were directed towards implementing reform: religious minorities, civil rights, local government and peasant affairs were all the direct concern of his department. Stolypin also introduced a coherence into the reform programme, which had hitherto been lacking. His reforms were firmly peasant-based, constructed around the idea of the creation of a class of small independent landowners, once the peasant had been released from the constrictions of the commune. The reorganization of the agrarian structure of the Russian countryside was the foundation of Stolypin's policy, but he was also insistent on the need to legislate for the social and political consequences of this major reform. The Russian peasant had to be fully integrated into the structure of society. The Great Reforms of the 1860s had begun the process by emancipating the peasant from serfdom, but Stolypin's reforms were intended to end the isolation of the peasant and place the peasantry on the same level as every other Russian subject. The changes that the government envisaged in the systems of local government and justice, the extension of civil liberties, and the development of education would all enable the peasant to play a greater part in Russian society and would close the gap that had existed between rural dwellers and educated society.

Stolypin realized that Russia could not be reformed overnight and he spoke of the need for 20 years of peace in which his plans could be realized.[97] In the aftermath of the 1905 revolution, he and the government as a whole needed to act quickly to deal with the divisions in Russian society, but the process of social transformation that Stolypin wanted to bring about could only happen slowly. The agrarian reform alone required a very substantial period of time to be implemented, as the process of severance from the commune, with its attendant land surveys and negotiations, was time-consuming and took time to show any concrete results in terms of greater yields. By 1915, the last full year of land settlements before the revolution, only some ten per cent of eligible peasants had taken advantage of the 1906 agrarian legislation and set up independent farms, but only one-quarter of these had taken the final step and actually left the village to move their dwellings onto their farmland.[98] Russia was faced with a situation that required rapid action to ameliorate it, but the changes Stolypin believed were needed would take a long period to implement.

There was a further problem in instituting change in the wake of the constitutional reforms of 1905. Stolypin proclaimed on a number of occasions that he intended to establish a state based on law, a *Rechtsstaat*. The establishment of the Duma, together with the granting of civil rights to Russian subjects – their transformation from subjects to citizens – meant that this new ethos had a firm and cogent basis. Once the government had granted these concessions, it was very difficult for them to be removed or modified, but the regime found it difficult to live with these new attitudes and the old ways continued to occupy an important place in Russian government. The root of the problem was that after 1905 the underlying political ethos of Russia was confused. Was Russia still governed by an autocratic monarch, as Nicholas II himself and many of his advisers continued to believe? Or were there now absolute legal standards that governed the conduct of the entire population, including the tsar and his ministers? The regime acted at times as if the monarch still possessed absolute power: in June 1907, when the electoral law was unilaterally amended by the government, this action was justified with a reference to the power entrusted to the tsar by God, rather than being based on any law.[99] Arbitrary actions by the government and its local agents continued; the widespread imposition of a state of emergency across the empire meant that local authorities could take such measures as they felt necessary to maintain order. One contemporary observer remarked that this was leading to a situation where each region of Russia had its own local laws, with the only common feature being that they were all aimed at the pacification of the country.[100] The government was also prepared to use Article 87 of the Fundamental Laws to implement legislation for long periods, even though the original purpose of the article had been to allow the promulgation of laws in an emergency while the Duma was in recess. The process of inculcating a new ethos into the administrative structure and personnel of the Russian Empire was not one that could happen overnight, especially at a time when the government was still having to deal with severe outbreaks of unrest. The traditional methods by which Russian governments had kept control over the population – exceptional law, the delegation of wide powers to local authorities and swift and severe punishment for offenders – were still widely used during Stolypin's premiership and were in direct conflict with his intention to see Russia become a state governed by law. While confusion about the role of law remained at the very heart of Russian government, there was little chance that new standards of behaviour could become established deep in the Russian countryside.

The crisis that Stolypin inherited when he became prime minister had been generations in the making and had been exacerbated by the unwillingness of the tsarist regime to relieve tensions among the population at all levels. The revolution of 1905 meant that the regime had to act to quell discontent in both town and country, and the concessions that it made to aid this helped to arouse expectations of further change. Both government and society recognized that reform was needed in the Russian Empire. The problem that Stolypin's government faced, however, was how to implement reform quickly, both to defuse the still-present tensions in Russian society, and to satisfy the expectations that had developed in the wake of 1905. This was a very difficult situation for any government to face, but was doubly challenging for Stolypin. Reform in Russia at the beginning of the twentieth century was intended to deal with a mass of intractable and deep-seated problems, but the ground rules for the operation of the new post-1905 system of government had not yet been established. Stolypin faced a formidable task.

## CHAPTER 3

# Institutional failure: the paralysis of parliament

### Reform and legislature

The government declaration of August 1906 and Stolypin's speech to the Second Duma in March 1907 had listed the legislative proposals that the government intended to introduce into the Duma. Seven key areas were identified for reform: agriculture, local government, the legal system, civil rights, workers' insurance, education and religious rights. Stolypin's government prepared bills to implement reform in each of these fields and introduced them into the Duma during 1906 and 1907. By the time of Stolypin's assassination in September 1911, however, his government's legislative achievements were very limited. The only major piece of legislation to have been enacted was the agrarian reform. Some of the government's proposals were rejected by the legislative bodies. Others were so radically amended that they ended up bearing little resemblance to the government's original plans. The government itself withdrew some bills from consideration in the Duma and the State Council. Most of the promises of change that Stolypin made upon his appointment came to naught.[1] The high hopes the Prime Minister had entertained when he came into office that he would be able to "renew" Russia, and thus sustain the tsarist regime, proved to be misguided. The process by which reform disappeared from Stolypin's agenda was complex. The new legislative structure of Russia proved to be ineffective in bringing about reform, while a resurgent conservatism was able to exert decisive influence. At the same time, Stolypin himself came to realize that the contours of the Russian political scene made change very difficult to achieve. Stolypin recognized that continuing to hold reformist ideals was not going to provide a basis on which he could remain in office and, by 1909, reform had almost disappeared from his agenda.

The agrarian reform was successful in gaining the approval of the three parts of the legislative process – Duma, State Council and tsar – in June 1910, when it finally became law after more than three years' debate.[2] The progress of the reform through the legislative institutions was, however, rather artificial since it had already been enacted in November 1906 under Article 87 of the Fundamental Laws. At the same time as the Duma and State Council were debating the government's agrarian reform, therefore, the measure was already being implemented in the Russian countryside. By the end of 1910 nearly 1.5 million peasant households had already left the commune and had consolidated landholdings of perhaps 10 million hectares.[3] Even though implementation of the reform was proceeding as it was being debated, political parties took the Duma's consideration of the bill with great seriousness and took every opportunity to propound their own solutions to the agrarian problem.[4] The rejection of the bill would probably have had little effect on the actual conduct of the government's agrarian policy, since it would have been extremely difficult to reverse the changes that had taken place in the organization of Russian agriculture in the four years between the initial enactment of the November 1906 edict and the eventual passage of the law in the summer of 1910.

The government's bill did command genuine support among a wide section of the population; especially important was the relative lack of opposition from the landowning class, for it was they who had been hard hit by the peasant disturbances of 1905 and they had the potential to block proposals with which they did not agree. The United Nobility stressed the inviolability of private property and they condemned any proposals that would involve the compulsory expropriation of land.[5] At their second congress in November 1906, immediately after the publication of the agrarian edict, they resolved that there was no need to make any special representations to the government over the agrarian policy that it was following,[6] for the principle of private property that they supported was being upheld by the government. The gentry sympathized with Stolypin's hope that a new class of small landowners could be created that would act as support for the government against the groups that wanted to encourage revolution. They shared with Stolypin's government the belief that private property was the best guarantee of stability, and its extension to a previously restless section of the population would serve the interests of the landowning gentry as well as those of the government. Parts of the bill did meet with opposition however, especially when it came to be debated in the State Council in 1910. There was particular discontent with a provision of the reform, not included in the original 1906 edict, that would automatically abolish communal holding of land in all communes where land had not been repartitioned during the previous 24 years. On the right, there was concern that this forcible approach had resonances of the demands for compulsory expropriation of land heard earlier. A. A. Manuilov, a prominent Kadet and rector of Moscow University, argued that compelling peasants to leave the commune would bring no benefits.[7] The State Council approved this section of the legislation by a majority of only two votes.

It has been argued that Stolypin's agrarian policy provides a key to the political "system" that came into being as a result of the June 1907 changes to the Duma franchise, since it provided a subject on which agreement was possible between the government, the Octobrists, the Duma right, the State Council and the gentry.[8] The agrarian policy was, however, exceptional: it was the only issue on which all these groups could reach agreement. Stolypin did not set out to pursue policies that would appeal to all these sections of the political spectrum, as his proposals for the reform of local government amply demonstrate. His ideas on the future local structures for Russia suggest that he was determined to lessen the influence of the gentry and that he did not expect political support from that quarter. It was only in 1909, after the gentry had shown the strength of their opposition to this part of the reform programme and had demonstrated the extent of their political influence, that Stolypin made assiduous efforts to lessen their hostility to his government. The outstanding feature of the political scene in Russia during Stolypin's period of office was precisely that there was no one group that was prepared to back the whole programme of reform put forward by the government, so that to speak of the "3rd of June alliance" as Hosking does, is to refer to a situation that only existed in relation to one bill. Although Stolypin stated that the agrarian reform was the foundation on which his other reforms were to be built, there is no evidence of careful calculation on his part as to the attitudes that would be adopted by the various political factions towards the rest of the programme. The agrarian reform may have been part of a larger system as far as Stolypin was concerned, but this interpretation was not shared by most of those who supported it.

This helps to explain the wholesale lack of support for Stolypin's other reforms. His plans to reform local government attracted substantial criticism. Even before the bills had been introduced into the Duma, two right-wing members of the State Council, A. S. Stishinskii and A. A. Naryshkin, attempted to persuade Stolypin not to proceed further with his proposals since they believed that the bills' enactment would lead to a growth in the influence of "politically unreliable elements" in the countryside.[9] Over the following months and years, the nobility was able to exert huge pressure on the government. The congress of the United Nobility, meeting at the end of March 1907, declared that Stolypin's proposals would "completely destroy the significance of the gentry in the provinces" and pressed for the local government bills to be distributed for discussion by the *zemstva* and by local noble assemblies.[10] The weight of gentry opinion persuaded Stolypin that it would be politically prudent to seek the views of provincial leaders on his proposals. But, rather than ask individual local organizations to consider his bills, he decided to implement an idea originally conceived by V. K. Pleve, minister of internal affairs from 1902 to 1904: the creation of a council on the affairs of the local economy. This council met for the first time in March 1908 and its membership included nearly 50 representatives of the *zemstva* along with 20 central government officials.[11] Stolypin viewed the council as a "pre-Duma" and he admitted that, as the Russian Empire was so vast and contained such wide regional variations, central government could only work out the theoretical foundations of reform and there was then a need for an intermediary body to "bring life" to the government's proposals.[12]

At the same time as the council on the local economy was beginning its debates, the United Nobility were holding their fourth congress. This meeting accepted a report by F. D. Samarin, brother of the Moscow provincial marshal of the nobility, that questioned the need for any type of local government reform. Samarin argued that it was dangerous to undertake reform at a time when unrest was continuing, and he suggested that the new legislative institutions were as yet too inexperienced to deal with the weight of legislation that Stolypin's reform programme entailed. His analysis of the local government proposals concluded that they would not achieve the aim of bringing unity to the structures of Russian local government and, in particular, that there was no sensible justification for reducing the role of the gentry in local administration.[13] The congress decided to send a deputation to the tsar to protest at Stolypin's proposals and it was heartened by Nicholas II's response as he assured the nobles that the marshals of the nobility would lose none of their rights.[14] Stolypin tried to placate the gentry by declaring that the government's intention was "to preserve the influence and significance in the *zemstva* of the most cultured and the most educated element . . . that is, the class of local landowners" and the government did make some concessions to noble opinion, especially in the area of the *zemstvo* franchise.[15] Further concessions came in the autumn of 1908, when Stolypin withdrew his proposal that the provincial governor should have control over all government agencies in the province and restricted his jurisdiction to authority over officials of the ministry of internal affairs. Furthermore, Stolypin declared that the marshal of the nobility would always be the government's first choice to head the *uezd* administration and gave a clear indication of his willingness to listen to criticisms of the government's proposals by suggesting that the bills submitted to the council for the affairs of the local economy were only first drafts and that they would be revised in the light of the council's conclusions.[16] These substantial moves towards the gentry's viewpoint resulted in other difficulties for the government. The industrial and commercial lobby also voiced disquiet about the reform of local government: in the spring of 1908 the national congress of trade and industry protested about the preferential treatment that the government was giving to the views of the landowning nobility and demanded representation for itself in the council for the affairs of the local economy.[17]

The government introduced two of its local government bills into the Duma in December 1908 – those dealing with the village and *uchastok* structures. Neither ever became law: legislative congestion meant that the Duma only discussed the *uchastok* proposals in full session in February 1911. It was a further three years before the State Council got round to debating the bill and, even though it had been amended to give the landowning nobility very considerable say in the running of the new *zemstvo*, the bill was rejected by the Council. The village bill met an even more ignominious fate, as it was sent back to the ministry of internal affairs in 1913 without ever having been debated in full session in the Duma. None of the government's other proposals to reform local government even got as far as being submitted to the Duma for consideration.

The bill to reform the administration of justice in the villages, by establishing a local court with jurisdiction over all sections of the population, was discussed in the Duma in the autumn of 1910. It had been introduced into both the First and Second Dumas, but had fallen when each of these were dissolved and was eventually introduced into the Third Duma at the end of November 1907. While the Octobrists approved of the principles on which the bill was constructed, there was substantial opposition from the right. The United Nobility did not believe that the defects that were present in the peasant court system warranted a full-scale reconstruction of the institution; but rather they felt that modifications to the existing court would be sufficient. A report to the fourth Congress of the United Nobility in March 1908 summed up the points of disagreement: it was felt that the government would be unable to find the requisite number of competent people to become JPs, since local landowners would be unlikely to be able to devote the necessary time to the job, and qualified people with a legal education would be able to earn more money elsewhere.[18]

When the bill was debated in the Duma, many deputies expressed their opposition to outsiders – especially "intellectuals" – becoming judges in the local court. They supported amendments that reduced the property qualification needed to become a judge and that ensured that the *uezd* assembly of justices would be able to elect its own chairman. These amendments found support both from the right and from sections of the Octobrist party. When the bill came to be considered by the State Council, the right was able to reverse these changes and to incorporate recommendations that were mainly the work of the United Nobility: this largely negated the whole purpose of the bill. The State Council decided that the court should be retained as a purely peasant institution with peasant judges, but it made a small concession to the government's wishes by giving JPs a role as part of a higher rural district court that would hear appeals from the peasant court.[19]

The government did little to support the terms of its original bill. The State Council debates on the bill took place in 1911, by which time Stolypin had lost interest in his reform programme, and by the time the bill was approved by the State Council in March 1912 Stolypin was dead. The changed political atmosphere after Stolypin's assassination is shown by the fact that when the bill was returned to the Duma for consideration in May 1912, after the State Council amendments had been made,[20] the Duma passed it with few alterations. Those political parties that had previously pressed for radical reform were aware that the government had no intention of resurrecting its original bill, and therefore made no attempt to return the bill to its original form. The opposition to the bill had been largely motivated by the same considerations as had determined the right's attitude to the local government reforms: they feared that the authority of the landowning gentry would be diminished and that their influence in local judicial affairs would be replaced by that of more liberal and, to them, undesirable elements. While the gentry were ready to see the extension of the principle of private property to the peasantry, they were not prepared to accept the political and social consequences of such a move. Stolypin wanted to see the peasantry become an integrated part of Russian society, able to take part in local government and to have access to justice on the same basis as everyone else. The gentry believed that even if the peasantry was to be able to consolidate its allotment land into its private property, this was no reason for ending its isolation as a class. The Russian nobility believed that the peasant was a world away from them and that the landowning gentry – as the most reliable and cultured elements in the countryside – deserved to continue their dominance of the rural world.

The government's measures to introduce a system of workers' insurance were introduced in the Duma in June 1908 and were debated in May 1909. Although they had been approved by the government in the summer of 1907, the death of D. A. Filosofov, the minister of trade and industry, in January 1908, resulted in the new minister, I. P. Shipov, submitting them for discussion at another special conference under the chairmanship of the deputy minister, N. A. Ostrogradskii, in April 1908.[21] Here the industrial lobby was successful in reducing the contribution that employers would have to make to the insurance funds, both by having the workers' contribution increased and by curtailing the scope of the benefits that would be provided.[22] The Duma commission that dealt with the bill was chaired by an industrialist, the textile magnate Baron E. E. Tizengauzen, and it was sympathetic to the wishes of the factory owners. The changes that were made to the bill during the Duma debates were motivated largely by the pressures that were exerted by the industrial and commercial lobby; they were concerned about the expenditure that would be necessary on their part to establish and run insurance schemes at a time when Russia's economic position was weak, especially since the workers themselves would exercise considerable control over the insurance funds. The factory owners were also worried at the lack of consultation in the preparation of the bill, and after making representations to the ministry of trade and industry, it was agreed that they would be allowed to make comments on the bills directly to the Duma.[23] This was a disingenuous argument: workers' insurance had been under serious discussion inside the government since 1903 and there had been wide opportunities for the industrial lobby to put its point of view. There was also pressure from the ministry of internal affairs to alter the proposals that had been made by the ministry of trade and industry, for the interior ministry was worried that the government would have insufficient control over the activities of the insurance funds, and that revolutionary parties might penetrate them. It therefore took steps to extend police powers over the proposed insurance funds.[24] The bill that emerged from the Duma was much more conservative than the government had originally proposed. The insurance schemes were to be more limited in their scope and would require a greater contribution to be made by the workers themselves, while government control over the activities of the funds was strengthened. Although the measure to introduce accident insurance became law in the spring of 1911, it was a year later before the main bill introducing sickness insurance was approved by the tsar.

The government's bill to introduce universal primary education in the Russian Empire was initially submitted to the Second Duma early in 1907, but had to be reintroduced into the Third Duma when it met. The Duma commission that examined the bill took nearly three years to prepare its report. The commission amended the government's bill to speed up the pace of the introduction of primary education, and to give local authorities a greater say in the organization of the process in their areas. While the government had rejected the idea of setting a target date for the system to be fully operative, the commission wanted the process of providing universal primary education to be completed within ten years and it also wanted to see a considerable increase in government expenditure on education. It was intended that spending should rise by 10 million rubles a year until the introduction of primary education was complete, and the commission wanted the new district education boards to draw the majority of their members from the *zemstvo*. The district marshal of nobility should not automatically become chairman of the board, but the chairman should be elected by the district *zemstvo*, and it would be the district board that would have direct control over the schools in its area. As a result, the provincial authorities would have no direct part in the process, and only hear appeals against decisions of the lower board.[25] The Duma in general approved the commission's recommendations, although the government had tried to prevent a commitment to an annual fixed increase in expenditure being included in the bill:[26] it was passed in February 1911 and sent to the State Council. Not surprisingly, the Duma's amendments were looked upon with some disfavour by the

Council, and it moved to ensure that the membership of the local school boards would consist mainly of gentry. There was also argument over the place that church schools would occupy in the new system: the State Council was unwilling to see them subordinated to lay authorities and rejected this part of the bill: so the church schools would continue as a separate body outside the new system. The Holy Synod and the United Nobility had exerted pressure in favour of this exclusion,[27] but this amendment, together with the others made by the Council, was unacceptable to the Duma when the bill was discussed in the conciliatory commission. Neither side was willing to compromise over the bill and it was declared to be rejected in June 1912.

The centrepiece of Stolypin's attempts to extend civil rights was legislation to reduce the discrimination suffered by non-Orthodox religions. It was difficult for these religious groups to build churches, their ministers did not enjoy the same legal status as Orthodox priests and they were not protected by the blasphemy laws. Discrimination extended to individuals: adherence to a non-Orthodox religion could bring civil and political disabilities, while marriages between the Orthodox and those from other faiths were made very difficult. Opposition to Stolypin's proposals had been voiced while the council of ministers was still considering the bills: the chief procurator of the Holy Synod – the senior official of the Orthodox Church – tried to insist that the legislation should not proceed until the views of the church had been sought and, when his argument was rejected by the council, the chief procurator P. P. Izvol'skii, refused to approve the minutes of the council's meeting.[28] The Holy Synod was only able to consider the proposals for religious reform once they had been introduced into the Duma, and it adopted a twin approach to the government's plans. The Synod itself concentrated on providing a critique of the government's bills by demonstrating how they would diminish the position of the Orthodox Church. At the same time, however, right-wing parties in the country began to mount a concerted campaign in support of the Orthodox Church and against Stolypin's proposals. During 1908, the Synod received many expressions of support from branches of the Union of the Russian People and the Russian Assembly, groups both on the far right of the Russian political spectrum, and strong links developed between local clergy and these organizations in some parts of the country. The national impact of these links was confirmed when the Synod agreed to allow the banners of the Union of the Russian People to be carried in religious processions, and messages of support from the Union were read at the Church's missionary congress in the summer of 1908.[29]

Although there was some disquiet at the highest levels of the Orthodox Church about the involvement of the church in partisan politics,[30] the church's supporters made strenuous efforts to influence the course of discussion in the Duma. Bishop Mitrofan of Gomel' insisted that the bill dealing with the extension of the rights of Old Believers should be considered not just by the commission established to deal specifically with the bill, but also by the Duma commission on the Orthodox Church. The government was successful by just one vote in this commission in getting approval for the section of its bill that would allow the Old Believers to engage in proselytization. Supporters of the Orthodox Church also put up a determined fight to try to prevent Old Believer ministers being granted the title of priest, and to ensure that each application by Old Believers to open a parish should be dealt with individually by provincial governors.[31] The leadership of the church was not able to maintain a monolithic stance in dealing with the bill, since some priests who were Duma deputies were prepared to countenance the extension of the rights of Old Believers.[32] The Duma as a whole supported the Old Believer bill, encouraged by the strong ties between the Octobrist party and the Old Believer community, but when the Duma considered the bill that would make it easier for an individual to change religion, Stolypin delivered a clear warning about the political obstacles that the bill would have to clear if it was to become law. Speaking in May 1909, he reminded the Duma that the manifesto establishing it had stated that the Duma should be "Russian in spirit" and that if the Duma should make a mistake in amending the religious reform bills, "something which is always possible, then the bill goes for examination by the State Council and after that for the judgement of the monarch, who, according to our law, is the defender of the Orthodox Church and the custodian of its dogmas".[33] It was evident from the prime minister's tone that the conservative political atmosphere that permeated the higher reaches of the Russian establishment was not conducive to passing legislation that was perceived as unfavourable to the Orthodox Church. During the late summer and autumn of 1909, the government moved to moderate its proposals: three bills were withdrawn from the Duma "so that they can be made to correspond to the canon law of the Orthodox Church and to its position as the established church of the state".[34] But none of them was ever reintroduced into the Duma. The bill dealing with Old Believers was considered in a commission of the State Council and then debated by the full Council in May 1910. P. N. Durnovo, who had chaired the commission, attacked both the government's original bill and the Duma's amendments to it: he upheld the position of the Orthodox Church and sought to remove as many as possible of the rights that the bill granted to Old Believers. The Council passed the bill in this very conservative form and, since the State Council's conclusions differed so dramatically from those of the Duma, the bill was sent for consideration by a conciliation commission consisting of members from both chambers. The Old Believer bill never emerged from this commission.[35]

While this bill got as far as the State Council, the government's bill on personal inviolability foundered in the Duma. It was sent for discussion in commission at the end of 1907, but the report that it submitted was considered to be unsatisfactory by the Duma as a whole, as the commission had amended the bill to make it less liberal than the government's original proposals. The Duma therefore decided that a new commission should examine the bill, and an attempt to produce a version that was more in line with the wishes of the Duma as a whole was made. But the discussions never came to a conclusion. The chairman of the new commission explained that this was because, by the time that his group began work on the bill, the government had lost all enthusiasm for the measure and was unwilling to see any law enacted to protect personal freedoms.[36] Thus, by the time of Stolypin's assassination, his legislative achievement was small. Even taking into account the two bills that had originated during his premiership, but were only approved in 1912, the only measure that was enacted in line with the promises made by Stolypin in 1906 was that of agrarian reform.

## The workings of parliament

The problems that Stolypin experienced in trying to implement his reform programme had their roots in the changed political situation in Russia after 1905. The introduction of national representative institutions was a fundamental break with Russia's traditional political culture. Successive tsars had resisted attempts to reduce their prerogatives by allowing the population to participate in national government. Even proposals to give a role in national decision-making to the landed nobility – perceived as the most reliable members of Russian society – had been rejected. The volte-face of 1905, when Nicholas II granted first a consultative national assembly, and then in October a fully-fledged parliament, was as radical as it was wholly unexpected and was far from unreservedly accepted by members of Russia's ruling elite. The Duma came into being, therefore, in an atmosphere where important sections of the government and the court disapproved of its very existence. Even though the Russian public had, by 1905, experienced 40 years of participation in local political affairs through the *zemstva*, the transition to involvement in national government represented a considerable leap in the scale of their responsibilities. The deputies who were elected to the Duma had no experience of legislating and, even if they had served in the *zemstva*, the work that they encountered there had been on a much smaller scale. Furthermore, before 1905 Russian society had lacked any open forum for proper political debate so that the new Duma legislators came to their task without any experience of operating in an open political environment. Political parties had been illegal in the Russian Empire until 1905, censorship had severely restricted the circulation of ideas and the apparatus of the state had been directed towards ensuring that political opinion was only expressed in a way that was approved by the regime. The culture of Russian politics in the nineteenth century, both inside the government and in wider society, was conspiratorial. The structure of the government, in which ministers needed to work individually to persuade the tsar to support their position, gave official politics an atmosphere of secrecy; while the only way for the Russian public to engage in political activity and debate was with a degree of caution unnecessary in the states of western Europe. The transformation in Russia's political structures that was represented by the introduction of the Duma was matched by the change in political attitudes that both government and the public had to undergo if the system was to work.

Although the irreconcilable differences of opinion between members of the legislative institutions and between the legislature and the government played an important part in bringing about the collapse of Stolypin's reform programme, the structure and mechanics of the institutions, especially the Duma, were also significant. The problems that were encountered in steering a piece of legislation through the Duma stemmed partly from the workload that the government placed upon the new parliament. During the Third Duma's first session, the government introduced 610 bills, of which only 332 were approved during that session, leaving the remainder to be dealt with later. During the five years of the Third Duma's life, over 2,500 measures were submitted to it by the government and 90 per cent of them were eventually approved.[37] Most of these bills, however, were of the so-called "vermicelli" variety, which legislated for very minor matters but did take up valuable time. The government was unable to draw any distinction between matters that needed primary legislation and those that, in other parliamentary regimes, were dealt with by government regulation. At the beginning of 1909 the pressure of time on the Duma was so severe that the number of full sessions had to be increased from three to four per week, solely to deal with this minor business.[38] But in the autumn of 1909 there was a return to three sessions weekly, not because the amount of work had decreased, but because the increased number of full sessions meant that Duma deputies were unable to devote sufficient time to the examination of bills in committee.[39]

The burden of legislation was intensified by the lack of any fixed timetable for the progress of legislation through the Duma. The main stumbling block was the commissions that were established to examine each bill: those dealing with major bills had 66 members, while less significant measures were debated by commissions of 33. These unwieldy bodies were intended to allow the party structure of the Duma to be reproduced in miniature, but made proper discussion very difficult indeed.[40] There was no requirement that a commission finish its work within a specified period and, when dealing with a major piece of reform legislation, it was not uncommon for a commission to take 18 months over its deliberations.[41] The lack of fixed procedure for a commission's work was replicated when a bill came to be debated in the full session of the Duma. There was no provision for a timetable to be set out for a bill's passage through the Duma, and no mechanism that the government could use to speed up the bill's progress. There was no means of introducing a "guillotine" motion that would allow the government to set a time limit for debates on a particular measure. In certain cases, the Duma itself voted to restrict the length of speeches, but this was only resorted to in exceptional circumstances.[42] The decision to limit debate rested with the Duma itself rather than with the government, and there was little incentive for the Duma to conclude its deliberations quickly.

Many of the government's major bills were introduced into the Duma at the very beginning of the 1907–8 session and this paved the way for severe legislative congestion. Each bill's passage through the commissions took at least a year and it was impossible to predict when a commission would complete its work of examining a bill and it would be ready for consideration by the full session of the Duma. Although in the autumn of 1908 Stolypin tried to influence the chairman of the Duma to take the local government measures first,[43] it was decided by the leaders of the different parties in the Duma that the order of business should be determined according to the preferences of the Duma parties themselves.[44] An informal committee consisting of 16 representatives from the political groupings in the Duma had been established by N. A. Khomiakov, the Duma chairman, so that "they could become acquainted with the opinions which existed in different groups concerning the various questions of Duma activity, and so achieve as much agreement as possible".[45] It was this committee that was responsible for deciding the pattern of the Duma's work. There was no agreement between the different parties on the order in which bills should be debated. The situation was further complicated by the inability of commissions to conclude their examination of bills to coincide with the Duma leaders' preferences. Discussion of the agrarian measures occupied the Duma for much of 1909, but there was no consensus on what should be dealt with afterwards. Suggestions by Guchkov that two bills could be debated in parallel were rejected because it was felt that the complexity of the measures he suggested – the local court and personal inviolability – would make this impractical.[46] It was decided to debate the local court bill first, but when Guchkov became the Duma chairman in the spring of 1910, he abandoned the meetings of the committee, believing that they served no useful purpose and that the views that were expressed could just as easily be put on the floor of the Duma. This lack of effective organization in arranging the Duma's timetable had a serious effect on the government's legislative programme, for it meant that the amount of time devoted to different bills could vary considerably. More than six months of the 1909 session were given over to the agrarian legislation, whereas the bill dealing with Finland was considered in a single week in 1910. Political parties could delay or speed up a bill as a political manoeuvre, and the government remained powerless in such a situation: relations between the government and the Duma had not reached the stage where informal contacts could ensure the smooth passage of legislation. It is clear that the leaders of the Duma parties themselves found their lack of control over the work of parliament to be frustrating, for it meant that it was difficult to plan any sort of reliable legislative timetable and the Duma parties could not be sure that their preferred reforms received priority. The government too was adversely affected by the delays in the legislative programme, for opposition to its proposals was given time to crystallize and organize itself, thus making the government's task much more difficult.

The delays that a bill encountered in the Duma had their roots in the fundamental relationship that existed between the government and the legislative institutions. The Russian Duma was not controlled by a government party and the government was therefore unable to guarantee that its legislation would become law. No party in the Duma was under any imperative to see a bill approved, for as there was no governing party, a party's position did not depend on its ability to see a piece of legislation successfully through parliament. The government was placed in the role of an observer, with little power to influence the course of events in the Duma, while the political parties had little power to lose by opposing or delaying government bills. The Octobrist party did try to demonstrate that it had special links with Stolypin's government, but this did nothing to persuade members of the party to present a united front in support of the government and splits developed within the party.[47] The Octobrists were as willing as any other party to criticize government policy: it was Octobrist amendments, for example, that substantially altered the bill to regularize the position of the Old Believers. Other parties maintained much more consistent opposition to the government. On the left, the Kadet party continued to voice fierce antagonism towards the government: during 1908 and 1909, other political parties came to believe that the Kadets were simply using the Duma as a tribune from which they could attack the government. Kadets certainly took a leading role in putting down interpellations to ministers that concentrated on laying bare the government's record on civil rights: in December 1908 they invited the Duma to condemn the widening use of the death penalty against participants in the revolutionary movement. When their proposal was rejected, the Kadets walked out of the session, along with Trudovik and Social Democrat deputies.[48] The attitude of parties on the right towards the government was overwhelmingly negative, since the influence of interest groups, such as the United Nobility and the Orthodox Church, at this end of the political spectrum was very considerable. Stolypin himself had said that he expected the Third Duma to display moderate opposition to the government.[49] The government never expected to be able to work closely with the Duma, while no Duma party found itself able to offer wholehearted support to Stolypin's government. This friction between executive and legislature was not conducive to the enactment of a major programme of reform.

From the beginning of its existence, the Duma saw its task as being to keep a watch on the activities of the government and to prevent the administration from overstepping the limits that each party saw as correct. This attitude dated from the Duma's first convocation: the first chairman of the Duma, S. A. Muromtsev, saw himself as being the most important political figure in Russia after the tsar. He would only use his right to report to the monarch if he was summoned by Nicholas II, and met the tsar only twice during the First Duma's session. Muromtsev also kept his distance from the government itself and took no steps to meet Goremykin, the prime minister, to help in establishing workable relations between executive and legislature. As contemporary observers noted, Muromtsev failed to take the opportunity to establish himself as the intermediary between the new parliament and the tsarist regime.[50] Assessments of the government's area of competence varied from party to party, but every party believed that there was some way in which the government's performance was unsatisfactory. The right was concerned that Stolypin was moving too quickly away from the traditional basis of Russian government; the Octobrists believed that not enough was being done to implement the provisions of the October Manifesto; the Kadets felt that the government should move beyond the manifesto and introduce more liberal measures. The suspicion with which the political parties viewed the government was reflected in the government's attitude to the Duma, for after the experience of the first two Dumas there was little confidence in the Duma's ability to do constructive work, and the constant criticism that emanated from the Duma in the form of interpellations and bills only served to increase the hostility that was felt in some sections of the government towards the Duma.[51]

The powers of investigation that the Duma possessed were very limited: deputies could put down interpellations to ministers and the Duma was able to debate the state budget. Interpellations – questions about any aspect of a minister's duties – could be submitted on any topic, and while initiated by individual deputies, they were put down in the name of the Duma as a whole. The government rarely refused to respond to Duma interpellations and, even though it was outside the Duma's competence to address questions directly to the chairman of the council of ministers in his capacity as head of the government, Stolypin took advantage of these opportunities to defend the government's policies. In March 1910, he replied to an interpellation about the army by mounting a vigorous defence of the government's policy to quell revolution and insisting that he did lead a reforming administration.[52] Deputies were not, however, always successful in bringing ministers to the Duma to answer interpellations: it proved exceptionally difficult to frame questions in such a way that the minister of justice could be brought to the Duma to answer deputies' concerns about the administration of justice, while any area that was declared to lie within the monarch's jurisdiction could not be the subject of interpellation.[53] The Duma's rights over the state budget were also limited. It could not interfere in any provision that had been made in the 1906 state budget, thus giving the government protection for most of its expenditure plans. The Russian state's spending did, of course, increase each year, and the Duma was able to examine the government's new annual appropriations in some detail. Each ministry's budget was discussed by a Duma commission and the deputies were able to use their scrutiny of expenditure plans to embark on detailed discussion of a department's policy as a whole. Some areas of the government's budget were, however, "iron-clad" and exempt from any examination by the Duma. These included the expenditure of the imperial court, as well as military and naval spending. The Duma was able to circumvent these restrictions on debate about the armed forces' budgets by taking advantage of the need for annual legislation to regulate the size of the armed forces.[54] The yearly debates on this topic gave the Duma deputies wide scope for discussion of military policy and the government did not always offer resistance to this, sometimes seeing the Duma as performing a useful function in pressing for the modernization of the empire's military capabilities.[55] After the problems that arose over the Duma's discussions of the naval general staff during 1908 and 1909, the right in the State Council moved to resist what it perceived as government support for an extension of the Duma's prerogatives. Even though the disputed legislation establishing a naval general staff had been introduced by the government and was passed by both Duma and State Council, the tsar decided to reject the bill as he believed it impinged on his own powers. The Duma's attempts to extend its own power met with a severe rebuff, and Stolypin's own authority was badly dented by Nicholas II's refusal to accept the views of both government and legislature.

Much of the significant legislation that Stolypin was able to enact was passed by means of Article 87 of the Fundamental Laws, thereby avoiding the necessity of relying on the Duma. The agrarian reform was the most substantial measure treated in this way; the 1910 Finnish bill was preceded by a regulation that laid down the bones of a new legislative procedure and the western *zemstvo* measure of 1911 was only implemented through Article 87 after its rejection by the State Council.[56] Stolypin was aware of the problems that the Duma posed for a government that was used to promulgating legislation as it fancied, but he was reluctant to use the extraordinary legislative procedure too frequently, believing that to do so in the face of opposition from the legislative institutions would be the clearest possible way of displaying the government's contempt for them.[57] Stolypin was not ready to use Article 87 deliberately to flout the wishes of the majorities in the legislative institutions, but rather to enact bills that he felt were of the greatest importance and required implementation immediately, without waiting for the lengthy process of examination by the Duma and State Council to be concluded. Article 87 was also a tool that could be utilized to frustrate what Stolypin saw as intrigue that was not representative of the real intentions of the Duma and State Council. Stolypin had to strike a careful balance between the desire to see his reforms implemented and the likely attitude of the legislative institutions; in most cases he was successful in seeing measures that were enacted under Article 87 later being approved by the Duma and State Council. Where there was some doubt that a measure would be approved, as in the case of the field courts-martial bill in 1906, the government preferred not to risk the possibility of defeat and did not even introduce the measure into the Duma. It was not a practical option to implement every bill using this procedure, since this would have been tantamount to ignoring the existence of the Duma. The experience of the western *zemstvo* measure demonstrated that even though the Duma may have been in agreement on the content of a bill, this was no guarantee that the other parts of the legislative process – State Council and tsar – would add their consent. The mere existence of a representative institution in the Russian Empire was no guarantee that it was able to complete any useful work.

Although the government wanted to see the Duma work effectively, and most of the parties inside the Duma intended that it should be seen to justify its existence by bringing benefit to Russia, the Duma was never able to find a satisfactory system for its prime purpose of legislating. The conscientious approach that many Duma members adopted to their job did not help in pushing reform through: deputies were, in the main, unwilling to approve legislation without having first examined and discussed it fully, and this process often involved much time being spent on research into the subject.[58] In the full sessions of the Duma, members were eager to speak, often at considerable length, and showed great reluctance to shorten speeches, either by the imposition of a time limit or by allowing only a given number of speakers on an issue. The problems that the Duma encountered were those produced by having a set of inexperienced legislators attempting to deal with an overfull programme of bills without a clear set of procedural rules to guide them, so causing delays that neither the Duma nor the government had the power or will to avoid. If Stolypin had been able to legislate without the Duma, his proposals would undoubtedly have had more success in becoming law, but the existence of the Duma – brought into being following widespread popular pressure – succeeded in slowing down the reform progress. It is ironic that an institution that was created to bring about reform actually acted to slow down the reform process, and ultimately to delay Stolypin's bills so much that organized opposition was able to defeat them.

CHAPTER 4

# The mobilization of conservative opinion

## Perceptions of reform

Institutional problems helped to defeat reform, but it was the underlying political atmosphere in the Russian Empire that enabled the legislative paralysis to become fatal. The reformist aims that Stolypin espoused proved to have weak roots. The commitment to reform that the prime minister demonstrated was shared by only a small segment of politically influential Russian society and Stolypin found that it was extremely difficult to persuade the majority of the Russian elites of the merits of change. The enthusiasm for reform itself that the tsarist regime had appeared to show during 1905 did not last long, and the traditional conservatism of the governing strata and their social allies soon made a powerful resurgence.

A crucial element in the waning of enthusiasm for reform was the success of the government's policy in dealing with the threat of revolution. The level of popular discontent during 1905 had been sufficient to bring the tsarist regime to its knees and to force the pace of change so dramatically that the regime's long-standing resistance to a national representative institution had been quickly overcome. During 1905 itself there had been more than

3,000 separate incidents of peasant discontent that had been severe enough to warrant the authorities sending in troops. This rural revolution involved peasants burning and destroying land-owners' estates, along with strikes by agricultural labourers and the seizure of pasture land and meadows. In the industrial cities of the empire, strike action had been widespread. In the aftermath of the "Bloody Sunday" shootings in January 1905, when a peaceful demonstration by St Petersburg workers had been met by troops firing on them and killing more than 130 people, over 400,000 people had taken part in strikes. The winter industrial unrest subsided during the spring and summer, but emerged again with even greater force in the autumn. In October 1905 nearly half a million workers went on strike, and this urban discontent was instrumental in pushing the regime towards making concessions. The disturbances of 1905 affected much of the empire. Action by industrial workers was especially severe in the urban centres of Poland: more than 90 per cent of all Polish workers went on strike at some stage during the year. Rural disturbances were widespread, and were especially common in those areas where the economic pressure on the peasantry was severe. This included both areas in the heartland of European Russia, as well as regions on the periphery of the empire. National tensions were accentuated as, for example, Estonian and Latvian peasants rebelled against the Baltic German nobles who dominated their lives. The resources of the imperial government were barely sufficient to contain these levels of discontent: many of the troops involved in fighting the Russo-Japanese War were still on their way back from the Far East and, even with the full military might of the empire at its disposal, the government would still have had difficulty in quelling the rebellions that were erupting right across the empire. The concessions that the regime made in October 1905 had some effect in reducing the level of unrest, particularly by satisfying the demands that were made by social elites; but the situation had gone too far for the widespread popular revolts to be suppressed by the intangible benefits that the October Manifesto promised.

The government had, therefore, to take determined action to restore its own authority. P. N. Durnovo, a noted conservative, was appointed as minister of internal affairs immediately after the

October Manifesto was issued and he embarked upon a policy of severe repression. In December 1905, the great uprising in Moscow was put down with harsh brutality by the authorities, leaving more than 1,000 civilians dead. This approach was adopted elsewhere in the empire. Punitive detachments of troops were sent to deal with uprisings early in 1906. The most vicious repression was visited upon the Baltic provinces where peasant revolts were suppressed with little regard for legal niceties: more than 1,100 people were killed by these troops in the first six months of 1906. Similar tactics were utilized by the government in other areas of the empire, especially in the Caucasus and the Ukraine, although troops were less ferocious in these regions than they were in the Baltic provinces. By the time Stolypin was appointed to head the interior ministry in April 1906, the government had clearly regained control of the empire and revolution no longer threatened the very existence of the regime. Nonetheless, the level of unrest was still high. In particular, the government was faced with a serious problem of terrorism, rather than mass demonstrations of popular unrest, and needed to take action to try to prevent its spread.

The use of field courts-martial, the imposition of states of emergency and attempts to prevent the expression of anti-government ideas all helped to contribute to a strengthening of the regime's position. Even though terrorist assassinations continued right through Stolypin's premiership, the government was never threatened by rebellion on the scale of 1905. This had an important effect on the perception of the need for reform, which had pushed the governing elite and its supporters into making concessions during 1905. As it became clear that the regime was being successful in reasserting its authority, so elements of the social and political elites became convinced that they could ride out the remnants of the storm without making further reforms. This perception that change was now unnecessary was heightened by the nature of the reforms that Stolypin proposed. The basis of Stolypin's programme was to bring about profound social change in Russia by transforming the position of the peasantry. Agrarian reform would give property rights to the peasant, and the accompanying package of change to other areas of rural life would consolidate the peasant's position as a full member of Russian society. The implications that this had for other social groups were immense. The emancipation of the serfs in 1861 had served substantially to weaken the importance of the landowning nobility in the Russian countryside, by removing the gentry's responsibility for exercising control over the peasant population. In the 40 years after emancipation, the economic position of the nobility in the countryside changed dramatically as the landowning gentry divested themselves of 40 per cent of their land. The proposals that Stolypin made after 1905 sought to recognize the reduced economic and social importance of the nobility in the rural environment and legislated to lessen the role that they played in the formal structures of government and administration in the provinces. The government's reforms would enshrine in law the economic revolution that had overtaken the gentry by significantly diminishing the political, judicial and social authority that they possessed. This was a bitter blow to the landed nobility: their traditional role had altered over the previous half century, but they had succeeded in retaining their formal authority in the countryside. Depriving the gentry of their jobs as local administrators and judges would, for many provincial nobles, represent the final acknowledgement that the Russian nobility had lost its independence and power and that its members could no longer obtain influence simply through their social position. Stolypin's reforms would ensure that the gentry could only occupy positions of importance in the government of the provinces if they were judged to be of sufficient merit. The assault that Stolypin was mounting on the gentry represented a logical conclusion to the process of economic and social change that had befallen them but, perhaps because it was a final and formal recognition of the long process of decline, it provoked the Russian gentry to make one last defence of their interests.

The conservative backlash that greeted Stolypin's reform programme represented an attempt to defend the traditional political structures and culture of tsarist Russia. The prime minister's attempts to enhance the legal position of the peasantry were resented because their concomitant was a reduction in the authority of the landed gentry. The autocratic political culture of the Russian state was also directly challenged by Stolypin's policies. The population of the empire possessed almost no rights before

1905. This very weak legal status had helped to keep the Russian people in check and the lack of redress that ordinary people could exact against their masters made their position even more difficult. From the government's point of view, arbitrary administration was the norm. Until 1905, the autocracy had been able to act more or less as it wished without any form of legal restraint. The autocratic ethos stretched right down into the depths of the Russian countryside: local officials were able to do their jobs and to impose penalties upon the population with little fear that their activities would be checked. The land captains were particularly noted for their arbitrary style of administration, and their habit of imposing fines on the peasantry or imprisoning them for short periods without any involvement by the courts, was wholly in line with the political culture of the autocracy. Stolypin's insistence that arbitrary government must come to an end, and that the Russian state at all levels must operate according to law, represented a fundamental change in the way the tsarist regime had worked. The buttressing of this commitment to a *Rechtsstaat* by promises to implement wide-ranging civil rights suggested a major shift in the political culture of tsarism. The introduction of a legislative Duma meant that the tsar's powers were no longer absolute, although the restrictions that the government had placed on the Duma's activities by reforming the State Council and issuing new Fundamental Laws early in 1906 had helped, it seemed to conservatives, to limit the damage.

Stolypin's appointment in April 1906 as minister of internal affairs and then chairman of the council of ministers in July, however, seemed to represent a return to the reforming atmosphere of late 1905. After he became prime minister, Stolypin displayed real enthusiasm for reform. The constitutional changes of 1905 had been forced upon the tsarist regime by the real threat of revolution, but Stolypin appeared ready to make far-reaching reforms without the pressure of imminent disaster facing the empire. While Goremykin, during his brief tenure of the chairmanship of the council of ministers, had sought to isolate the Duma and to demonstrate that its introduction had made no real difference to the way in which the Russian Empire was governed, Stolypin was keen to acknowledge the change that the introduction of a parliament represented, and to see it as only one part of a radical change in Russian political culture. Stolypin's ministry worked hard to produce legislation that would put flesh on the bones of the very general commitments to civil rights that had been made during 1905, and it was clear to the traditional supporters of tsarism that the prime minister intended to press ahead to change the underlying philosophy on which the regime rested. Stolypin envisaged a transformation in the ethos of the tsarist government that would put an end to arbitrary actions by officials and would ensure that law – enacted by the Duma and State Council – held primacy through every part of the state. This was a trend that deeply perturbed much of the Russian political establishment, since the change in attitude represented by Stolypin's reforms posed a severe threat to their traditional sources of power. Under serfdom, the landowning gentry had been able to behave as they wished towards the serf population, with almost no fear of interference from the state. This method of control continued to inform the arbitrary style of government after 1861: the governing elite was accustomed to treating the empire's subjects as it wished; law was seen as secondary to the need of the state to be able to continue to act in this manner. Stolypin's insistence that law should be the touchstone for the actions of every part of the empire's administration was intended to ensure that even the most lowly official should behave in a way that could be upheld in the courts, thus removing much of the latitude that the gentry who staffed the local administration possessed in the performance of their duties. This approach was perceived as a further attack on the role of the landed gentry: not only was their right of participation in local administration being challenged but, even if they were able to obtain an official post, they would be wholly subservient to the law of the state and unable to exercise autonomous authority.

The Stolypin reforms represented a major assault on the traditional political and social structures of the Russian Empire. In conjunction with the constitutional changes of 1905, they would have transformed the political landscape of the state. The autocratic base of the empire had been crucially undermined by the introduction of a representative legislature: even though Nicholas II wanted to believe that his authority remained undiminished, the intervention of the Duma and the State Council in the legislative process severely reduced the monarch's freedom of action. Stolypin's reforms would further undermine the traditional politics of the empire by changing the social composition of a vital cohort of local officials and by significantly reducing the reliance of the autocracy on the empire's noble social elite. Allowing and encouraging other social groups to play key roles in the local government of the Russian Empire was a radical step, and its importance was hugely magnified by the emphasis that Stolypin placed on civil rights and on the place that the peasantry should play in the empire's economy and society. Each of these innovations by itself represented an important attack on traditional structures, but taken altogether, they promised nothing less than a revolution in Russian society. It is not surprising, therefore, that Stolypin's reforms were resisted by much of the "establishment" of the empire with the same vigour as they had put into opposing the direct threat of revolution in 1905.

## Political elite and political culture

Conservatism was inherent in the structures of Russian politics. It stemmed from the position of the monarch who owed his duty only to God. Even on the eve of his abdication in 1917, Nicholas II still asserted that, "I am responsible to God and to Russia for everything that has happened and will happen."[1] Each Russian ruler believed that they held the Russian Empire in trust and that they must bequeath it to their successors intact and with the monarch's prerogatives unaltered. Even though successive tsars had acknowledged that change had to take place, and had recognized that they had to take account of the opinions of the nobility – the social elite – if they were to be able to rule effectively, the underlying assumption of Russian monarchs was that reform should be avoided if at all possible. Change was rarely seen as a positive move, rather it was an option to be embarked upon only as a response to difficult political or economic conditions. Even the Great Reforms of the 1860s had been perceived by Alexander II as a means of restoring Russia's military and economic strength after the débâcle of the Crimean War, rather than as a deliberate attempt to restructure Russian society. Tsars saw the role of government as being to reflect the prevailing social structures of society, rather than deliberately to reshape Russia. The ethos of tsardom was, therefore, deeply conservative. This was accentuated by the personalities of the last Romanov monarchs themselves.

After Alexander II's assassination in 1881, his son and successor Alexander III imprinted a deeply traditional stamp on Russian government and society. The new tsar's immediate abandonment of plans to involve representatives of society in the consideration of legislation set the tone for his reign. Alexander III ensured that his own children were educated in a manner that reflected his own views. The future Nicholas II was given a comprehensive programme of studies in history and, in particular, military matters. He was schooled in constitutional law by Konstantin Pobedonostsev, who had himself been his father's tutor and had continued to be one of Alexander III's chief advisers. Grand Duke Alexander Mikhailovich commented that Pobedonostsev's "cynical mind influenced the young emperor in ways designed to teach him to fear any innovation".[2] The characteristics that Nicholas II displayed from the moment of his accession to the throne in 1894 served to confirm his adherence to the views espoused by his father and Alexander's advisers. Nicholas reproached representatives of the *zemstva* who had gathered to offer congratulations on the new tsar's marriage for their "senseless dreams" of participation in national government. The tsar possessed an almost mystical view of his role and of the way in which he should govern Russia. Responding to Stolypin in 1906 over proposals to remove some of the restrictions on the Jewish population of the empire, Nicholas wrote that:

> Despite very convincing arguments in favour of approving this matter, my inner voice tells me ever more insistently that I must not take this decision upon myself. Until now my conscience has never deceived me and I therefore intend to follow its dictates in this case . . . I know that you also believe that "the tsar's heart is in God's hands".[3]

Bolstered by the attitude of the tsarina, the German-born Alexandra Fedorovna, who had adopted the Orthodox religion upon her marriage to Nicholas and had embraced its more mystical elements with all the fervour of the convert, Nicholas was able to draw on his innate belief in the immutability of the Russian autocracy to resist calls for reform.

The tsar harboured a deep distrust of advisers and ministers who tried to pressure him into taking steps that he believed conflicted with his God-given mission to rule the Russian Empire. This was especially evident in Nicholas's attitude towards Witte. The constitutional changes of October 1905 were only wrung from the tsar with the greatest difficulty. He wrote to one of his closest advisers that "Yes, Russia is being granted a constitution. There were not many of us who fought against it. But support in this struggle was to be found nowhere."[4] Two days after the October Manifesto was issued, Nicholas wrote to his mother, the Dowager Empress Maria Fedorovna that:

> There was no other way out than to cross myself and to grant what everybody was asking for. My only consolation is the hope that such is God's will, that this grave decision will lead my dear Russia out of the intolerable chaos in which she has found herself for almost a year.[5]

After Witte had performed his final service for the Russian state by negotiating a sizeable loan for the government from French investors, the tsar was happy to comply with Witte's request to resign as chairman of the council of ministers in April 1906. Nicholas's letter of thanks to Witte for his services to the state was perfunctory in the extreme, and the ex-prime minister received few of the privileges that were traditionally granted to distinguished senior bureaucrats. The tsar's resentment at being, as he saw it, pushed into abandoning his conservative principles was real and long-lasting.

The relationship between Nicholas and Stolypin was not always easy. After his experience with Witte, the tsar was very wary of the intentions of his chief ministers and he tried hard to make Stolypin aware of his own views and of the sort of policy that he wanted the government to pursue. As well as his regular meetings with Stolypin, Nicholas kept up a sustained correspondence with his prime minister. The tsar's rejection of the participation of "public figures" in the government in the summer of 1906 was only the first example of the monarch's desire to play a full part in the government of the empire during Stolypin's premiership. The tsar continued to suggest individuals whom he considered appropriate for appointment as ministers, but he also pressed his views on policy matters on Stolypin. In August 1906, Nicholas complained to his prime minister about the continuing anarchy in the empire and the spate of terrorist assassinations. He called for exceptional legislation to be enacted to counter revolutionary activity and asked for Stolypin's proposals on the subject. Within a week, field courts-martial were introduced.[6] The tsar commented to Stolypin that the behaviour of the left in the Second Duma was "characteristic, not to say undignified", and later warned that the tone of the speeches made in the Duma on the agrarian question was so extreme as to threaten the peace of the countryside, since reports of the Duma's proceedings were so widely distributed.[7]

The first serious tension between tsar and prime minister arose in 1909 over the naval general staff question. During 1908 Nicholas II had expressed his unhappiness with the Duma's refusal to vote credits for the reconstruction of the fleet, and he continued to be very wary of the Duma's attitude to naval questions. Even though the government had made proposals to establish a naval general staff and the Duma and State Council had approved these plans, Nicholas felt that this infringed his prerogatives and he wrote to Stolypin to say that he intended to reject the legislation. The tsar was well aware that his prime minister would regard this decision as a severe rebuff. Stolypin had written to him at the end of March to say that:

> The affair of the naval general staff has caused a colossal stir: everyone has forgotten what the argument is really about and is just talking about a struggle against the government . . . I foresee excessive and insurmountable difficulties which would arise for me if the Naval general staff bill was rejected. This would create unrealisable duties for the government in its present composition.[8]

When Nicholas decided at the end of April that he would refuse to confirm the bill, he tried to soften the blow by assuring Stolypin that:

> There can be no talk of trust or lack of trust. This is my will. Remember that we live in Russia, and not abroad or in Finland (Senate) and therefore I will not allow any thought of anyone's resignation . . . I warn that I will categorically refuse any request by you or anyone else to be relieved of their duties.[9]

This episode helped to make the relationship between the tsar and Stolypin much less easy. The prime minister was already well aware of Nicholas II's predilection for vacillation, since this had caused Stolypin some difficulty when it came to dealing with appointments as the monarch was extremely unwilling to firmly commit himself.[10] Stolypin's influence with the tsar was becoming less strong even before the naval general staff dispute: in the first months of 1909, the prime minister had seen the monarch reject several of his preferred candidates for appointment to ministerial jobs. The tsar's own personal political views were all too clear to Stolypin who, in the aftermath of the naval general staff débâcle, wrote to Nicholas that "Your Majesty clearly wants to rely on the extreme right, even though you have a moderate cabinet."[11] Despite the introduction of the Duma, the tsar was still the final arbiter in Russian politics and the government had to take his views into account if it wanted to survive. During 1910, the government's policies turned towards placating the conservative opinions of the tsar and of groups that had the monarch's ear. The promotion of Russian nationalism by Stolypin's government, particularly in Finland, helped to maintain a workable relationship between the prime minister and the tsar, but this apparent change in policy could not wholly mask the mistrust that by then existed between the two men.

Tensions emerged into the open again at the beginning of 1911, when problems arose over a bill to introduce *zemstva* into the western provinces of European Russia. When the bill reached the State Council, the right perceived that it offered an opportunity to dislodge Stolypin from office and, therefore, decided to vote against the measure. Even though this was a government bill,

Nicholas II was persuaded by V. F. Trepov and P. N. Durnovo to offer his support to the right against his own government. In March 1911, buoyed up by the tsar's views, the State Council rejected the section of the bill that imposed national *curiae* for elections to the western *zemstva*. The tsar's extraordinary behaviour in supporting an extreme political faction against the government infuriated Stolypin and the prime minister requested that he be allowed to resign. The resulting meeting between the tsar and his prime minister was lengthy and dramatic. Stolypin later described the "energetic reproaches" that he directed at Nicholas II but the tsar failed to respond to his prime minister, instead "bursting into tears and embracing [Stolypin]". The prime minister forcefully put it that the right were simply carrying on an intrigue against him and reminded the tsar that this presented dangers to Nicholas too, since it was difficult "to separate [the tsar and the prime minister] in the same way that it was difficult to separate master and servant". Stolypin reminded the tsar of the service he felt he had performed to the state by suppressing revolution, but continued to press for his resignation to be accepted.[12] Four days after this meeting, Nicholas wrote to Stolypin, stressing that he did not want to see his prime minister resign. The tsar praised Stolypin's courage and his devotion to duty, and declared that "my trust in you is as complete as it was in 1906".[13] The outcome of this crisis was unsatisfactory for both Stolypin and Nicholas. Stolypin felt able to set out a series of conditions for his remaining in office: he demanded, despite the right's triumph, that the western *zemstvo* bill be enacted under the emergency provisions of Article 87 and that the legislative institutions be closed for three days so that this could occur. The prime minister was also determined to teach a severe lesson to the people whom he perceived as instigating the right's revolt in the State Council: he demanded that V. F. Trepov and P. N. Durnovo be suspended from the State Council for an indefinite period. Nicholas reluctantly agreed to these conditions, fearful of losing his prime minister in such acrimonious circumstances. By this time, Stolypin was so mistrustful of the tsar's actions that he insisted Nicholas write down the terms that they had agreed on.[14]

Relations between the tsar and his prime minister cooled very quickly after this débâcle. In general, Nicholas II found it very difficult to confront his ministers, much preferring to avoid awkward personal interviews and to give unpleasant news in writing. Within six weeks of the suspension of Durnovo and Trepov from the State Council, Nicholas wrote to Stolypin to suggest that Durnovo be allowed to take his seat again. Although Stolypin avoided the acidity of his earlier discussions with the monarch on the topic, the prime minister's reaction was carefully couched to indicate to the tsar that he was implacably opposed to such a move. He reminded Nicholas of their agreement that had enabled Stolypin to stay in office and noted that Durnovo was continuing to obstruct the work of the government by producing inflammatory pamphlets. As Durnovo was about to depart for a visit abroad, Stolypin argued that no practical point would be served by allowing him to return to the State Council, other than demonstrating to the country at large that a policy shift had taken place. After making what was, eventually, a most forceful statement of his view, Stolypin concluded by assuring the tsar that he "least of all wanted to influence the freedom of your decision". Durnovo remained suspended from the State Council.[15]

The attitude that the tsar adopted towards Stolypin in the spring and summer of 1911 was redolent of the way in which he had treated Witte after the issuing of the October Manifesto in 1905. Nicholas deeply resented that he had been pushed into adopting a course of action that had resulted in two of his *confidants* receiving a public humiliation, and that Stolypin's threat of resignation had forced the tsar to act in a way that he found deeply uncomfortable. Alexander Krivoshein, the minister of agriculture, wrote that "the Sovereign never forgave [Stolypin] for this".[16] Contact between the two men after this incident was limited: Stolypin spent much of the summer on his estates in the country and, when a monument to Alexander III was unveiled in Kiev at the beginning of September, his part in the proceedings was minimal. It was at a performance in the Kiev Opera House to mark this occasion that Stolypin was shot and fatally wounded by an assassin: Nicholas's attempt to visit his prime minister in hospital was rebuffed by Stolypin's wife and he was able to pay his respects only after Stolypin's death, three days later.

Nicholas displayed a continual readiness to listen to the views of the right. In December 1905 the tsar had wished the Union of the Russian People well in its efforts to unite loyal Russians, and had accepted the organization's badge from its chairman, Dubrovin. In June 1907, after the dissolution of the Second Duma and the proclamation of the new electoral law, the tsar sent Dubrovin a telegram in which he expressed "his heartfelt gratitude [to the Union's members] for their devotion and readiness to serve the throne and the welfare of our dear homeland".[17] Witnesses testifying to the commission that investigated the activity of the right after the collapse of tsarism in 1917 confirmed that Nicholas II looked with sympathy on the Union of the Russian People.[18] The tsar made a point of enquiring of Stolypin in 1908, at the height of the controversy over the government's religious reforms, how many telegrams had been received from the Union of the Russian People and asked for a summary of the views that they contained.[19] Accustomed to determining the policy of the government, the tsar found it impossible to alter his behaviour once his place in the political structure of Russia changed after 1905. He was never able to play the role of an impartial arbiter standing above party politics, which was demanded by the new constitutional structures of Russia. Nicholas was unable to suppress his own political views and made no secret of the sympathy that he felt with the most conservative sections of Russian society. Stolypin therefore faced a monarch whose political views were significantly more conservative than his own and who was unafraid of using his power to influence government policy to favour the right.

The people who surrounded the tsar at court were very much of his cast of political mind. The monarch's relations with his ministers were in general formal and business-like, and Nicholas rarely sought to rely on them for day-to-day discussion of politics and policy. Instead, he listened to a range of courtiers and, of course, to his wife, Empress Alexandra. The tsarina's political views were at least as conservative as those of her husband. She was involved in some of the key decisions that Nicholas took, meeting Witte together with the tsar in October 1905 to hear Witte's analysis of the situation facing the empire and his proposals for constitutional change.[20] During the First World War, when Nicholas was based at headquarters for much of the time, the letters that tsar and tsarina wrote to each other demonstrate how accustomed Alexandra was to advising her husband on political matters. The empress advised Nicholas "to stand firm" in 1916 and to remember that "it is the tsar who rules, not the Duma".[21]

Others in the tsar's circle were of equally determined views. The minister of the imperial court from 1897 until 1917 – responsible for the management of the imperial family's activities and finances – was Count V. B. Frederycksz who "had for the Emperor the devotion of an old servant"[22] and who supported the tsar in his concept of his duty and responsibilities. Frederycksz was treated much as a member of the family by the tsar and his wife and he took part in many of the meetings at which the reforms of 1905 were debated, often acting as a conduit for the tsar's views and transmitting them to ministers. Nicholas placed especial trust in General Dmitrii Trepov who had been both governor of Moscow and then governor-general of St Petersburg during 1905. At the height of the turmoil of October 1905, the tsar wrote to Trepov to tell him that, "You are the only one of my servants on whom I can rely completely. I thank you with all my heart for your devotion to me, for zealous service to the motherland and for rare honesty and straightforwardness."[23] Trepov represented a more politically active and sophisticated tradition: he was prepared to make positive suggestions for political change, rather than simply supporting the status quo as Frederycksz did. In 1905 Trepov argued that the conservative nature of the autocracy needed to be strengthened and that the tsarist regime should go on the offensive to regenerate itself. Trepov wanted the government to promote the formation of a conservative party that would offer support to the regime in the Duma and also stressed the need for the government itself to ensure that its programme was properly reported and publicized. The press, Trepov believed, should be harnessed by the regime to bring its views to the notice of the people, especially the population in the provinces who could make the difference between the survival of the regime and its collapse. Trepov resigned from his government responsibilities late in October 1905 since his views were fundamentally at odds with those of Witte, but Nicholas was not willing to see Trepov disappear from a position of influence; he appointed him to be palace commandant, in charge of ensuring the security of the imperial family. For the remaining year of Trepov's life, he enjoyed exceptional access to the tsar and was able to establish something approximating to a personal secretariat for the monarch, providing advice on government matters and managing the tsar's appointments.[24]

The advice that Nicholas sought at the time of the greatest threat to Stolypin's position – the western *zemstvo* crisis – gives further evidence of the conservative circle that surrounded the tsar. In the critical days in March 1911 when Nicholas was considering his response to the prime minister's request to resign, the tsar met Prince A. A. Shirinskii-Shikhmatov – no friend of Stolypin's – who had been removed from his post as Chief Procurator of the Holy Synod when Stolypin became prime minister. As the crisis was developing, the tsar met I. G. Shcheglovitov, the deeply conservative minister of justice, whose department was noted for its attempts to undermine the rule of law and to champion the utility of administrative measures, rather than insisting on the primacy of the courts.[25] M. G. Akimov, the chairman of the State Council, was another of Nicholas's conservative advisers at this critical time. Not all the members of the monarch's circle were, however, of such views. The tsar's mother, the Danish-born Dowager Empress Maria Fedorovna, offered a different perspective on events. When the Russification of Finland was being discussed, Maria Fedorovna played an important part in trying to persuade her son to moderate the government's policies. In 1902 she had written to Nicholas that, "Those who tell you that the crushing of [Finland] is your history's noblest page are blackguards. Here and throughout Europe, indeed everywhere, enraged voices can be heard."[26] Maria Fedorovna also played an important part in the 1911 discussions concerning Stolypin's future, and her pressure was instrumental in persuading the tsar to refuse Stolypin's resignation.[27] Nicholas's mother represented, however, an isolated example of moderation among her son's courtiers: the overall tone of the imperial Russian court was deeply conservative and suspicious of attempts at change. Stolypin's programme of reform met with little sympathy among those who surrounded the tsar.

The progress of Stolypin's reform programme was also affected by the attitude adopted by the rest of the government. The traditional rivalry between the interior ministry and the ministry of finance continued throughout Stolypin's period in office, and V. N. Kokovtsov, the minister of finance, emerged as the most consistent and thorough critic of Stolypin's policies within the government. Although some of his criticism, such as his comments on proposals for workers' insurance, was based on his departmental experience as minister of finance,[28] Kokovtsov attempted to demonstrate the practical difficulties that would result from the implementation of Stolypin's bills. He tried to show that the interior ministry's plans for the reform of local government were confused and would be awkward to put into practice and accurately predicted the adverse reaction to the Finnish legislation from the Finns.[29] Kokovtsov had taken a sceptical approach to reform since the very beginning of Stolypin's period in office: in November 1906 the disagreements between the two men went so far that the minister of finance offered his resignation over the proposal to allow the ministry of internal affairs to distribute funds to *zemstva* without the sanction of the finance ministry.[30] Stolypin, however, persuaded him to stay on and insisted that his opinions were greatly valued.[31] At the beginning of 1907 the finance minister wrote to Stolypin setting out his detailed objections to other sections of the local government reforms: Kokovtsov declared that he and Filosofov, the minister for trade and industry, were willing to make compromises except where they conflicted with their deepest convictions. He wrote that Stolypin "was mistaken in seeking a compromise between your views and mine . . . just to keep me in the cabinet".[32] Kokovtsov's cynical assessment of Stolypin's motives remained strong and, when he testified to the 1917 commission investigating the collapse of tsarism, he was highly disparaging about Stolypin's political judgement and ability.[33]

The council of ministers as a whole became less inclined to accept proposals for reform as Stolypin's premiership proceeded. During 1909, the composition of the council of ministers became less favourable to Stolypin: V. I. Timiriazev, the new minister of trade and industry, S. V. Rukhlov, appointed to the ministry of communications and S. A. Voevodskii, the new naval minister, were all out of sympathy with the premier's reform goals. In addition, Stolypin's close colleague in the ministry of internal affairs, A. A. Makarov, was appointed as a state secretary, and his replacement, P. G. Kurlov, had rightist views that were well known.[34] It is significant that Stolypin was unable to see his views prevail in the appointment of ministers. Nicholas II was inclined to seek advice from the court in making ministerial appointments and to follow his own instincts in selecting men for government posts, rather than rely on the views of his prime minister. After 1909, the council of ministers was dominated by men whose first instincts were to resist reform. But even in 1906, when Stolypin first entered the government, enthusiasm for reform among his fellow ministers had been limited. Stolypin's own ministry was responsible for developing the majority of the proposals for change that his government introduced: it was the ministry of internal affairs that was responsible for the agrarian reform, for the proposals to reform local government and for bills extending civil rights and to allow greater religious freedom. Other ministries therefore played only a minor part in the preparation of reform. Furthermore, Kokovtsov's tenure at the head of the finance ministry and Shcheglovitov's tutelage of the justice ministry throughout Stolypin's premiership ensured that the cabinet always contained men of considerable political weight whose views were out of line with the premier. The ministerial colleagues with whom Stolypin had to work were far from being enthusiasts for wide-ranging reform and their more traditional approach to the government of the empire helped to constrain the prime minister in his drive to implement reform.

It was not just ministers themselves who were able to exert a considerable influence on government from the inside. The senior bureaucratic officials who staffed the highest levels of the government machine played a vital part in determining policy and helped provide a continuity to government policy that the often rapid turnover of ministers did not allow. The senior civil servants of the Russian Empire represented diverse strands of opinion. A substantial proportion of the senior bureaucrats in the ministry of internal affairs in the capital owned land,[35] but perhaps more importantly, more than two-thirds of provincial governors were landowners.[36] The social composition of the upper echelons of the Russian government machine meant that the changes represented by Stolypin's reform proposals would have a deep effect on the governing elite of the empire. When the council for the local economy met, the representatives of the provincial governors were overwhelmingly opposed to the government's proposals to reform local government.[37] An analysis of the reasons for their opposition prepared by I. Ia. Gurliand, one of Stolypin's closest bureaucratic assistants, showed that the governors were motivated by exactly the same concerns as the United Nobility had already expressed.[38] Similarly, Stolypin's proposals to reduce the authority of the district marshal of the nobility found little sympathy with the provincial representatives who debated them. The council's commission examining the government's bill wanted to limit the new district commandant's powers to dealing with police and taxation matters and made a very vigorous defence of the position of the marshal of the nobility. It declared that attempts to reduce the marshal's influence were not only "an injury to the interests of the noble estate, but most significantly, pushed the *zemstvo* ideal – the ideal of local initiative – into the background".[39] As Stolypin's plans in these vital areas were actively opposed by men who were responsible to him as interior minister, it is clear that the degree of support for his reforms, especially among provincial officialdom, was far from universal. Central government officials were also ambivalent about the merits of Stolypin's plans. S. E. Kryzhanovskii, the assistant minister of the interior who had been responsible for drafting many of the reform bills, argued that it would be more appropriate to take a more gradual approach to change in the structures of government of the state. He wanted to see a progressive democratization of local government and, even though Kryzhanovskii believed that the case for reducing noble involvement in local government was indisputable, he recognized that the outright assault on the gentry's position that Stolypin was undertaking meant that the reform proposals could not proceed further.[40]

High-level officials both inside and outside the central government establishment openly showed their lack of sympathy with Stolypin's aims and policies. The extreme right-wing parties, and especially the Union of the Russian People, had significant support among officials. The St Petersburg city governor, V. A. Dediulin, recommended people to the Union,[41] while the Samara deputy governor, S. P. Beletskii, attended right-wing ceremonies in his official capacity; in his previous post as head of the Vilno provincial chancellery he had been a member of the local council of the Russian Assembly.[42] Beletskii was brought to the capital in 1909 by Stolypin to take up the post of deputy director of the department of police. One of the empire's other most senior police officials, P. I. Rachkovskii, believed that the Union of the Russian People represented the most effective opposition to revolution and sought to encourage its growth as a means of countering the activities of revolutionary groups.[43] This pattern was repeated throughout the empire.[44] Many of the men who staffed the Russian government held no brief to support the prime minister: neither the council of ministers nor senior provincial officials offered sustained support to Stolypin. Even more significantly, the prime minister was unable to ensure that government officials would not indulge in active opposition to his policies. This resulted from the nature of the Russian political process: government servants saw their responsibility as being to the monarch and, in some indefinite way, to Russia itself. They did not identify with the post-1905 reformed government in the same way, and did not feel that they owed loyalty to Stolypin and his policies. Even though a council of ministers had been set up in 1905, this did not extend to the adoption of collective cabinet responsibility and this extended down into the lower reaches of the administration. Officials in the Russian provinces did not believe that they possessed any duty to support the policies being pursued by the government: instead, the nebulous conception that they had of the interests of the tsar and Russia as a whole allowed them to promote a variety of positions.

## The nobility revitalized

Alongside "establishment" reservations about the progress of reform, Stolypin faced opposition to his plans from important social groups that were able to make their views known to the governing elite. The resurgence of conservatism and waning of support for reform in Russia after 1906 were not just consequences of the specific measures that Stolypin proposed to take, but were also a result of the effects that the events of 1905 had on the country. While the revolutionary disturbances and strikes were in full spate, it was relatively easy for the government to introduce the large-scale constitutional reforms that were implemented during the latter part of 1905. The fear of a full-scale revolution motivated the governing and landowning classes to, albeit grudgingly, accept these reforms that allowed a degree of popular participation in government, for it was they who had the most to lose if they continued to resist reform. The option of continued conservatism was likely to lead only to an intensification of rebellion and posed the very real risk that the apparatus of the state and its supporters would be unable to quell the outbreaks of violence and discontent. The seriousness with which the highest reaches of the government treated the 1905 disturbances is shown by the tsar's advice to his mother, the dowager empress, not to return to Russia as her safety could not be guaranteed.[45]

After the introduction of a representative legislative body and the promise of the extension of civil liberties there were complaints from the gentry that the government had gone too far.[46] It was felt that the electoral law offered too great a scope to "unreliable" elements, and this opinion was strengthened by the results of elections to the first two Dumas. The majority of the nobility accepted that the new political institutions could not be abolished, but there was a great reluctance to countenance any reduction in the political power that the gentry had traditionally wielded. The nobility wanted to see elections on an estate basis, so that they themselves would gain an influence vastly disproportionate to their numerical strength. They quickly grasped the nature of the threat that reform posed to their position. During the spring of 1905, provoked by the 18 February announcement that a national assembly was to be convened, a small group of conservative nobles began to meet in St Petersburg to discuss how they could exert influence on the government to ensure that proper account was taken of noble views. This group comprised some of the most influential members of the noble estate: A. S. Stishinskii and B. V. Sturmer were members of the State Council – Sturmer would become prime minister for ten months during 1916; A. A. Shirinskii-Shikhmatov was assistant chief procurator of the Holy Synod; V. I. Gurko was head of the land section of the ministry of internal affairs; Count A. A. Bobrinskii was chairman of the St Petersburg provincial *zemstvo* and a former provincial marshal of the nobility; and A. A. Naryshkin was a *zemstvo* activist from Orel province.[47] The initial participants in this group were essentially bureaucrats whose links to the apparatus of government were very close indeed. In April 1905 they formally established the Patriotic Union, but took care to ensure that its leadership included a significant proportion of nobles who had only limited contact with the St Petersburg apparatus. This was not the only organization that was seeking to represent the views of the noble elite: the Union of Russian Men came into being in March 1905 and included members of some of Russia's greatest landowning families. Count Pavel Sheremetev and Prince A. G. Shcherbatov were joined by the marshals of the nobility for both St Petersburg and Moscow, Count V. V. Gudovich and Prince P. N. Trubetskoi. The Russian Men wanted to draw support from a wider spectrum of people than the Patriotic Union and placed more stress on publicizing its work among local noble groups and the *zemstva*.

The Russian nobility found other outlets for its views during 1905. Provincial nobles in the province of Saratov took the initiative in setting up a local union of landowners in September 1905, and their example was soon followed by gentry across Russia. At the end of November 1905, the first national congress of landowners took place in Moscow, attracting 227 representatives from 33 different provinces. A second congress took place three months later, and declared itself firmly opposed to a plan for expropriating noble land, albeit with compensation, which was circulating inside the government and which appeared to have Witte's approval.[48] The variety of political groupings on the conservative wing of Russian politics was unsurprising, given the novelty of the open political environment, but it also represented real differences in the views of the nobility. A national conference of marshals of the nobility took place in January 1906: the marshals adopted a stance akin to the Octobrist party, but they were also very keen to maintain their own position as the traditional leaders of the noble estate and to prevent other groups encroaching on their authority.[49] By the late spring of 1906, however, most of the local noble groups were in favour of establishing a single umbrella organization that would speak for the noble estate. At the end of April a steering committee assembled in Moscow to bring unity to the nobles. This proved to be dominated by conservatives, clearly demonstrated by the brisk replacement of Prince P. N. Trubetskoi as chairman of the committee by N. F. Kasatkin-Rostovskii, a member of the Patriotic Union.[50]

The following month, the first national congress of the United Nobility took place. The organization was dominated by conservative nobles, and its congresses succeeded in attracting representatives from only half of the provincial noble assemblies. Nevertheless, the United Nobility came to play a critically important part in the opposition to reform. This was, in part, due to the strength of the influence that could be exerted by the great nobles who played the most significant role in the organization. This section of the noble estate enjoyed privileged access to the political structures of the empire: Count Aleksei Bobrinskii, the chairman of the United Nobility, was an appointed member of the State Council, as were other leading lights in the organization, such as A. P. Strukov, O. R. Ekesparre, F. D. Samarin, A. A. Naryshkin and Prince Kasatkin-Rostovskii. In all, more than 30 per cent of the Council's membership between 1906 and 1914 belonged to the United Nobility. These men made full use of debates in the State Council to ensure that the nobility's point of view was heard, and the Council eventually became the chief forum for the articulation of conservative political views. These men had an existing entrée to the seats of power in Russia. State Council membership meant that ministers would receive these men: the first congress of the United Nobility in May 1906 was held in the building of the agriculture department by the invitation of its head, A. S. Stishinskii. Naryshkin was able to meet Stolypin in the winter of 1907 to personally express the disquiet of the United Nobility about the government's proposals to reform local government. Links between the regime and the nobility were also personally close. Stolypin's brother-in-law, Aleksei Neidgart, was a member of the permanent council of the United Nobility from its inception until after Stolypin's death – and also a member of the State Council. The leaders of the United Nobility had significant experience of the work of government and were able to put this to good effect. V. I.

Gurko, a member of the permanent council from 1908 onwards, had been a senior civil servant, reaching the post of deputy minister of the interior in 1906 before being forced to resign as a result of scandal. His knowledge of government thinking on rural matters – he had been responsible for much of the work on land reform – made his contributions to the nobility's debates exceptionally valuable. Added to this was a deep dislike of Stolypin, fuelled by the prime minister's insistence that Gurko resign, which sharpened the former bureaucrat's distaste for the government's policies.

The congresses of the United Nobility that met annually during Stolypin's premiership each attracted more than 125 representatives. The nobility adopted a sceptical attitude to the government's plans from the start: at their second congress in November 1906, a proposal to mark their approval of the government's programme, in a telegram congratulating Stolypin on his escape from the August explosion that wrecked his home, was rejected. Instead, the congress took the view that, "To express approval of the prime minister's programme is premature, since its content is not yet clear. The work of the congress will show how far we consider that the government's programme is worthy of full commendation."[51] The United Nobility also provided a platform for political parties on the right to publicize their views. V. M. Purishkevich, a prominent member of the Union of the Russian People, spoke at the second congress and painted a very rosy picture of the Union's work, suggesting that it had attracted more than three million members in 205 branches and had printed 13 million pamphlets during 1906.[52] The anti-government tone of the congresses was most clearly seen in March 1908 when F. D. Samarin delivered his report criticizing the entire basis of the reform programme. The willingness of the tsar to meet a deputation from the United Nobility gave further evidence of the influence that the organization enjoyed and the report on the audience gave the United Nobility great cause for satisfaction. The congress was assured that the deputation had heard:

A reassurance from the Sovereign that the district marshals of the nobility and their rights would not be impinged upon and that the marshals were as close to the heart of the

Emperor as they were to our own . . . we were instructed to
express the monarch's thanks to the congress for its work.[53]

The United Nobility took an interest in all the chief political
issues that Stolypin's government was addressing, but its atten-
tions had most impact on the local government and legal reforms.
The United Nobility had only very limited representation in the
Third Duma, with only 20 or so men elected to the 500-strong
assembly, but it was able to exercise considerable influence
through the council for the local economy. The nobility were able
to achieve some success here, seeing the village *zemstvo* bill
defeated in 1909 and registering substantial minorities against the
government's proposals for district administration. The proposal
to reduce the powers of the marshal of the nobility by establishing a post of district commandant was approved by a majority of
39 votes to 30, but the supporters of the nobility's position presented a substantial minority report and requested an adjourn-
ment, so that they could draft a bill in line with their views.[54]
The United Nobility were also successful in getting the government's proposals for a new local court abandoned by launching a
severe attack on them in the State Council and it also saw the
government's bill to introduce a village *zemstvo* defeated. The
direct extent of the United Nobility's pressure is not easy to
judge, since other pressures were working on Stolypin. But the
extent to which the nobility's views were received sympathetically
at the highest levels of Russian government suggests that this
pressure group played a vital part in countering Stolypin's reform
programme.

## Church and state

Other traditional forces played an important part in articulating
opposition to radical reform. Most of the leadership of the
Orthodox Church believed that the government's proposals to
extend religious freedoms posed a direct threat to its own position. Religious life in Russia was dominated by the Orthodox
Church, which enjoyed a status that gave it enormous privileges.
Orthodoxy was the religion of the state; the 1906 Fundamental

Laws defined the Orthodox Church as "pre-eminent and predominant". The church's position was strengthened by its relationship with the imperial family since the monarch had to belong to it, as did any woman who married into the family – Nicholas II's fiancée was received into the church shortly before her marriage in 1894. Before 1905 the Orthodox Church had the exclusive right to carry out missionary work among the peoples of the empire, while it was an offence for an individual to leave the church and join another sect or religion. Ecclesiastical censorship also helped to protect the church's position, since printers were prohibited from producing books about the Orthodox Church without the permission of the church's own censorship committee. The links between spiritual and temporal powers were made even closer by the way in which the Orthodox Church was governed. Since the time of Peter the Great, the church had been administered by a lay official, the chief procurator, who headed the Holy Synod, which was comprised of senior clerics. While the Synod had met infrequently under Pobedonostsev, leaving the day-to-day administration of the church in the hands of the chief procurator and his lay assistants, the events of 1905 had not left the church untouched. By the autumn of 1907, the metropolitan of St Petersburg was writing to one of his fellow bishops that, "In the present troubled times, the more the full sessions of the Synod the better: the steadier will be the general direction of affairs. And there is a great deal of business . . . since October [1906] we have been meeting twice a week, this week three times."[55]

The reforms that Stolypin proposed would allow other religions to gain substantial parity with the Orthodox Church and this provoked enormous resentment in the established church. The Orthodox religion already had institutional channels that enabled it to make its views known at the highest levels of the Russian state. The chief procurator of the Holy Synod sat as a member of the council of ministers and this offered him a unique position – as the representative of a sectional group – to express the church's opinions. Often, however, the chief procurator ended up expressing his own views or represented only one part of the full spectrum of ecclesiastical opinion. Nevertheless, the chief procurator's status as a quasi-minister gave him direct right of access to the tsar, and Pobedonostsev's particular intimacy with both Alexander III and Nicholas II while he was the administrative head of the church had made this link especially valuable. The tradition of church and state working very closely together received a jolt, however, in 1905 when there was pressure from Orthodox clerics for the process of reform to be extended to the church itself. The Holy Synod itself appealed to the tsar over the head of Pobedonostsev for a church council to be summoned, and the bishops began to agitate for the level of state control of the church to be reduced.[56] Nicholas II rejected the idea of a church council, but the seeds of discontent had been sown among priests and bishops. When Stolypin made proposals that were intended to give considerable rights to non-Orthodox believers and, by implication, to reduce the privileged position of the Orthodox Church itself, the church felt itself under threat and responded with great vigour.

The church used all the means at its disposal to counter Stolypin's plans for reform. Although the Holy Synod occupied a position that gave it both spiritual and temporal authority, the Synod bore no responsibility for government policy towards other religious faiths. This was in the jurisdiction of the ministry of internal affairs and Stolypin's department was keen to promote greater civil rights for the non-Orthodox to fulfil the commitments made by the government to extend religious toleration. There was also a political motivation for the policy as, by improving the lot of these groups, the government hoped that it would be rewarded with increased support. The Holy Synod was aghast when it realized the extent to which other religions were to be given parity with the Orthodox Church, and the chief procurator used his position in the council of ministers to press the church's case. The Synod argued that the government had no business concerning itself with the extension of freedom of conscience to non-Orthodox religions, since this was a matter of canonical significance and, therefore, came within the jurisdiction of the Synod itself. This argument was designed to stop the reform process in its tracks by challenging the validity of any temporal involvement in reforming the status of religions in the empire, but while the council of ministers agreed that strictly canonical questions must remain under the Synod's jurisdiction, it did not accept that these religious reforms fell into this category.

The Synod prepared detailed objections to the content of the various bills to extend religious freedoms, but its objections were swept aside by the government in October 1906.[57] The church was not prepared to give up the fight over what it regarded as extremely harmful proposals. When the council of ministers considered the second set of bills on religious toleration in February 1907, the chief procurator argued that the government's proposals far exceeded the provisions of the April 1905 edict that had promised greater religious toleration, and that Stolypin's bills would effectively disestablish the Orthodox Church. The council of ministers rejected this argument too, but did agree that the Synod's views on the religious bills should be considered, although this must not be allowed to delay the bills' progress. The Church was invited to formulate its detailed response to the proposals at the same time as they were being considered by the Duma, and the council of ministers agreed that any amendments that were needed as a result of the Synod's representations could be introduced at an appropriate stage in the Duma's proceedings.[58]

The chief procurator, P. P. Izvol'skii, was not without ministerial allies in his fight to protect the Church's position. In February 1907, P. Kh. von Shvanebakh, the deeply conservative state comptroller, argued that there was no need for new legislation to bring about greater religious freedom since most of what was being proposed was not specifically prohibited by law and could, therefore, be enacted by means of senate interpretations of existing legislation. This approach was aimed at limiting the extent of reform since von Shvanebakh believed that it would be much more difficult to introduce change without actual legislation and that, if bills were introduced into the Duma, there was a strong chance that the elected legislators would seek to go further than the government in liberalizing the position of non-Orthodox believers. The minister of transport, N. K. Schaffhausen, also tried to obstruct Stolypin's proposals by voicing his disagreement with the bill that would make mixed marriages easier. These arguments found no greater favour with the council of ministers and the majority of ministers agreed that freedom of conscience needed to be guaranteed by legislation, although they accepted that the Jewish question remained a special case that needed separate discussion.[59] It is perhaps not surprising that the church was unable to see its views prevail in the first year of Stolypin's premiership: the strength of feeling in favour of reform among ministers was still substantial, and the government was committed to implementing measures that would put flesh on the bones of the general commitments to extending civil rights made during 1904 and 1905.

The Orthodox Church was not prepared, however, to let the situation rest: it was able to voice its concerns through a wide variety of channels. The church's network of parishes and monasteries gave it a level of contact with the population of the empire that was unmatched by any other organization. More than 100,000 priests staffed the church and, while this provided Orthodoxy with the means to communicate with its flock, it also presented problems of control for the church's bishops. Once the Synod's opposition to the government's proposals became clear, local priests were able to voice their concern in a variety of ways, and were also able to enlist support from other organizations to press the church's case. The Moscow missionary I. Aivazov wrote that "Stolypin was constantly working against Orthodoxy" and this perception was widespread among the ordinary clergy.[60] The Pochaev monastery in the province of Volynia, a well-known centre of conservative ideas, was particularly active in trying to drum up popular opposition to the government's Bills. It produced printed petition forms for submission to the tsar as a supplement to its daily newspaper, *Pochaevskie izvestiia* (Pochaev News), each with space for some 150 signatures, asking Nicholas II not to confirm the bill allowing non-Orthodox religions to undertake proselytization.[61] The local bishop approved these tactics, and petitions containing more than 44,000 signatures were sent to Nicholas II at the end of 1909.[62] The Chief Procurator identified a number of individual priests, including Bishop Hermogen of Saratov, Archpriest Vostorgov of Moscow and the monk Illiodor, who were especially active in fomenting discontent against the government's bills. These priests – and others – were identified as having close links with right-wing political organizations and these political groups were often recruited to add extra weight to the church's own protestations. The Tambov and Iaroslavl' branches of the Union of the Russian People congratulated the Holy Synod on its stand, as did the Kiev branch of the

Russian Assembly.[63] The involvement of the Orthodox Church in overtly political matters, and the development of campaigns by political groups that were deeply opposed to the tenor of Stolypin's government, gave both spiritual and temporal powers cause for concern. While the Synod wanted to press its case with vigour, the chief procurator recognized the dangers that were inherent in the church becoming openly involved in the political arena. The creation of antagonism between the spiritual and temporal powers would only lead to a diminution of the church's power and influence, Izvol'skii realized, and he set out to try to limit the extent of political involvement in church affairs.[64]

This was not within the power of the church's hierarchy to achieve, however, and during late 1908 and 1909 the pressure from the political right to amend the religious toleration legislation increased. The tsar was one of the chief targets for petitions and the like from the political right: Nicholas II's deep attachment to Orthodoxy meant that he was ready to listen to concerns expressed by the church and was especially sympathetic if he felt that the special position of Orthodoxy was being undermined.[65] Religious questions were the centre of discussion at various salons attended by courtiers. Countess S. S. Ignat'eva, a well-known society hostess, assembled around her men such as Bishop Hermogen, the Synod officials V. K. Sabler and A. P. Rogovich and the conservative politicians B. V. Sturmer and A. A. Shirinskii-Shikhmatov. The State Council member, Count S. D. Sheremetev, held regular gatherings at which court favourites such as A. S. Stishinskii and Count S. A. Tol' were present.[66] These meeting-places acted as a conduit by which views could be transmitted to the tsar's circle and to the monarch himself. Nicholas II found it reassuring that there was significant support for the Orthodox Church among sections of the political elite and among the population as a whole, and this helped to strengthen his own resolve to support the church. Stolypin's reminder to the Duma in 1909 that Russia was ruled by an "Orthodox Tsar" was as much a recognition by the prime minister of Nicholas II's support for the church as it was a warning to the Duma of the consequences of liberalizing the religious bills.

The Synod devoted substantial energies to presenting its position in the Duma when the bills came to be debated there. It also continued its pressure on Stolypin himself to shift his position. The appearance of the assistant chief procurator, A. P. Rogovich, before the Duma in the spring of 1909 demonstrated that the church's position remained as firm as ever and he declared that if the ministry of internal affairs continued to insist on supporting a bill, "which is out of line with the judgements of the Holy Synod . . . then new ways will have to be found to defend the independence and power of the Church".[67] The new chief procurator, S. M. Luk'ianov, kept up the pressure on Stolypin as the government's proposals were being debated in the Duma. He continued to insist that the Synod would not compromise and intended to hold out to ensure that the church's position remained untouched. It is clear that, by the spring of 1909, the Synod had a clear perception of the direction in which the political wind was blowing in St Petersburg. Stolypin's reform programme was running into difficulties on a number of fronts, and the Synod and its conservative supporters could scent the prospect of victory.

The success of the Orthodox Church in preventing reform that would have affected its own position only indirectly was further evidence of the power that the traditional conservative bulwarks of Russian society were able to wield. The twin pillars of the old regime – nobility and church – proved extremely resilient and resistant to accepting reform in any guise. This resistance to change can be seen as symptomatic of the weakness of both nobles and clergy in early twentieth-century Russia. The economic decline of the nobility since emancipation was paralleled by the ossification of the structures of the Orthodox Church. Pobedonostsev's long tenure as chief procurator had helped to prevent the development of initiatives inside the Orthodox Church to cope with the changing social structures of the Russian Empire, and had tied the church even more closely to the state. In the growing cities of the empire, the church's role was uncertain and hindered by factional dispute and a concern to counter the influence of other religions.[68] Even though the numbers of Orthodox believers far outnumbered adherents to other religions in the empire, the resentment of the Orthodox authorities when improvements to the position of other religions were being considered, indicated a lack of confidence in their own church's ability to weather the process of extending freedom of conscience.

The refusal of the tsar and his advisers to permit a church council in 1905 put a further obstacle in the way of revitalizing Orthodoxy. The response of the Orthodox Church to Stolypin's proposals for reform demonstrated how unsure the church was of its own position, but it still retained the power to influence the political elite of the empire.

Even though both the nobility and the Orthodox Church were trying to protect weak positions, the political structures of the post-1905 Russian Empire preserved the traditional power and influence of these groups. The State Council, with its inbuilt conservative majority, provided a forum in which they could articulate their opinions and the constitutional reforms of 1905 and 1906 had ensured that the Council could block legislation that was not to its taste. Conservative Russia was, therefore, provided with a very powerful legislative weapon in its struggle to survive. The position of the monarch – the empire's chief nobleman and the protector of Orthodoxy – and his veto over legislation that he disliked further enhanced the power of the traditionally powerful elements of Russian society. Stolypin was, therefore, trying to implement his reforms in a political environment that was fundamentally hostile to them. The dramatic social changes that Stolypin envisaged as vital for the renewal of Russia had to be enacted through a legislative system where conservative influence could exert a decisive influence over two of the system's three stages. The post-1905 political structures of imperial Russia were reformed in form only; the ethos of Russian politics remained firmly opposed to change.

# CHAPTER 5

# *Reform defeated*

## Politics and public opinion

After 1905 the Russian political environment provided considerable challenges for a reforming government. The need to see legislation approved by Duma, State Council and tsar meant that the
government actively needed to seek support for its plans to
ensure that each section of the tripartite legislative process was
prepared to offer its endorsement of the government's bills.
Russian governments had never before needed to justify their
policies to such a wide spectrum of opinion and the introduction
of this more transparent political system forced Stolypin's government to think carefully about effective methods of gaining
support. This process was made more difficult by the emergence
of political parties in the Russian Empire and the rapid development of a full-blown party structure at the same time as the new
legislature was coming into existence. The government therefore
had to deal with a twin constituency in seeking support: it needed
to work with political parties to try to ensure their support, especially in the Duma, but it also had to address itself to the voting
population of the empire to try to encourage support for those
political parties that the government believed would help in the
passage of its programme.

The government's task was made more difficult by the embryonic nature of the new political system. Before the first set of Duma elections took place early in 1906, political groupings were fluid and unclear. Political parties had hardly had time to develop full programmes and, even where they had articulated their aspirations, the problems of communication across the empire made it difficult for the voting population to be fully aware of the positions adopted by the different parties. Many of the deputies who were elected to the First Duma arrived in St Petersburg in April 1906 without any definite party affiliation and with only hazy ideas of what each party stood for. Government attempts to influence the outcome of the elections to the First Duma were, therefore, doomed to failure. The political instincts of the government in the winter of 1905 proved, in any case, to be unsure. The regime's reliance on the peasantry to deliver a moderate majority in the Duma was misplaced and it was only with the convocation of the First Duma, and the realization that its political complexion was far from conservative, that the government began to pay serious attention to influencing political opinion.

Even before Stolypin's appointment as minister of internal affairs in April 1906, his predecessor P. N. Durnovo had sought the views of provincial governors in trying to analyze the Duma election results and to explain the unexpected success of the parties on the left, and especially the Kadets. Durnovo's analysis identified the unpopularity of the government as crucial in persuading people to vote for the Kadet party: society was discontented in the wake of the Russo-Japanese War and the loss of government authority during 1905. The government's hesitant policy during 1905 had contributed to its loss of authority, and the regime's attempts to reassert its position by using repressive measures had further alienated public opinion. Durnovo argued that the success of the Kadets was not so much a product of the party's own intrinsic strength, but rather a reflection of the weakness of every other political group. The Kadets' energy and broad programme contrasted particularly with the disunity and poor organization of the Octobrists. The provincial governors reached no consensus about the effect of the electoral system itself, and Durnovo left open the question of how far the details of the franchise had helped radical parties to triumph.[1] Stolypin himself undertook a much more detailed examination of the electoral system when he took over the ministry of internal affairs. The size of each electoral constituency – usually a province – meant that it was difficult for the more conservative elements to exert their influence over the voters, but it was clear to Stolypin that the weight given to the peasants' votes was the chief reason for the radicalism of the First Duma. Stolypin admitted that the government had badly misjudged the mood of the peasantry by believing that they were the most reliable supporters of the existing order. Also, conservative representation in the Duma had been reduced by the disadvantageous position occupied by the Russian population in the borderlands – especially the Polish provinces of the empire. The new prime minister was clear that popular discontent with the government could only be reduced by the promotion of social and economic reform, but Stolypin did argue that the government should play a much more active part during the next election campaign. In his report to the tsar he declared that:

> The government must abandon its indifference to the outcome of the elections . . . It must use all the means at its disposal to support the moderate press, both nationally and locally . . . It must quickly identify those candidates, whether from the moderate parties or else independents, whose election would be most desirable from the government's point of view and support them during the election campaign by every means that is not prohibited by law. It is vital that the government explains to all those who are connected with the administration that it is their duty to support the government in this task . . . We must support pro-government agitators in opposition parties . . . We must encourage all those people who may prove useful to the government during the elections, but we must exercise the greatest care in eliminating from the elections candidates who are unsympathetic to the government; no violence or police restraint can be allowed.[2]

Stolypin was prepared to see the elections for the Second Duma carried out on the same franchise as had produced the radical First Duma, but was determined to adopt a much more interventionist approach. In the run-up to the new elections, the prime minister instructed provincial governors to publicize the government's legislative plans and to ensure that they countered anti-government propaganda. While the governors were reminded that they must not interfere in the party political arena, Stolypin wanted them to make it plain that the government hoped to co-operate with the Duma and that it was determined to adhere strictly to the principles of legality.[3] The government tried to influence public opinion through subsidizing newspapers and by arranging for the publication of pamphlets that explained govern-ment policy, but these practices were still in their infancy in Russia.[4] Stolypin identified three additional ways in which the government could affect the Duma elections without the need for any change in the electoral law: clerks should be provided to help illiterate voters, lessening the chances of their being influenced by others; there should be a prohibition on the distribution of pre-marked ballot papers;[5] and there ought to be a reduction in the number of electoral meetings at which Duma deputies were actu-ally chosen, to allow more influence to be exerted on the peasan-try by more reliable members of the meeting.[6] The Second Duma turned out, however, to be of much the same political complexion as its predecessor and it was clear that the government's measures to influence the outcome of the elections had been unsuccessful.

The government, therefore, had to consider manipulating the franchise if it wanted to see a Duma elected that might take a more helpful attitude to the government's reforms. Stolypin was realistic, however, about the extent to which the altered franchise could change the composition of the Duma. He accepted that a gerrymandered assembly, with its membership restricted to the traditional elites of the empire, would have no credibility now that the population had experienced a much more representative assembly. More importantly, however, Stolypin had to tread a careful line if he wished to implement reform. A Duma that was similar in political outlook to the conservative State Council would hardly help in the implementation of reforms, so Stolypin had to be careful to ensure that the new Duma contained a sub-stantial proportion of deputies who were fundamentally in favour of reform. Although Stolypin expressed the wish that the new electoral law should ensure the representation in the Duma of the "best classes" of Russia, meaning those who had material inter-ests at stake, he did not want to wholly exclude the Kadets from participation in the legislative institutions. Discussion about a new electoral law took place inside the government during the spring of 1907 and Kryzhanovskii, the assistant minister of internal affairs, prepared three different proposals for consideration by the council of ministers.

The first option was to set out in advance the number of Duma deputies that would come from each social group; the second was to ensure that landowners dominated the electoral system; the last was to have the national Duma elected by members of the district *zemstva*. The council of ministers approved the second alternative and, at the same time as the Second Duma was dissolved, a new electoral law was issued on 3 June 1907.[7] The new electoral law also gave the interior minister considerable discretion in the precise organization of electoral meetings, and this allowed arrangements to be made to increase Russian voting strength in areas where there was a mixture of nationalities. The government took full advantage of this power to organize separate meetings for Russians, especially in the western borderlands, where the number of seats available to the national minorities was substantially reduced.[8] These measures had the desired effect, and when the Third Duma assembled in 1907, its composition was more agreeable to Stolypin and his fellow ministers. The prime minister still did not believe that the government would receive unconditional support from the newly elected assembly and he expected that, overall, the Third Duma would be in moderate opposition to the government.[9] This proved to be a realistic assessment of the prospects for co-operation between government and legislature. While government and Duma were able to exist together with reasonable equanimity, in the long term the Third Duma proved hardly more malleable than its two predecessors.

At the same time as the government was considering how to maximize its support among the public, it was also attempting to establish good relations with political parties. When Stolypin assumed the chairmanship of the council of ministers in the summer of 1906, he attempted to form a government that would include public figures with liberal views, especially members of the Kadet party, as well as traditional bureaucrats. Stolypin was unable to persuade the liberals to join the council of ministers as they imposed conditions on their participation: the government

should make commitments in advance to implement all the promises of the manifesto of 17 October 1905 and the liberal public
figures should receive half of the cabinet posts, including the
interior ministry.[10] This rebuff immediately put Stolypin on his
guard when dealing with the Kadets and he was subsequently
unwilling to rely on them to provide support for the government
in the Duma. This attitude was strongly reinforced by the behaviour that the Kadets had adopted at the dissolution of the First
Duma, immediately before Stolypin's appointment as prime minister. A substantial section of the Kadet party condemned the
Duma's dissolution as illegal and, meeting in Vyborg in Finland,
issued the Vyborg Appeal, which called on the population of the
empire to refuse to pay taxes or to perform military service. Stolypin took what he saw as irresponsible behaviour by the Kadets as
evidence that the liberals were not yet ready to take a part in government.[11]

This rejection of the Kadet party by the government helped to
weaken the government's position in the Duma. Although the
Kadets occupied a much less prominent position in the Third
Duma than they had in the first two, their 54 deputies could still
have been useful to the government in its attempts to push
through reform. Stolypin, however, refused to seek their support
and the Kadet Duma group became increasingly disunited and
disillusioned.[12] Having turned away from the Kadets, Stolypin
focused his attention on the Octobrist party. This appeared to be
a much more promising source of support for the government.
The party's choice of name – The Union of 17th October –
demonstrated its support for the new order and showed that it
accepted the foundations of the new Russia. This alone marked
out the Octobrists as more likely allies for Stolypin's government,
since they were one of the very few Russian political parties that
accepted the 1905 reforms and did not demand further radical
institutional change. By basing their party's aims on the wholehearted acceptance of the new order that had been implemented
by the October Manifesto, the Octobrists showed that they were
prepared to work within the new legislative framework. Within
these limits the Octobrists wanted reform, but this was to be
founded on the principles laid down in the October Manifesto. It
was therefore easy for the government to see them as reliable sup-

porters who would provide a solid base in the Duma on which to build a majority, and this belief was strengthened by the public pronouncements made by Alexander Guchkov, the party's leader, in the months following Stolypin's appointment as chairman of the council of ministers. Shortly after Stolypin's statement of his government's policy was published in August 1906, Guchkov gave a newspaper interview and stated, "I have great faith in P. A. Stolypin. We have not had such talented and able people in power before. I am convinced that he will use all his energies to fulfil his programme. I believe that his intentions are honest and that he has a deep love for our suffering motherland."[13] The Octobrist party based its programme on the promises that had been contained in the manifesto of 17 October 1905, and this gave them the clearest possible affinity with Stolypin himself. After the dissolution of the First Duma, Guchkov had reflected on the reasons for the failure of government and Duma to co-operate. He criticized the composition of Goremykin's government, seeing its domination by "old bureaucrats" as one of the chief reasons for relations between government and Duma reaching an impasse. More importantly, however, Guchkov condemned Goremykin's administration for having no definite programme of reform and he set out a list of items that he believed should form part of the new government's programme. Guchkov wanted to see an agrarian reform that would increase peasant landholding; a reform of local self-government; the implementation of the freedoms of assembly, association, conscience and the press; and he specifically called for the easing of restrictions on Jews.[14]

The legislative priorities of the Octobrist party were strikingly similar to the government's own intentions and Guchkov commented approvingly on the August 1906 declaration of government policy, noting that "the government has not retreated from the principles which it defended in its conversations with public figures [early in 1906]". Even though the dissolution of the Duma might have prompted the government to abandon any idea of reform, Guchkov congratulated it for "not making this mistake and promising to prepare reforms . . . and to work together with the Duma".[15] Stolypin took every opportunity to try to maintain the support of the Octobrists by stressing that his government intended to make liberal reforms. He stated that the government would act "in the name of the projected reforms without retreating a single step"[16] and in a number of interviews with the British ambassador he confirmed the government's commitment to "enlightened reform".[17] Stolypin felt that if a sufficient number of Octobrists could be elected to the Duma, this would be extremely advantageous for the government: and so the revised electoral law enacted in June 1907 was aimed at increasing the representation of social groups that might elect Octobrists. The greater weight given to landowners and to industrialists had the desired effect, increasing Octobrist strength from 42 deputies in the Second Duma to more than 150 – 35 per cent of the Duma's total membership – in the new Duma that met in November 1907. The right-wing parties also made gains, and the combined strength of the extreme and moderate right exceeded the Kadets' strength. As the government had intended, the losers in the elections were the parties to the left of the Octobrists: the Kadets, the Polish nationalist party, the Trudoviki and the Social Democrats all had their representation reduced.

Although the government had succeeded in its chief aim of ensuring a more agreeable legislature, the Octobrist Duma party was unable to provide the consistent backing that Stolypin needed if his reform bills were to be approved by the Duma. The coherence of the party was vital for the government, since any Duma majority had to include the Octobrists. The parliamentary arithmetic meant that the left could not achieve a majority on its own and, while by 1909 parties on the right could muster almost as many votes as the Octobrists, a majority was still beyond their grasp if at least some of the Octobrists were not prepared to offer their support. The Octobrist party in the Duma came from a restricted background: more than 65 per cent of its deputies were propertied men, although the party's leadership was drawn from urban deputies. The Octobrist deputies were highly educated and more than half had a university degree, making them a close second to the Kadet deputies in terms of education. The party had a limited geographical base, since two-thirds of its deputies came from the central provinces of European Russia, and more than 90 per cent were Orthodox believers.[18] This social uniformity was not, however, a guarantee of political cohesion. Not all the deputies who became Octobrists once the Duma met were members of the party before the elections, but had been persuaded to join when they arrived in St Petersburg for the Duma session. Despite the Octobrists' claims to the contrary, their national organization hardly existed. Police reports in the autumn of 1907 indicated that the influence and significance of the Octobrists in the provinces "had declined mainly as a result of the lack of activity of [the party's] leaders" and that after the Duma elections were completed "local activity by the party was almost invisible".[19] It was easy for deputies to feel that they existed in a political vacuum, seeing the Duma as being the whole political world and indulging in internal bickering. Without an established organization in the countryside, it was very difficult for the Duma party to feel that it should remain completely homogeneous, since there was little pressure from members outside the cities to adhere to an agreed political line.

During the first months of the Third Duma, the Octobrists took a major part in the formation of the permanent commissions that were to examine legislation before it was submitted to the full session of the Duma for discussion and, for the first year of the Duma's existence, it appeared as if the legislative institutions might be able to offer useful support to the government. Much of the Third Duma's first session was taken up with debating the agrarian reform. This commanded wide support and did not provoke the socially motivated controversy that the local government and religious bills were to bring. The Octobrists were careful to avoid giving their backing to measures that might cast doubt on the responsibility of the Duma and so call its very existence into question, for they were convinced that the basis of the new order was the establishment of representative legislative institutions and they had no desire to do anything that would threaten their stability. At the same time, the Duma party had to develop its own discipline, and Octobrist deputies had to be reminded that disagreements in commissions had to be reported to the party as a whole for discussion.[20]

During the second session of the Duma, however, the tensions within the Octobrist party began to come out into the open. Proposals to hold a party conference had been circulating since the spring of 1908, but Guchkov himself was opposed to the idea, fearing that divisions in the party would come out into the open at such a gathering. Although the left of the party succeeded in getting an assurance that the conference would take place by the beginning of 1909, Guchkov was able to delay its meeting until October 1909.[21] The lack of internal party discipline was clearly demonstrated in February 1909 by the Gololobov incident. Ia. G. Gololobov, the reporter for the Duma commission on interpellations and one of those who had joined the party only after his election to the Duma, presented a report on a Kadet interpellation and opposed the official Octobrist view.[22] After prolonged discussion within the Duma party, it was decided to censure Gololobov for his conduct, but the incident was symptomatic of widespread tensions within the party. There were widespread rumours at the time that the party was on the verge of splitting and that those on the right of the party were about to leave the Octobrists and join the Moderate Right group in the Duma.[23] Even though one of the legislative proposals closest to the heart of the Octobrist party – the bill to give more rights to the Old Believers – was running into trouble, this did not prompt the party into sustaining its unity.

While these internal party squabbles weakened the discipline of the Octobrists, a much more serious setback for the party was the naval general staff crisis. This challenged the whole basis on which the Octobrists existed, since it showed the weakness of the constitutional structure established by the manifesto of 17 October 1905. The tsar's refusal to confirm a piece of legislation that had been approved by both Duma and State Council suggested that the popularly elected legislature was far from dominant in the law-making process. The Octobrist party had gained its legitimacy from upholding the new constitutional order, but the evidence of the naval general staff affair suggested that the new order was not so different from the pre-1905 political structures of the empire. The power of the tsar was still able to override the wishes of the elected Duma. This débâcle weakened the coherence of the Octobrist party by demonstrating the party's impotence, since it showed the power of the extra-parliamentary right, and gave all elements of the party reason to be concerned about its effectiveness. By the autumn of 1909, the party was in disarray. It lost a Duma by-election in what was regarded as the

Octobrist heartland of Moscow, as urban voters turned to the Kadets as a means of registering their discontent with the slow pace of reform.[24] The congress that eventually met at the beginning of October included only 156 delegates and it was reported that more than 40 per cent of the party's 150 local organizations had ceased to exist.[25] The congress also sparked off the long-promised split in the party: eleven members, including Gololobov, left to form their own Right Octobrist group.

The naval general staff crisis also showed that reform itself was under threat. The inability of the prime minister to get his own legislation accepted by the tsar boded ill for the raft of reforms that were making their way through the Duma. This dismayed both Stolypin and the Octobrists, for it showed that their collaboration was insufficient to overcome the pressures that could be exerted by the right. The response of the prime minister to this was to begin to edge away from the wholehearted commitments that he had made to reform at the beginning of his term of office. The Octobrists seriously contemplated whether their interests were best served by continuing to ally themselves with Stolypin. They had, however, little choice. The party's whole *raison d'être* was to bring about the transformation of Russia on the basis of the October Manifesto and moving to oppose Stolypin's administration would deprive the Octobrists of whatever degree of influence they possessed. Guchkov therefore stood firm behind the prime minister. The Octobrist leader met Stolypin at the end of October 1909 to discuss the work of the forthcoming Duma session and the Duma party discussed how the local court bill could be supported when it came to be debated.[26]

The party's position changed early in 1910. The chairmanship of the Duma became vacant on the resignation of N. A. Khomiakov and Stolypin was instrumental in persuading Guchkov to take the job. The Prime Minister wrote to Guchkov – after unsuccessfully trying to reach him by telephone – to say that "it would be to the benefit of business if the Chairman of the State Duma was to be A. I. Guchkov".[27] Stolypin believed that if Guchkov were to be chairman of the Duma, this would give the government a greater chance of legislative success, for he hoped that Guchkov would be able to use his influence to persuade the Octobrists to give more consistent support to the government's measures, even if they did not always seem to be in line with the promises made in the October Manifesto. Giving the chairmanship to the leader of the Octobrists would also demonstrate the value that the government placed on Octobrist opinion and thus, Stolypin hoped, reinforce the party's support for his administration. Stolypin also hoped that, as the Duma chairman had the right of access to the tsar, Guchkov would be able to counter the influence of the right at court and would act as a defender of the government's policies in that milieu.[28] This was, however, a miscalculation since Nicholas II was suspicious of Guchkov's attempts to extend the Duma's influence over military matters.[29] Guchkov's move to the Duma chairmanship was, therefore, designed to counter both the institutional weakness of the Duma and the growing influence of conservatism.

Guchkov's speech on assuming the Duma chairmanship showed distinct signs of having been agreed with the prime minister. Guchkov attacked the external obstacles to the Duma's efforts, which he characterized as "slowing down our work or distorting its outcome";[30] but he enjoyed limited support inside the Duma. Only the Octobrists, Nationalists and Progressists voted in favour of his assuming the chairmanship, with the parties both on the left and right failing to endorse his candidature. The effect on the Octobrist party of Guchkov's elevation was, however, exactly the opposite of what Stolypin had hoped. Instead of the party becoming more united, there was considerable dispute over who should become the new leader, and this resulted in any decision being postponed until the autumn of 1910, leaving the Duma party leaderless during the debates on the bill to introduce *zemstva* into the western provinces of the empire. It was only late in 1910 that M. V. Rodzianko was elected to lead the party, after months of infighting. The Octobrist party failed to display any coherent attitude towards this piece of legislation, as was obvious from the differing attitudes that members of the party displayed about the bill in the Duma, and this resulted in many Octobrist deputies voting against amendments tabled by the party as a whole.

By the beginning of 1910, Stolypin was looking elsewhere in the political spectrum for support. He recognized the weakness of his own political position and had come to appreciate that reliance on the Octobrists could not provide him with any guarantee of political success. The conservative landowning nobility had been flexing their political muscles not just in the Duma and through the United Nobility, but also in the provincial *zemstva*. The 1907 national *zemstvo* congress proved to be deeply conservative in nature and this was reflected in changes to the political control of individual *zemstva*. Between 1906 and 1909 the overall profile of *zemstvo* political control shifted rightwards as the number of *zemstva* dominated by the right tripled.[31] At the same time, new organizations committed to promoting Russian national values were being established, largely by members of the nobility. The Russian Borderland Society, the Kiev Club of Russian National-ists and the All-Russian National Union were the most durable of these groups.[32] Their geographical focus was firmly in the west and southwest of European Russia, a region with a complex ethnic mix where the Russian population existed alongside Polish, Jewish and Ukrainian communities. National divisions in the region were paralleled by social differences. Even though more than 70 per cent of the population of the nine western pro-vinces were Russian, the landowning nobility of the area was tra-ditionally overwhelmingly Polish, even though Poles and Lithuanians comprised less than 15 per cent of the region's popu-lation. This had important political consequences, especially in determining the region's representation in the State Council. As the western provinces did not have *zemstva*, which were else-where responsible for electing a proportion of the Council's members, the region's representatives were chosen by its nobility and were all Poles. In these circumstances the development of Russian national groups, determined to improve their own posi-tion, was unsurprising. The supporters of these nationalist groups included both senior political figures, such as S. V. Rukhlov who became minister of transport in 1909, and D. I. Pikhno, an appointed member of the State Council, as well as men of more modest status. By the early summer of 1908, the organizers of the most significant of these nationalist groups had concluded that they should move one step further and embark on the formation of a fully fledged political party.

At the same time, there was movement on the extreme right in the Duma. More than 20 deputies broke away from the Right group at the beginning of 1908 and formed the National group under the leadership of Prince A. P. Urusov, who also played a vital part in the All-Russian National Union. The new Nationalist party's first congress took place in June 1908 and declared that the party's chief aim was to ensure that Russian interests were protected in the empire's borderlands. This was much in line with the programme of the small Moderate Right group in the Duma and offered the prospect of substantial parliamentary influence for the Nationalists. During 1909, as the Octobrist party began to lose its coherence, and the government signalled that its commitment to reform was diminishing, the importance of the Moderate Right group and the Nationalist party grew significantly. Between them, these two groups could amass nearly 100 Duma deputies and Stolypin began to see this sizeable voting bloc as having the potential to provide important support for his government.

In the spring of 1909 the prime minister accepted Pikhno's proposal for changes to State Council representation from the western provinces. This question had been debated in the Kiev Club of Russian Nationalists and other nationalist groups in the first months of the year, and they concluded that the franchise should be adjusted to guarantee that Russians would occupy the majority of the seats from the region. The influence of these groups became clear when they quickly succeeded in gaining audiences with both Stolypin and Nicholas II to press their case. Some on the right hoped that this move would embarrass Stolypin and that the prime minister would be unable to support the proposal as it would probably result in the replacement of moderate Polish members of the State Council by conservative Russian land-owners.[33] When Stolypin received the Nationalist deputation, however, he immediately agreed to support the Pikhno plan and introduced a bill into the legislature at the beginning of May 1909. This set the pattern for the second part of Stolypin's premiership. The key parts of the government's programme during the last 30 months of Stolypin's premiership were not radical reforms but measures to enhance Russian nationalism. The Duma Nationalist party became the government's main bulwark in the Duma.

While Stolypin recognized that support from political parties was critical if he was to be able to control the Duma and State

Council, he also appreciated the importance of influencing public opinion more widely. Faced with opposition to its reform programme from many sides, Stolypin's government made considerable attempts to mobilize public opinion in favour of its policies. The government wanted to see its reform proposals explained to the population and to establish a popular atmosphere sympathetic to the government's aims. In particular, government propaganda was aimed at the middle levels of society, at the village priests and teachers who were literate and who were in a position to explain government actions to the largely illiterate peasantry. The ministry of internal affairs set up an organization to arrange the distribution of pro-government material to everyone who held some sort of public office, no matter how lowly. Stolypin was especially concerned to ensure that the government's case was publicized outside the immediate government circles in St Petersburg and Moscow, and considerable sums of money were expended on trying to influence provincial opinion. Special attention was paid to agrarian issues, and the merits of the government's agrarian policy were vigorously emphasized. Pamphlets were written by civil servants, usually under pseudonyms, with such titles as *The truth about the Kadets* and *Our socialists* and were published either by the government itself, or by using a publishing house owned by a relative of Stolypin, S. S. Podolanskii.[34]

The main thrust of the government's propaganda efforts, however, was devoted to influencing the periodical press. Central to this effort was I. Ia. Gurliand, a senior civil servant in the interior ministry and one of Stolypin's closest collaborators, described as "intelligent . . . but very cunning",[35] and who displayed considerable journalistic talent. Stolypin believed that a national newspaper should be established to express the government's point of view and act as a semi-official government organ; *Rossiia* (Russia), under Gurliand's editorship, began to fulfil this role from late 1906. Stolypin regarded *Rossiia* as a means by which government policy could be explained to the population and he frequently instructed Gurliand on material to include in the paper and what approach to adopt on particular issues.[36] There was no question of *Rossiia* having to pay its way on a commercial basis and the interior ministry made substantial amounts of money available to support it: Kryzhanovskii estimated that the paper received more than 200,000 rubles in subsidies during Stolypin's period of office.[37] The government evidently considered that the results obtained from publishing the newspaper justified the expenditure, for although politically informed circles were well aware of *Rossiia*'s bias and took this into account when reading it, opinion in the provinces may well have been more influenced by it.[38] Other national newspapers were also the recipients of government subsidy: *Russkoe znamia* (The Russian Banner) received more than 30,000 rubles and *Zemshchina* (The Populace) was allocated more than 10,000 rubles a month. Both papers supported the far right.

The government also took steps to influence the local press right across the empire, using financial subsidy as its main weapon. Kryzhanovskii, the assistant minister of the interior, was closely questioned about his activities in this area in 1917 by the commission that investigated the collapse of tsarism: he stated that the records that Stolypin had kept had disappeared, while he had destroyed his own papers in 1917.[39] Despite this, Kryzhanovskii was able to detail the destination of considerable sums of money: he estimated that between 1908 and 1911 more than 600,000 rubles a year were distributed through him to the press. The majority of this money was sent directly by telegraph to local newspapers, but in some cases there were specific intermediaries who passed money on from the government to the paper concerned; these were usually local officials such as provincial governors and marshals of the nobility, although in one case a bishop, Mikhail of Minsk, was involved. The Voronezh paper *Natsionalisticheskii vestnik* (Nationalist Messenger) received 3,000 rubles a month, the Vitebsk provincial governor disbursed funds to the local *Vitebskie vedomosti* (Vitebsk News), while more than 2,000 rubles a month was sent directly to the editor of *Kazanskii telegraf* (Kazan Telegraph).[40] Some money was set aside specifically to support journals that dealt with agrarian issues; about 300,000 rubles was spent on two periodicals, *Zerno* (Grain) and *Khlebopashets* (Tiller of the Soil). The government also believed that it was also vitally important that its policies were presented in the best possible light to foreign audiences and the ministry of foreign affairs had a special fund to use on subsidizing the foreign press. Money was also made available to translate Stolypin's speeches into foreign languages.[41] The government was clearly not convinced that all the money that it disbursed was actually used to support Stolypin's policies in print, but in nearly all cases the subsidies to individual newspapers were continued throughout Stolypin's period in office.

In addition to the campaign to influence public opinion through the press, Stolypin also attempted to affect directly the policies adopted by certain of the extreme right-wing parties. Stolypin believed that these groups presented the greatest threat to his government at the beginning of its existence, since they were able to mobilize popular support in a way that no other group could. Even though they had been responsible for carrying out pogroms that had resulted in the murder of Jews in several cities in Russia, Stolypin felt that the government might be able to harness their energies in its support, and he saw the most effective way of achieving this as being through the provision of financial aid to right-wing parties. In return for these subventions, Stolypin hoped that the right would moderate its attacks on the government, and would perhaps be willing to give the new order its support. It was completely unrealistic for Stolypin to imagine that groups such as the Union of the Russian People could be converted to offer wholehearted acceptance of the government's views by what was effectively bribery, and it is difficult to believe that this was the prime minister's aim. Rather, he hoped that by making them partially dependent on the government for funds, this might reduce some of the excesses that these groups had committed and persuade them to offer nothing more than moderate opposition to the government. N. E. Markov, a leading member of the Union of the Russian People and a deputy in the Third Duma, stated that he believed that Stolypin wanted to prevent the Union from becoming too strong, and that this could be achieved by making it dependent on the government for its funds.[42] Markov saw nothing wrong in accepting subsidies from the government, arguing that "ideals cannot exist without money",[43] and from 1909 onwards he received 12,000 rubles a month to be used to support right-wing organizations and publications.[44] Other members of the Union estimated that half of the organization's annual budget, a sum of 30,000 rubles, was provided by the government,[45] but this was substantially lower than the sums that were alleged to have been provided in 1905 and 1906. At that time, before the split in the Union that resulted in the party's leader, A. I. Dubrovin, setting up his own organization, the government was reported to have given the Union more than 75,000 rubles a year. This was used mainly to finance the party's election campaign to the First Duma, with a large proportion of the money going to assist in the election of V. M. Purishkevich in Kishinev.

Distribution of the money to the right-wing parties was made through Kryzhanovskii or else by Stolypin himself, but there were doubts in the interior ministry as to whether the funds were being used in a way that was beneficial to the government. Markov stated that he did not feel any compulsion to use the subsidies as Stolypin had instructed and it is clear that this attitude was wide-spread in the Union. There was no sign that the party's represen-tatives in the Duma were prepared to offer the government their support and the party press, including such papers as *Zemshchina* and *Russkoe znamia*, which received separate government subsi-dies, continued to attack the government for its lack of vigour in combating terrorism and for making concessions to the liberals.[46] Inside the Duma, Purishkevich and Markov were consistent and vociferous opponents of Stolypin's reform bills. They took parti-cular exception to the proposals to allow greater religious freedom and remained close to the regime's traditional principles of orthodoxy, autocracy and nationality, showing great enthu-siasm for Stolypin's nationalist policy when it emerged in 1909.[47] The government's attempts to get guaranteed support from politi-cal parties were largely unsuccessful: Stolypin had not been able to persuade liberal "public figures" to join his government in 1906 and he was equally unsuccessful in trying to neutralize the opposition of the extreme right-wing parties. Neither liberals nor extreme right were prepared to abide by the conditions that Stoly-pin wanted to impose on them. In the case of the liberals, this led to their refusal to play a part in Stolypin's cabinet and to their adopting an attitude of deep scepticism towards the government. Payments to the Union of the Russian People produced no guar-antee of support, and it was only when government policy moved to the right in 1909 that parties on the right moderated their opposition to the government.

The government's attempts to influence public opinion were unsophisticated. Operating in a new political environment, Stolypin and his colleagues had little idea of the motors of public opinion and found it difficult to target their efforts effectively. While the new electoral law of June 1907 did produce what appeared at first sight to be a more compliant Duma, the government soon came to realize that the mere presence of sympathetic deputies was not sufficient to guarantee a smooth passage for its legislation. Pouring money into local and national newspapers was a very crude tactic that may simply have resulted in sections of the Russian press enjoying an unaccustomed prosperity. Stolypin's subsidies did nothing to moderate the attacks that the right mounted on his government and its policies. In trying to build a base of popular support from zero, the government was faced with an uphill struggle. Stolypin was attempting to create a general sense of approval for the government's reforms, but he proved unable to compete with the closely targeted and well-focused campaigns that conservative Russia mounted against him. The strategy of trying to win over public opinion that Stolypin adopted needed a long period to become successful. The prime minister did not have time on his side.

## Nationalism and the reshaping of Russian politics

The transformation of Russian politics that took place during 1909 involved change to the political parties and to the government's own views. This process was motivated on both sides by the realization that reform was going to be very difficult to achieve. For the Octobrists this meant that their party, shorn of real influence, began to disintegrate. At the same time, Stolypin recognized that he would have to move towards the right if he wished to remain in power and to achieve any positive results. Russian nationalism provided an area where government and legislature could agree. Nationalist policies could come close to producing a Duma majority with the support of the Right, the Moderate Right and the Nationalists. The Octobrist party, which was as committed to maintaining Russia's prestige and international standing as it was to the principles of the October Manifesto, would also provide support for such measures. The conservative political complexion of the State Council and the tsar's personal political views provided further encouragement for Stolypin that nationalist politics would provide a basis for unity across the Russian political establishment.

Russia's international situation also affected the government's domestic policies. Even though Russia had concluded agreements with France in 1894 and with Britain in 1907, Japan's emphatic victory over Russia in the war of 1904–5 had demonstrated the weakness of the tsarist state. In 1907 Stolypin had argued that internal difficulties did not allow Russia to pursue an aggressive foreign policy,[48] but the continued evidence of Russia's international vulnerability made nationalism a more attractive course of action for the prime minister. Russia had been unable to prevent Austria's annexation of Bosnia in 1908, and Stolypin's apparent abandonment of the Slav population of the Balkans made it all the more important for him to demonstrate to the right that he was concerned to promote Russian interests at home.

The prime minister was faced with difficult decisions in 1909. His programme of reform had run into the sands, effectively stalled by the resurgence of traditional Russian conservatism. It was clear to everybody, and not least Stolypin himself, that the extensive reformist aspirations that his government had entertained when he first came to power would have to be substantially moderated. Stolypin was faced with a choice: he could accept that his hopes of changing the social and political structures of Russia were doomed to failure and resign, or else he could adapt his policies to blend with the prevailing conservative ethos of the empire's social elites. The prime minister chose the second course. Nicholas II had insisted that there was no question of Stolypin resigning in the wake of the naval general staff crisis and the prime minister did remain in office, gradually letting most of his reform proposals fall by the wayside. The agrarian reform did continue on its passage through the legislature and the government maintained its support for this centrepiece of its programme, confident that this bill would eventually become law. Stolypin perhaps believed that his reform proposals could be resurrected later and that he was merely deferring his ambitions until the political atmosphere was once again more congenial.

The government did not make any formal declaration of a change in policy, and withdrew relatively few bills from the Duma, preferring to let its proposals slide gently into oblivion. Ministers failed to turn up to defend their bills in the Duma, and stopped trying to push for rapid consideration of their proposals either by Duma commissions or in its full session. The indications are that Stolypin still entertained some hope of reform at the end of 1909. This is evident in his enquiry of one of his senior officials at the end of November whether all the disagreements between the government and the Orthodox Church over the religious bills making their way through the Duma had now been resolved.[49]

The balance of the government's programme shifted during 1909 and 1910 as Stolypin and his ministers used their energies actively to promote policies that asserted the rights of Russians over those of other nationalities. Russian nationalism was a traditional component of the imperial government's ethos, but from 1909 onwards it came to occupy the vacuum that was left as reform was gradually abandoned and to stand as the main plank of government policy. This was a new departure for the imperial government: Alexander III's Russification measures had been part of a wider programme to extend the authority of the St Petersburg regime, and had sprung from an ideological conviction that the autocracy needed to be invigorated and its impact extended. In contrast, Stolypin's nationalist ambitions were based on pragmatic political considerations and were motivated largely by his desire to remain in power. The policy that the government pursued after 1909 was designed to ensure that political support was forthcoming and to neutralize the forces that had wreaked havoc with Stolypin's reforms. The government paid particular attention to the position on the western edge of the empire: in Finland and in the western provinces of European Russia itself. These were regions that appeared to conservative opinion to represent the greatest affront to the empire's Russian nature. The dominance of a Polish social elite in the western borderlands was a situation that conservative opinion wanted to see changed, while the imperial government had earlier made significant attempts to reduce Finland's autonomy and bring the region under the direct control of St Petersburg. This policy, pursued with especial vigour by Governor-General Bobrikov from 1898 until his assassination in 1904, had provoked great opposition from the Finns and they had been able to take advantage of the disturbances of 1905 to wrest back some of their autonomy.[50]

Finland had concerned Stolypin's government since the autumn of 1907 when a special committee had been established to screen matters relating to Finland before they were debated in the council of ministers itself. In May 1908 Stolypin had announced to the Duma that he would introduce a bill to regulate the position of Finland in the empire, intended, "not to contravene any of the rights of little Finland, but to protect that which is dearest and closest to us – the historic, sovereign rights of Russia".[51] It was only at the very end of 1908, however, that the government seriously began to address itself to the issue by seeking to curb once and for all the powers of the local Finnish administration. This exercise was designed to define which areas of policy should remain under the autonomous control of the Finns themselves, and which matters were of imperial significance and should therefore be under the jurisdiction of the St Petersburg government. Matters still moved very slowly, suggesting that this was yet not a priority for the government. The Kharitonov commission that was to determine the details of this policy did not meet until the autumn of 1909 but, once it commenced its work, the process of imposing the imperial will on Finland accelerated. The commission that carried out the work of defining which matters fell under imperial, rather than Finnish control identified 19 separate subjects as being outside the jurisdiction of the Finnish authorities. These included all the most significant areas of policy such as customs, education, defence and transport. It also, however, reserved to the St Petersburg government the right of adding other subjects to the list as it saw fit, thus giving the imperial authorities complete control over the affairs of Finland.[52]

As a result of these deliberations, the government prepared a bill to change the position of Finland inside the empire. The nationalist tone of the measure did not, however, win the wholehearted support of Stolypin's ministerial colleagues when they discussed the new Finnish policy. Kokovtsov, the minister of finance, consistently pressed for the government to take a more moderate line and to allow the Finns to retain a degree of autonomy. He argued that the proposed changes to the

administration of Finland would only serve to increase opposition to the Russian government in Finland, and that it would
be more sensible to allow the governor-general – a Russian
resident in Finland – to have the power to decide which items
of legislation should fall under St Petersburg's jurisdiction.[53]
The minister of foreign affairs, A. P. Izvol'skii, also harboured
significant reservations about the imposition of Russian administration on Finland. He too was concerned about the adverse
reaction that the reform was likely to produce from the Finns
and argued that, in view of the difficult European international
situation, Russia should avoid measures that might lead to
further internal difficulties.[54] The council of ministers as a
whole, however, rejected these views and saw no reason to
tone down the bill to placate Finnish opinion. Once the proposals had been approved by the cabinet, they were quickly introduced into the Duma in the spring of 1910. The sclerosis that
the Duma had displayed in dealing with the government's
reform bills disappeared when it came to the measure to reduce
Finnish autonomy. There was little significant opposition to the
Finnish bill: even sections of the Kadet party were prepared to
support the measure. In contrast to the lengthy and detailed
examination that the Duma had given to other measures, the
Finnish bill completed all its stages in the Duma in a single
week in May 1910. The State Council's conservative majority
approved the bill without demur and it became law in June
1910. The changed tenor of the Russian political scene was
evident from this episode. The contrast between the reception
given to the Finnish bill and to the government's earlier reform
measures could not have been sharper. If Stolypin wished to
remain as prime minister, he had to follow a political path that
included Russian nationalism as its most significant element.

At the same time as the government was taking steps to reduce
the autonomy of Finland, it was moving to increase the influence
of the Russian population in the western borderlands of European
Russia itself.[55] Stolypin's own background as a landowner and
local official in this region gave him particular interest in the
topic. The prime minister's declarations of policy at the beginning
of his period in office had stressed that he intended to introduce
*zemstva* into the nine western provinces.[56] The original *zemstvo*

statute of 1864 had ensured that elected local councils would only be established in provinces with a strong Russian nobility, which would guarantee that the new institutions would be dominated by the empire's political elite. This clearly excluded the western provinces, while the government's reluctance to countenance giving even limited power to the Polish elite of the region was made more resolute by the Polish rebellion of 1863. Debates had taken place inside the government during the half century after the original *zemstvo* statute over whether the western provinces could be included in the scheme, and in 1903 an adulterated form of *zemstvo* had been introduced. This gave the western border-lands appointed councils, but these bodies were despised by almost every section of society and served only to increase the pressure for elected *zemstva* to be introduced. Only six months after Stolypin's appointment as minister of internal affairs, he pre-sented a proposal to the council of ministers to establish elected *zemstva* in the region and for this measure to be introduced under Article 87 of the Fundamental Laws – thus allowing for its immediate implementation – only making its way through the Duma and State Council once they met again. The council of ministers turned down Stolypin's proposal to use this procedure and the question then disappeared back into the depths of the interior ministry. When the government began to demonstrate greater sympathy with the nationalist cause, however, the subject of the western *zemstvo* came back onto the political agenda.

It was D. I. Pikhno's proposal about State Council representa-tion from the region that brought the matter to the forefront of political concern again. When Stolypin gave his approval to Pikh-no's bill, he resurrected the idea of establishing *zemstva* in the western provinces. The political advantages of the project for the government in the changed environment of 1909 and 1910 were obvious. It offered a further opportunity to cement nationalist support for Stolypin's administration, but the practical difficulties of devising a satisfactory structure for the new *zemstva* and their electoral system proved to be considerable. The main problem came in defining the *zemstvo* franchise: although the larger part of the region's population was Russian, this was mainly made up of peasants and the government could not, therefore, rely upon them to elect deputies who would support the government. A property qualification for the franchise was also out of the question, since this would result in the elections being dominated by the Polish landowners. Stolypin therefore proposed that a complex system of calculating the number of *zemstvo* members from the two national groups should be established, so that both the amount of property owned and the numerical strength of each group should be taken into account. Even though most of the Jewish population of the empire lived in this region, Jews were not to be allowed either to vote or to stand for election to the *zemstva*. Russian Orthodox priests would be given significantly greater representation in the region's *zemstva* than they enjoyed elsewhere in the empire, while each *zemstvo*'s chairman and his deputy, as well as the chairman of each *zemstvo* commission, had to come from the Russian population. Even after these carefully circumscribed rules had been worked out, the government recognized that they could not guarantee a Russian majority if *zemstva* were established in the three northwestern provinces of Grodno, Kovno and Vilna and so the provinces were dropped from the scheme, leaving it to be implemented only in the six remaining western provinces.[57] The government's aims in promoting this piece of legislation were easy to divine. The convoluted electoral system that was proposed made it obvious that the whole project was not so much concerned with ensuring the good government of the region, as with making sure that political support would be forthcoming for the government in St Petersburg.[58]

The western *zemstvo* bill proved to be much more controversial than the Finnish legislation and it had an uneasy passage through the Duma. It was paralleled by another measure designed to extend Russian influence in the western part of the empire. Since the 1863 Polish rebellion, there had been repeated plans to create a new Russian-dominated province out of the easternmost parts of two of the Polish provinces of the empire – Lublin and Siedlce. In late 1906, the council of ministers had rejected Stolypin's proposal to detach the region and incorporate it into the province of Grodno, but the topic surfaced again at the beginning of 1909. A scheme to create a new province of Kholm was approved by the cabinet in January 1909: complex provision was made to ensure that the Russian and Orthodox population would have greater influence than the Polish and Roman Catholic segments, even though the Catholic population of the new province would outnumber the Orthodox.[59] The bill was introduced into the Duma in April 1909 and had a difficult passage, meeting prolonged opposition from Polish deputies. It was not until 1912 that it emerged from the Duma, but then very quickly gained the approval of both State Council and tsar and became law in June 1912.[60]

The western *zemstvo* bill was considered by the Duma in the spring of 1910. While the principle of introducing *zemstva* into the western provinces was approved by the majority of the Duma, there was severe argument over the detail of the government's proposals. The Duma commission that examined the measure ended up by rejecting its own bill, so contradictory were the changes that had been made to it. It was the qualification for voting that aroused the greatest passions and various amendments were passed that, when taken together, would have increased Polish representation in the new *zemstva*. When the bill came to be debated in full session by the Duma, the weakness of the Octobrist party and the effect that this could have upon the Duma became clear. The leaderless party proved unable to agree a clear position on the bill and, while the Nationalists and the Right were firm in support of the measure, many Octobrists declared that they could not vote for the government's bill as it was too blatant an attempt to manipulate the situation in favour of the Russian population of the region. Alterations were made to the electoral qualification and to various clauses concerning the nationality of the *zemstvo* board's personnel. These aroused strong feelings in the Duma and polarized opinion. On the right, there was explicit opposition to any amendment that would weaken the position of the Russian population of the region, but the Kadet party and sections of the Octobrists – many of them *zemstvo* activists themselves – drew back from supporting a bill that they recognized as being nothing more than a piece of political manoeuvring and that bore little resemblance to the ideals that the *zemstva* had come to represent in the years since 1864. The Duma passed the bill by a slim majority and it was sent to the State Council in May 1910.

The commission of the State Council that examined the bill in

March 1911 removed most of the amendments that the Duma had inserted, returning the bill almost to its original form. But this gave no hint of the upset that was to occur when it was debated in the full session. Although the rightist group in the State Council had itself proposed that the *zemstvo* franchise should be organized on a national basis, when this part of the bill was put to the vote, it was defeated. This was the result of the intrigue by P. N. Durnovo and V. F. Trepov aimed at reducing Stolypin's credibility with the tsar by demonstrating that even with his legislative programme shorn of its radical reforms, he was still unable to muster the necessary support in the legislative institutions. Durnovo and Trepov were able to persuade Nicholas II that he should indicate to the right that they could vote according to their conscience on the bill, without feeling that there was any pressure on them from "the highest spheres" to approve the measure. Stolypin was faced with his bill having gained the approval of the Duma, but being defeated in the State Council on the say-so of the tsar. As a result of this manoeuvring, relations between the tsar and his prime minister cooled almost to freezing point, but at least as significant was the uproar that the intrigue caused amongst Duma deputies and State Council members. Stolypin ensured that he obtained Nicholas II's approval briefly to suspend the Duma and State Council and to issue the western *zemstvo* legislation by using Article 87 of the Fundamental Laws, which allowed for the enactment of urgent laws while the legislative institutions were not in session. Durnovo and Trepov were also suspended from the State Council. The prime minister used Article 87 in this case simply as a means of circumventing the express decision of the State Council and demonstrating that the government could override the legislature's wishes.

The use of Article 87 was condemned by both the Duma and the State Council and the prime minister faced substantial criticism in both chambers. Stolypin's arguments that his action was justified because the bill met the needs of the western provinces, and that the dissolution of the legislative institutions when there was disagreement with the government was common in western Europe were not accepted and both chambers passed interpellations attacking the move.[61] The use of Article 87 was seen by the Octobrists as contrary to both the letter and spirit of the Fundamental Laws; Guchkov told Stolypin that although he approved the content of the western *zemstvo* bill, the way in which it had been enacted cast serious doubts on the level of support he felt able to give to Stolypin. Guchkov described the government's actions as "a step which would be fatal not only for you [Stolypin] personally . . . but also for the renewal of Russia", and resigned the chairmanship of the Duma.[62] Guchkov was well aware of the forces that were ranged against Stolypin and he foresaw that if the moderate groups in the legislative bodies withdrew their support for the government, Stolypin would be left without any power base. The Octobrists, however, were no longer prepared to support a government that had demonstrated its contempt for the new constitutional order established in 1905. After the western *zemstvo* affair, the Octobrists moved into open opposition to the government. Stolypin now could only hope for the support of the Nationalists and the Right, but the plotting of Durnovo and Trepov had demonstrated that the Right held no love for the prime minister and that their loyalty to him was almost non-existent. By the spring of 1911 Stolypin was unable to command any sort of majority in the Duma. He was an isolated figure, deserted by the Octobrists and no longer able even to command the support of the Right.

Guchkov's forecast turned out to be correct. After both Duma and State Council had shown their disapproval of the government's actions, Stolypin was left with only the tsar to support him. But the limits of Nicholas II's enthusiasm for his prime minister were all too clear. The tactics that Stolypin had adopted during the crisis over the western *zemstvo* bill rankled with Nicholas II, however, and it was not long before he began to go back on the agreement that he had made with Stolypin. At the beginning of May 1911 the tsar wrote to the prime minister suggesting that Durnovo and Trepov might be invited to return to their posts before the two-month period of their suspension was up, a move that would have shown publicly how fragile was the confidence that the tsar placed in Stolypin.[63] For much of the summer of 1911 Stolypin was out of St Petersburg,[64] leaving Kokovtsov as acting head of the government, and on his return to public life at the beginning of September, for the unveiling of a statue to Alexander III, he was almost ignored by the court.[65] On the evening of 1 September 1911, Stolypin was shot while attending a performance at the Kiev Opera House in the presence of the tsar. He died four days later. The assassin was D. G. Bogrov, a socialist revolutionary and former police agent: it seems very likely that the murder was carried out with the knowledge of high police officials, but even if this was not so Stolypin was removed from the scene at a time when his political career was over.[66] Rumours were rife during the summer of 1911 that he was to be moved to some other post – it was suggested that the vice-royalty of Siberia or of the Caucasus were the most likely alternatives. In any event, it is difficult to see how he could have continued as prime minister without the support of either the tsar or the legislative institutions.[67]

## Stolypin defeated

The problem that Stolypin faced in trying to mobilize backing for his government and its policies was that there was no natural source of support in Russia for the reforms that he was proposing. Although he could find disparate groups that were ready to give their backing to individual measures, there was no single political or social group that was able to provide complete support for the government's programme. The attempts that Stolypin made to gain different groups' approval all proved to be unsuccessful because his policies were aimed at creating a new social class of small, peasant landowners. The peasantry had demonstrated where their political sympathies lay in their votes for radical deputies to the First and Second Dumas and by their limited enthusiasm for Stolypin's agrarian reform, but the government had moved to limit the extent of their representation and to ensure the significant overrepresentation of the traditional social elite in the legislature. These groups were very sceptical about the merits of Stolypin's reforms and were determined to protect their own position. The agrarian reform was supported because it would ameliorate the conditions of both the large gentry landowners and the peasantry. But when it came to the political consequences of this measure, the bills that Stolypin introduced to reform local government and to increase the range of civil liberties available to the population as a whole were opposed by land-owning and conservative groups. They believed that their authority would be reduced, and that this new class of peasant landowners would be granted the same rights as they themselves enjoyed, which would devalue the position that they held in rural society. As established members of the Russian political scene, it was easy for them to make their views known and for them to exert pressure on the legislative institutions, especially in the Third Duma. As Stolypin's class of peasant landowners was hardly in existence, it was impossible for it to make its voice heard and, in any case, the government had shown its unwillingness to listen to the voice of the peasantry.

Stolypin made very considerable efforts to improve the links that existed between St Petersburg and the provinces, by supporting the local press and assiduously cultivating the contacts between central and local government.[68] The process of establishing a new class and then giving it a political voice was not, however, something that could be accomplished within the period of his premiership. Stolypin himself admitted that the agrarian reform required 20 years to be completely effective, but he did not realize that the success of the agrarian policy was a precondition for the success of his other bills. The fundamental task that Stolypin was trying to cope with – the transformation of the economic, political and social conditions of the Russian peasantry – was a problem of such magnitude that neither Stolypin, nor indeed any Russian politician of the period, was able to realize its full implications. It is hardly surprising that Stolypin was unable to find consistent support for his programme since his policies impinged on the interests of powerful groups and the people whom they would benefit possessed only a modest political voice. The failure of the government's attempts to gather support for its work among political parties and from the press was predictable. None of the political parties represented in the Third Duma could claim to speak for the peasantry. Instead, they overwhelmingly represented the traditional political order. The process of achieving a more pliant Duma had led the government to fall back on the Russian social elite and their instincts were to resist reform.

Stolypin's retreat from reform and his embracing of Russian

nationalism was a dead-end policy, adopted almost by default. The prime minister was forced into a corner by the much more experienced political figures of the conservative establishment. Stolypin's shift to the right reduced his credibility with the centre ground of Russian politics and made him appear as no more than an unprincipled figure, keen to curry favour with his conservative opponents. He failed to realize, however, that the opposition from the right would not be dissipated simply by a change of policy. The prime minister was not trusted by the right and, after they had succeeded in weakening the link between Stolypin and his Octobrist allies, their leaders aimed at forcing him from office. The groups that proclaimed their support for the new constitutional order hardly realized the seriousness of the situation and its implications for their ambitions for reform. Intent on maintaining their independence from the government and unwilling to provide any sort of united support for Stolypin's programme, the Kadets and the Octobrists allowed conservative Russia to overwhelm the reform programme. The right was able to use its traditional methods of influencing the monarch and his advisers, while the political parties of the left and centre did little more than create a storm of protest in the Duma, a forum that had almost no influence in the real seats of power in the Russian Empire. This failure of Stolypin's attempts to gather solid support around him was to doom his premiership.

## CHAPTER 6

# Conclusion: between two revolutions

Reforming an autocracy poses exceptional difficulties. By its very nature, an autocratic regime refuses to recognize the validity of popular opinion and is unwilling to respond to pressure for change from below. Reform is rarely a course of action that an autocracy undertakes with enthusiasm. The tsarist regime was no exception. It took a lost war and the fear of social unrest to persuade Alexander II to undertake change in the 1860s, and in 1905 a lost war and the reality of widespread revolt forced his grandson into reforming the Russian state. The concession of an elected legislature appeared to represent a fundamental change in attitude by the tsarist regime and offered the hope to Russian society that the pace of modernization would continue. The necessary ingredients for reform appeared to be falling into place: a legislative mechanism that allowed for popular participation had been established; political parties committed to change were formed; and, in the summer of 1906, a prime minister who was personally committed to reform came to power.

Peter Stolypin ultimately failed in his ambition of renewing Russia. His particular approach to politics played some part in this lack of success. Stolypin stood out in the rather colourless Russian political environment in the first decade of the twentieth century. He was physically imposing and projected a self-confident and authoritative image. The prime minister was able to use his physical characteristics to enhance his appearance: a spasm in his speech produced the effect of pent-up force, while the fact that he had largely lost the use of his right hand – the result of a damaged nerve – gave rise to rumours that he had been involved in a duel. Contemporaries recognized Stolypin's considerable oratorical power and his speeches in the Duma were delivered with force and passion.[1] The terrorist bomb that severely injured one of Stolypin's daughters and destroyed his home, only six weeks after his appointment as chairman of the council of ministers, provoked great sympathy for the new premier and helped to ensure a good reception for his reformist statement, published less than two weeks later. Contemporaries did not doubt Stolypin's determination and energy, although they did have reservations about his intellectual sharpness.[2] Some, including V. K. Pleve, who from his position as minister of internal affairs between 1902 and 1904 had observed Stolypin's progress as a provincial governor, saw in this energy and love of oratory merely "a tendency to strike poses and indulge in idle rhetoric".[3]

The experience that Stolypin had gained before his move to St Petersburg gave him a perspective on Russian government that was very different from most of his ministerial colleagues. He had spent more than 15 years living and working in the provinces, so that the move to head the ministry of internal affairs represented a radical change in direction. Stolypin's experience was even more untypical since his base was in the northwestern provinces of the empire. His family home was in the province of Kovno, an area where two-thirds of the population was Lithuanian and where Polish landowners retained great strength. Emancipation had been welcomed by these nobles, tired of the government's attempts to promote the interests of the Russian peasantry at their expense. The regime had, however, drawn back from introducing *zemstva* in 1864 in the province, wary of the type of assembly that would result from a population that was only seven per cent Russian. Stolypin's brief experience of governing Saratov between 1903 and 1906 was his only real exposure to the problems of a more typical province in which the population was almost exclusively Russian and where *zemstva* played a part in local government.

The premier's experience was not, however, as limited as the bones of his career might suggest. Stolypin and his wife did own estates in Russia proper, in Kazan, Penza and Nizhnii-Novgorod, and this gave him some exposure to the problems that faced the majority of the empire's population. Furthermore, Stolypin's own provincial roots concealed his family's links with the elite of Russian society. His father had served in the army, reaching the rank of general and had been appointed as adjutant to tsar Alexander II and then as governor-general of Eastern Rumelia, ending his career as commandant of the Moscow Kremlin. Stolypin's wife's family – the Neidgarts – was also part of Russia's social elite. Based in Moscow, they played an important part in the management of the city's charitable institutions and were welcome guests of the Moscow governor-general, Grand Duke Sergei. When Stolypin moved to the capital in 1906, therefore, he possessed the social background and connections that enabled him to fit easily into the St Petersburg environment, but lacked recent direct experience of the central government bureaucracy.

This did provide Stolypin with some advantages. He came to St Petersburg free from the burden of ministerial debate and dispute that had served to inhibit reform during the nineteenth century. His lack of ministerial experience meant that, in 1906, he was not perceived as attached to any particular faction or viewpoint, so that it was easier for him to set out a new course for the government. His extensive and direct experience of life in the provinces gave him a perspective on the tasks of the government that was rare. Stolypin's view of reform was focused on the needs of the empire's population, seeing attention to the conditions in which the people lived as providing the key that would ensure the durability of the tsarist regime itself. The reputation that he brought with him to the capital – as a firm opponent of rebellion – paradoxically gave the new premier an advantage in promoting reform. He was seen by the stalwarts of tsarism as devoted to the regime and committed to its preservation, and avoided the immediate antagonism that earlier reforming ministers, such as Sviatopolk-Mirskii, had succeeded in arousing. This did give Stolypin a breathing-space during which he was able to proceed with his reform programme, a period that proved too short to implement change before conservatism was able to mobilize its forces.

The problems that Stolypin faced as a relative outsider to the apparatus of central government were very substantial. Without ready allies among his ministerial colleagues, the prime minister found that he had to seek support from outside the government. Stolypin's attempts to recruit liberal figures to serve in his government and his later attempt at reliance on Guchkov and the Octobrist party indicated that his focus was set much wider than that of traditional bureaucrats. While this approach might have had more success if the new Russian parliamentary system possessed real power, Stolypin failed to recognize the extent of the authority that continued to rest with Russia's traditional conservative elites. By concentrating on Duma politics, the prime minister paid inadequate attention to his more immediate political environment. The council of ministers never provided a secure base of support for its chairman and after 1909, when men appointed to ministerial jobs were largely out of sympathy with Stolypin's views, the atmosphere inside the government gave no encouragement to him to continue with his reform programme. Stolypin's miscalculation in assessing the locus of political power in reformed Russia was to prove fatal to his reformist aspirations. The prime minister's lack of national political experience told particularly when opposition to his reform programme began to be voiced from the right. Faced with the intimate links between nobility, church and the Russian political establishment, Stolypin found his provincial background to be a severe disadvantage.

While the political skills of Stolypin himself provide some explanation for his eventual failure, the political culture of the Russian Empire also played an important part. By the beginning of the twentieth century, the social structure of imperial Russia was changing. The emancipation of the serfs in 1861 had helped to give the peasant population of the empire greater independence. More peasants began to work in the growing industrial cities as the ties between urban and rural Russia developed. The process of industrialization – particularly powerful during the 1890s – changed the urban landscape of the empire by bringing into existence a class of industrial workers, and by allowing the growth of entrepreneurial and professional groups. The establishment of *zemstva* in much of European Russia in 1864, along with the introduction of elected urban councils six years later, had pro-vided the opportunity for provincial figures to gain practical experience of governing their local region. *Zemstvo* involvement in education, social services, public health matters and the provi-sion of local infrastructure had laid the basis for the growth of employment opportunities right across European Russia for edu-cated professional people. The twin trends of industrial growth and the development of local self-government helped to give a sharp stimulus to the growth of a Russian middle class. Profes-sional bodies, industrial and commercial trade organizations and a wide variety of cultural societies were all coming into being by 1900. The greater freedom of association that was promised by the government during 1905 gave a further impetus to the estab-lishment of groups that brought together the nascent Russian middle class. A more heterogeneous press, together with a better system of education, contributed to the widening influence of the sector of Russian society that stood between the nobility and the peasantry. During the first decade of the twentieth century, the Russian Empire was undergoing a process of social diversifica-tion. The vacuum left by the declining power of the nobility was very gradually being filled by a vigorous and varied middle class.

This process of social change was not, however, reflected in the political structures of the empire. The traditional social elite con-tinued to retain power and influence, both in the formal legisla-tive institutions of Duma and State Council and in the informal channels through which much of the work of the imperial govern-ment was still done. The elections to the First and Second Dumas had allowed a wider constituency to play a part in the political process, but the outcome had proved unpalatable to the govern-ment. The 1907 franchise, while producing an easier relationship between government and Duma, had done so by restricting the participation of – in the government's view – the Duma's most awkward elements and by shifting the balance of the Duma firmly towards the right. The sections of Russian society that had the most to gain from the reform process found themselves heavily outnumbered in the post-1907 legislative system by those groups that had most to lose.

In particular, the growing middle classes found that their views were poorly represented. Even though the Octobrist party drew much of its support from urban voters, and might have been expected to reflect the views of the industrial and commercial populations of the great cities of the empire, the landowners who dominated the leadership of the party had divided loyalties. It was also true that in the first decade of the twentieth century, the level of development of the middle classes had hardly reached the stage where they saw themselves as having coherent political objectives. While the long-established merchants and industrialists of Moscow, St Petersburg and Nizhnii-Novgorod demonstrated a cohesiveness that allowed them to pursue political objectives, the growing professional and entrepreneurial classes had not yet achieved that degree of common purpose. The concerns of these people were expressed through their disparate sectional organizations and, as the formal political arena was barely open to these groups, their congresses became a vital forum for the articulation of their aspirations. The more open political environment after 1905 quickly helped to promote the discussion of matters of social and political concern. As the Duma failed to provide an appropriate arena for this debate, the varied congresses came to provide what one contemporary described as a "parliament of public opinion".[4] Even though meetings such as congresses on fire insurance, on alcoholism or of librarians could by no stretch of the imagination be described as overtly political, they – and many other gatherings – passed resolutions that addressed questions of political importance. There was little connection, however, between these unofficial expressions of opinion and the formal political institutions of the empire. Indeed, conservative newspapers attacked the holding of such congresses and called for government action to prevent meetings at which political questions were debated. Russian political life failed to live up to the expectations aroused by the upheaval of 1905. The new political structures ossified rapidly and failed properly to represent the transformations that Russian society was undergoing. The façade of reformed political institutions concealed an established political class that was intent on resisting real change.

The Romanov monarchs had proved highly successful in maintaining their position since their dynasty came to power in 1613. By 1900, the tsarist regime was exceptional among European states as it had proved able to resist reform. Monarchical power had been limited in England, Austria-Hungary and Germany and the monarchy eliminated in France. The Russian state's success in quelling the widespread popular discontent during 1905 served to confirm the regime's confidence in its own invincibility. Even though the Russian Empire had suffered repeated military or diplomatic reverses in the Crimea in the 1850s, in the Balkans in 1878 after the Russo-Turkish War and against Japan during 1905 itself, tsarism had retained sufficient power to put down internal threats to its authority. While the troubles of 1905 should have alerted the state apparatus to the deep crisis that faced it, the regime's ability to come through the year relatively unscathed served to reassure the tsar and his advisers that they were secure. The outcome of the 1905 revolution engendered a feeling of complacency among much of Russia's political and social elite: they had vanquished the most serious threat to their position for generations. This was, however, a superficial view of the security of the tsarist state. The experience of 1905 served to accelerate the disillusionment of much of Russian society with the government. The regime had not flinched from setting its troops against the population when revolt threatened and had used great brutality to put down rebellion in both city and countryside. Society's sympathy with tsarism was rapidly diminishing as its patriarchal structures disintegrated. The emancipation of the serfs had severed the link between noble and peasant and the rapid decline in noble land-owning after 1861 had accentuated this process. The inhabitants of the growing cities of the empire felt little loyalty to any other social group. The political opinions that were reflected in the elections to the first two Dumas give a clear indication of the disillusionment with the regime felt by much of the population, but the government could find no way of reaching a *modus vivendi* with these views.

Stolypin's government pursued a confused strategy in trying to promote reform. The prime minister needed to wrest power from the traditional noble elite that had dominated Russian politics, but he did not realize that the very groups from which he needed support were those that he had alienated in the early stage of his premiership. Stolypin was too easily seduced by the promise of a tranquil political life that he believed would ensue from a compliant Duma, but he failed to see that the Third Duma did not properly reflect the aspirations of the bulk of Russian society. This had a dual impact: there was insufficient support in the legislature for the radical reforms that he proposed, and it meant that the prime minister was relying for support on sections of society whose interests would be directly threatened by his measures. To carry through his transformation of Russian society, Stolypin needed to persuade the traditional political elites of the empire that the long-term interests of the state required them to forgo their power and privileges. This most difficult of political tasks had to be carried out in the post-1905 environment when the empire's elites were congratulating themselves on having survived revolution. Stolypin recognized, however, that revolution had not been defeated in 1905, merely held at bay, and he insisted that failure to make change would have the deepest dangers for the tsarist state. In the years immediately after 1905, Stolypin was one of very few voices in the political elite expressing such views. He understood that radical reform was vital if revolution was not to break out again: reform could prevent revolution. The difficulties of reforming an autocracy were highlighted by Stolypin's efforts. The regime's earlier resistance to reform meant that, by 1905, change was long overdue. Popular pressure for reform was intense but, even after the October Manifesto, the tsarist political establishment was determined to make as few concessions as it could. The Russian autocracy possessed no mechanism by which it could respond to social and economic change. The monarch remained in ultimate control, and Nicholas II and his coterie took a short-sighted view of Russia's future, believing that antiquated political structures could successfully cope with a society and economy that were rapidly modernizing.

The failure of the Russian state's political direction became clear all too quickly. By 1914 there were unexpected individuals who foresaw dark times ahead for the Russian Empire: in the year before war broke out in the summer of 1914, both Guchkov and Durnovo warned of the threat of rebellion and social upheaval. By this time, however, the situation had moved too far for reform to be a realistic option. After Stolypin's assassination in 1911, he was succeeded as chairman of the council of ministers by the cautious Kokovtsov who demonstrated no inclination to embark on radical change. The Fourth Duma, which met from

1912, continued along the lines set by its predecessor. Most of Russia's political elite went through the years after 1905 confident after having defeated the revolution of 1905 and having tamed the radicalism of the first two Dumas. Stolypin, however, saw clearly the knife-edge on which the edifice of tsarism rested. His first-hand experience of revolution in Saratov had shown him the fragility of the social stability of the empire. But he ultimately proved unable to convince his social peers of the seriousness of Russia's situation. Stolypin's vision of a renewed Russia held little appeal for a declining elite, clinging on to the remnants of its social and political power. Unable to comprehend the historical experience of the monarchical regimes of Europe, the tsar and the Russian nobility believed that they could continue to rule an unreformed Russia.

The ethos of autocracy proved too strong for the hopes of reform. The ambitions of the Duma were extinguished and reform was snuffed out. Stolypin himself was reduced to behaving as a traditional St Petersburg politician, pursuing policies that supported the customary role of autocracy. The outbreak of war in 1914 dealt a final and fatal blow to the hope of peaceful change in Russia. The tsarist regime showed itself incapable of successfully managing the war effort, but the grip that it retained on power meant that the political groups represented in the Duma could only rant in impotent rage as Russia slid further into disarray as the war progressed. Stolypin's programme of reform represented tsarism's last opportunity to modernize and thus sustain itself. The failure of his attempt was to doom the autocracy. The collapse of the Soviet state and the failure of the Bolshevik experiment show that there was no inevitability about the onset of revolution in 1917. In the critical years after 1905, the path of peaceful change was open. Standing between two revolutions, Stolypin recognized the lessons of 1905, but was unable to do enough to prevent Russia's drift towards the cataclysm of 1917.

# Notes

## Introduction

1. A. Ia. Avrekh, *Tsarizm i tret'eiiun'skaia sistema* (Moscow, 1968) and E. D. Chermenskii, *Burzhuaziia i tsarizm v revoliutsii 1905–7gg.* (Moscow, 1939) are examples of this genre.
2. M. P. Bok, *Vospominaniia o moem otse P. A. Stolypine* (New York, 1953).
3. See, for example, A. V. Zen'kovskii, *Pravda o Stolypine* (New York, 1956).
4. Even previously hostile historians began to take a more balanced view. See, for example, A. Ia. Avrekh, *P. A. Stolypin i sud'by reform v Rossii* (Moscow, 1991).
5. See S. Rybas & L. Tarakanova, *Reformator: zhizn' i smert' Stolypina* (Moscow, 1991) and I. V. Ostrovskii, *P. A. Stolypin i ego vremia* (Moscow, 1992).

## Chapter One

1. See T. Emmons, *The Russian landed gentry and the peasant emancipation of 1861* (Cambridge, 1968).
2. The activities of the *zemstva* are fully considered in T. Emmons & W. S. Vucinich (eds), *The zemstvo in Russia: an experiment in local self-government* (Cambridge, 1982).
3. F. A. Petrov, "Crowning the edifice. The zemstvo, local self-govern-

ment and the constitutional movement, 1864–1881", in *Russia's great reforms, 1855–1881*, B. Eklof, J. Bushnell, L. Zakharova (eds) (Bloomington, Indiana, 1994), pp. 204–5.

4. A. K. Afanas'ev "Jurors and jury trials in imperial Russia, 1866–1885", in *ibid.*, pp. 214–30.

5. R. S. Wortman, *The development of a Russian legal consciousness* (Chicago, 1976).

6. B. Eklof, *Russian peasant schools: officialdom, village culture and popular pedagogy, 1861–1914* (Berkeley, Calif., 1986), pp. 64–9 gives details of the measures.

7. See D. Balmuth, *Censorship in Russia, 1865–1905* (Washington DC, 1979), especially ch. 3.

8. F. A. Miller, *Dmitrii Miliutin and the reform era in Russia* (Nashville, 1968), especially pp. 182–230.

9. Loris-Melikov's proposal is reproduced in M. McCauley & P. Waldron, *The emergence of the modern Russian state, 1855–81* (Basingstoke, 1988), pp. 74–6.

10. The best analyses of Alexander III's reign are V. G. Chernukha, "Alexander III", in *The emperors and empresses of Russia*, D. J. Raleigh (ed.) (Armonk, New York, 1996), pp. 335–68 and P. A. Zaionchkovskii, *Rossiiskoe samoderzhavie v kontse XIX stoletiia* (Moscow, 1970).

11. Different view of this legislation are provided in J. Daly, "On the significance of emergency legislation in late imperial Russia", *Slavic Review* 54, 1995, pp. 602–29 and P. Waldron, "States of emergency: autocracy and extraordinary legislation, 1881–1917", *Revolutionary Russia* 8, 1995, pp. 1–25.

12. T. S. Pearson, "The origins of Alexander III's land captains: a reinterpretation", *Slavic Review* 40, 1981, pp. 384–403.

13. L. G. Zakharova, *Zemskaia kontrreforma 1890g.* (Moscow, 1968) gives a very detailed account of these changes.

14. S. G. Wheatcroft, "Crises and the condition of the peasantry in late imperial Russia", in *Peasant economy, culture and politics of European Russia, 1800–1921*, E. Kingston-Mann & T. Mixter (eds) (Princeton, New Jersey, 1991), pp. 133–5.

15. H. Balzer, "The problem of professions in imperial Russia", in *Between tsar and people: educated society and the quest for public identity in late imperial Russia*, E. W. Clowes, S. D. Kassow, J. L. West (eds) (Princeton, New Jersey, 1991), pp. 183–98 argues that the professions remained socially fragmented and were unable to articulate their demands. Evidence from, for example, the banquet campaign of 1904–5 does not support this. See L. Edmondson, "Was there a movement for civil rights in Russia in 1905?" in *Civil rights in imperial Russia*, O. Crisp & L. Edmondson (eds) (Oxford, 1989), especially pp. 265–7.

16. See I. Nish, *The origins of the Russo-Japanese War* (Harlow, 1985).

17. A. Ascher, *Russia in disarray*, vol. 1 of *The revolution of 1905* (Stanford, Calif., 1988), pp. 87–9.
18. M. Perrie, "The Russian peasant movement of 1905–7", in *The world of the Russian peasant: post-emancipation culture and society*, B. Eklof & S. P. Frank (eds) (Boston, Mass., 1990), pp. 196–8.
19. S. Galai, *The liberation movement in Russia 1900–1905* (Cambridge, 1973), pp. 232–6.
20. A. M. Verner, *The crisis of Russian autocracy: Nicholas II and the 1905 revolution* (Princeton, New Jersey, 1990), P. 236.
21. D. Lieven, *Nicholas II: emperor of all the Russias* (London, 1993), p. 141.
22. D. Lieven, *Russia's rulers under the old regime* (New Haven, Connecticut, 1989), ch. 2 sets out the nature of the State Council's membership.
23. V. G. Chernukha & B. V. Anan'ich, "Russia falls back, Russia catches up: three generations of Russian reformers", in *Reform in modern Russian history: progress or cycle?*, T. Taranovski (ed.) (Cambridge, 1995), p. 65.
24. K. L. Bermanskii, " 'Konstitutsionnye' proekty tsarstvovaniia Aleksandra II", *Vestnik Prava* 35, 1905, pp. 271–81; V. G. Chernukha, *Vnutrennaia politika tsarizma s serediny 50-kh do nachala 80-kh gg. XIX v.* (Leningrad, 1978), pp. 15–22.
25. T. Emmons, *The formation of political parties and the first national elections in Russia* (Cambridge, Mass., 1983), p. 240; H. D. Mehlinger & J. M. Thompson, *Count Witte and the tsarist government in the 1905 revolution* (Bloomington, Indiana, 1972), pp. 112–24.
26. M. Szeftel, *The Russian constitution of 23 April, 1906: political institutions of the Duma monarchy* (Brussels, 1976), pp. 84–109 provides a translation of the text of the document.
27. V. I. Startsev, *Russkaia burzhuaziia i samoderzhavie v 1905–1917 (Bor'ba vokrug "otvetstvennogo" ministerstva i "pravitel'stva doveriia")* (Leningrad, 1977), pp. 46–7.
28. *Gosudarstvennaia Duma. Stenograficheskie otchety* (hereafter GDSO), I Duma, vol. 1 (St Petersburg, 1906), cols 321–4.
29. See T. Fallows, "Governor Stolypin and the revolution of 1905 in Saratov", in *Politics and society in provincial Russia: Saratov, 1590–1917*, R. A. Wade & S. J. Seregny (eds) (Columbus, Ohio, 1989), pp. 160–90.
30. A telegram of 4 January 1906 from the tsar to Stolypin congratulated the Saratov governor on his "exemplary efficiency in sending troops to put down revolt". St Petersburg, Rossiiskii Gosudarstvennyi Istoricheskii Arkhiv (hereafter RGIA), fond (f.) 1276, opis' (op.) 3, delo (d.) 959, list (l.) 75.
31. "K istorii agrarnoi reformy Stolypina", *Krasnyi Arkhiv* 17, 1926, pp. 83–7; N. Karpov, *Agrarnaia politika Stolypina* (Leningrad, 1925), pp. 172–4.

32. P. A. Tverskoi, "K istoricheskim materialam o pokoinom P. A. Stolypine", *Vestnik Evropy* (1912, no. 4), p. 186.

## Chapter Two

1. See Emmons, *The formation of political parties*, esp. ch. 7.
2. V. V. Shelokhaev, *Kadety – glavnaia partiia liberal'noi burzhuazii v bor'be s revoliutsiei 1905–1907 gg.* (Moscow, 1983), pp. 92–6.
3. Emmons, *The formation of political parties*, pp. 206–33 offers a detailed analysis of the Octobrist party in its first months of existence.
4. D. C. Rawson, *Russian rightists and the revolution of 1905* (Cambridge, 1995), pp. 21–72 looks in detail at the formation of groups and parties on the right.
5. S. M. Sidel'nikov, *Agrarnaia politika samoderzhaviia v period imperializma* (Moscow, 1980), pp. 75–80.
6. *Polnoe sobranie zakonov Rossiiskoi imperii* (hereafter PSZ), vol. XXIII/I, no. 22581 and vol. XXIV/I, no. 25495.
7. GDSO, I Duma, vol. 1, pp. 321–4.
8. Kokovtsov, the minister of finance, described Goremykin as reading the speech "in a voice that was hardly audible . . . his hands shaking with agitation". V. N. Kokovtsov, *Out of my past* (Stanford, Calif., 1935), p. 140.
9. See A. Ascher, *Authority restored*, vol. 2 of *The revolution of 1905* (Stanford, Calif., 1992), pp. 171–3 for a detailed description of the various parties' proposals.
10. Kokovtsov, *Out of my past*, p. 143.
11. A. I. Guchkov, "Zapiska o reformakh, kotorye dolzhno provesti pravitel'stvo". Moscow, Gosudarstvennyi Arkhiv Rossiiskoi Federatsii (hereafter GARF), f. 555, op. 1, d. 17, l. 1.
12. V. I. Gurko, *Features and figures of the past: government and opinion in the reign of Nicholas II* (Stanford, Calif., 1939), p. 487.
13. D. N. Shipov, *Vospominaniia i dumy o perezhitom* (Moscow, 1918), pp. 445–7.
14. The tsar, after meeting the latter pair, wrote to Stolypin that "they would not be suitable as ministers . . . Therefore attempts to attract them into the government should stop. We must look closer to home." "Perepiska N. A. Romanova i P. A. Stolypina", *Krasnyi Arkhiv* 5, 1924, p. 102.
15. GDSO, II Duma, vol. 1, cols 167–9.
16. Tverskoi, "K istoricheskim materialam", p. 193. Although Stolypin had given this interview in 1907, this was its first publication as the interviewer felt that it raised too many doubts in his mind about Stolypin's intentions for publication immediately prior to the opening of the Second Duma.

17. *Ibid.*, p. 193.
18. Bok, *Vospominaniia o moem otse*, p. 144.
19. *Pravitel'stvennyi Vestnik*, 24 August 1906, p. 1.
20. GDSO, II Duma, vol. 1, cols 167–9.
21. A. Levin, *The Second Duma* (New Haven, Connecticut, 1940).
22. "Doklad Stolypina o khode i rezul'tatakh vyborov deputatov v Dumu", 15 July 1906. GARF, f. 601, op. 1, d. 912, ll. 1–25.
23. V. S. Diakin, "Chrezvychaino-ukaznoe zakonodatel'stvo v Rossii (1906–14)", *Vspomogatel'nye Istoricheskie Distsipliny* 7, Leningrad, 1976, pp. 240–71 analyzes the provenance and application of Article 87.
24. S. E. Kryzhanovskii's testimony in P. E. Shchegolev (ed.), *Padenie tsarskogo rezhima: stenograficheskie otchety doprosov i pokazanii, dannykh v 1917 g. v chrezvychainoi sledstvennoi kommissii Vremennogo Pravitel'stva*, vol. 2 (Leningrad and Moscow, 1925), pp. 381–91 sets out the government's thinking. Kryzhanovskii was the assistant minister of internal affairs who drafted the new electoral law.
25. GARF, f. 601, op. 1, d. 1352, l. 14. This is undated and in Stolypin's own handwriting and is clearly the document Kryzhanovskii refers to in Shchegolev (ed.), *Padenie tsarskogo rezhima*, vol. 1, p. 429.
26. S. E. Kryzhanovskii, *Vospominaniia* (Berlin, 1925), pp. 107–16.
27. "Report of interview between Stolypin and Mackenzie Wallace", London, Public Record Office (hereafter PRO), FO 418/38, p. 203.
28. PRO, FO 371/126, p. 163.
29. "Po voprosu ob uchrezhdenii voenno-polevykh sudov", Osobyi zhurnal soveta ministrov, 17 August 1906. RGIA, f. 1276, op. 20, d. 2, l. 105.
30. "Perepiska N. A. Romanova i P. A. Stolypina", p. 104.
31. GDSO, II Duma, vol. 1, col. 513.
32. PSZ, vol. XXVI/I, no. 28255.
33. "Po voprosu o sokrashchenii primeneniia zakona o voenno-polevykh sudakh", Osobyi zhurnal soveta ministrov, 9 February 1907. RGIA, f. 1276, op. 20, d. 8, ll. 51–2; A. A. Polivanov, *Iz dnevnikov i vospominanii po dolzhnosti voennogo ministra i ego pomoshchika, 1907–1916* (Moscow, 1924), pp. 18–19.
34. See Waldron, "States of emergency", pp. 1–25 for a full discussion of these powers.
35. *Zaprosy zhizni* (1912, no. 10), p. 22.
36. In 1895 a total of 8,699 titles were published in Russia, but by 1914 this had increased to 32,338. D. Balmuth, *Censorship in Russia, 1865–1905* (Washington, DC, 1979), p. 113 and B. Rigberg, "The efficacy of tsarist censorship operations, 1894–1917", *Jahrbücher für Geschichte Osteuropas* 14, 1966, p. 333.
37. V. S. Diakin, *Samoderzhavie, burzhuaziia i dvorianstvo v 1907–1911 gg.* (Leningrad, 1978), pp. 28–9.
38. "V gody reaktsii', *Krasnyi Arkhiv* 8, 1925, p. 242.

39. "Po proektu iskliuchitel'nogo polozheniia", Osobyi zhurnal soveta ministrov, 2 and 6 February 1907. RGIA, f. 1276, op. 20, d. 7, ll. 14–32.
40. Quoted in A. S. Izgoev, *P. A. Stolypin: ocherk zhizni i deiatel'nosti* (Moscow, 1912), p. 40.
41. "Vsepoddanneishii otchet saratovskogo gubernatora P. Stolypina za 1904 god", *Krasnyi Arkhiv* 17, 1926, pp. 83–7.
42. *PSZ*, vol. XXVII, no. 29240, pp. 319–20.
43. Speech at the opening of the council for the local economy (*Sovet po delam mestnogo khoziaistva*), 11 March 1908. RGIA, f. 1288, op. 1, d. 23, l. 3.
44. *GDSO*, III Duma, session 1, vol. 1, col. 354.
45. "Po zakonoproektam, kasaiushchimsia svobody sovesti", Osobyi zhurnal soveta ministrov, 3 and 17 February 1907. RGIA, f. 796, op. 188, d. 7620, l. 76.
46. See P. Waldron, "Stolypin and Finland", *Slavonic and East European Review* 63, 1985, pp. 41–55 and E. Chmielewski, *The Polish question in the Russian State Duma* (Knoxville, Tennessee, 1970).
47. *GDSO*, III Duma, session 1, vol. 1, col. 352.
48. RGIA, f. 1276, op. 3, d. 18, l. 41.
49. *GDSO*, II Duma, vol. 1, col. 107.
50. "Doklad Stolypina o khode i rezul'tatakh vyborov v Dumu", 15 July 1906. GARF, f. 601, op. 1, d. 912, l. 22.
51. *GDSO*, III Duma, session 1, vol. 1, col. 348.
52. *GDSO*, II Duma, vol. 1, col. 107.
53. *GDSO*, III Duma, session 1, vol. 1, col. 349.
54. K. A. Krivoshein, *A. V. Krivoshein (1857–1921)* (Paris, 1973), p. 49.
55. Gurko, *Features and figures*, pp. 157–61.
56. *PSZ*, vol. XXV/I, no. 26871, p. 790.
57. *GDSO*, II Duma, vol. 2, col. 440.
58. "O dopolnenii nekotorykh postanovlenii deistvuiushchego zakona, kasaiushchikhsia krest'ianskogo zemlevladeniia i zemlepolzovaniia", Osobyi zhurnal soveta ministrov, 10 October 1906. RGIA, f. 1276, op. 2, d. 406, ll. 138–45.
59. See D. A. J. Macey, *Government and peasant in Russia, 1861–1906: the prehistory of the Stolypin reforms* (DeKalb, Illinois, 1987) for a comprehensive analysis of the reform's origins.
60. See R. G. Robbins, *The tsar's viceroys: Russian provincial governors in the last years of the empire* (Ithaca, New York, 1987) and I. Blinov, *Gubernatory* (St Petersburg, 1905) for wide-ranging surveys of the governors' powers and responsibilities.
61. I. M. Strakhovskii, *Gubernskoe ustroistvo* (St Petersburg, 1913), p. 104.
62. Blinov, *Gubernatory*, p. 262 quoting K. A. Golovin.
63. S. A. Korf, "Predvoditel' dvorianstva, kak organ soslovnogo i zemskogo samoupravleniia", *Zhurnal ministerstva iustitsii* 3, 1902, p. 93.

64. *Svod zakonov rossiiskoi imperii*, vol. 9 (St Petersburg, 1899), pp. 76–9.
65. Bok, *Vospominaniia o moem otse*, p. 7.
66. A. Novikov, *Zapiski zemskogo nachal'nika* (St Petersburg, 1899), p. 52.
67. *Ibid.*, pp. 36–8.
68. D. M. Wallace, *Russia on the eve of war and revolution* (New York, 1961), p. 351.
69. G. A. Hosking, *The Russian constitutional experiment: government and Duma 1907–1914* (Cambridge, 1973), p. 151.
70. F. W. Wcislo, *Reforming rural Russia: state, local society and national politics 1855–1914* (Princeton, New Jersey, 1990), chs 2 & 3.
71. The committee's membership included two assistant ministers of internal affairs, A. A. Makarov and S. E. Kryzhanovskii, together with other senior civil servants and the St Petersburg provincial governor, A. D. Zinov'ev.
72. "Ob ustanovlenii glavnykh nachal ustroistva mestnogo upravleniia", Osobyi zhurnal soveta ministrov, 19 and 22 December 1906 and 3 and 6 January 1907. RGIA, f. 1405, op. 543, d. 909, l. 71. See N. B. Weissman, *Reform in tsarist Russia: the state bureaucracy and local government, 1900–1914* (New Brunswick, New Jersey, 1981), pp. 130–44.
73. "Vremennoe polozhenie o spravochnom otdele pri sovete mestnogo khoziaistva", RGIA, f. 1288, op. 1, d. 29, l. 75.
74. "Ob ustanovlenii glavnykh nachal ustroistva mestnogo upravleniia", RGIA, f. 1405, op. 543, d. 909, l. 1.
75. *Ibid.*, l. 2.
76. This was shown by the survey that the ministry of internal affairs undertook to look at the performance of duties by the marshals of the nobility. RGIA, f. 1288, op. 1, d. 3-1908, l. 20.
77. Osobyi zhurnal soveta ministrov, 20 and 27 January 1907. RGIA, f. 1405, op. 543, d. 909, ll. 66–70.
78. *Ibid.*, l. 77.
79. "Polozhenie ob uchastkovykh nachal'nikakh", RGIA, f. 1288, op. 1, d. 12, ll. 102–3.
80. "Ob ustanovlenii glavnykh osnovanii preobrazovaniia zemskikh i gorodskikh uchrezhdenii", RGIA, f. 1405, op. 543, d. 911, l. 85.
81. "Po proektu preobrazovaniia zemskikh i gorodskikh uchrezhdenii", Osobyi zhurnal soveta ministrov', 7 and 18 December 1907. RGIA, f. 1405, op. 543, d. 911, ll. 181–3.
82. See P. Czap, "Peasant-class courts and peasant customary justice in Russia, 1861–1912", *Journal of Social History* 1, 1967, pp. 149–78.
83. "Kratkaia ob"iasnitel'naia zapiska k proektu ministerstva iustitsii o preobrazovanii mestnogo suda", RGIA, f. 1288, op. 2, d. 326, ll. 437–41.
84. *Ibid.*, l. 443.
85. Osobyi zhurnal soveta ministrov, 19 and 23 January 1907. RGIA, f. 1276, op. 20, d. 7, l. 174.

86. See P. Waldron, "Religious reform after 1905: Old Believers and the Orthodox Church", *Oxford Slavonic Papers*, New Series 20, 1987, pp. 110–39.
87. "Pravila ob inoslavnykh i inovernykh religioznykh obshchestvakh", RGIA, f. 796, op. 188, d. 7620, l. 35.
88. GARF, f. 601, op. 1, d. 1125, ll. 10–11, 10 December 1906. Published in "Perepiska N. A. Romanova i P. A. Stolypina", p. 105. The United Nobility had also passed a resolution in May 1906 opposing the relaxation of restrictions on the Jews, since they argued that this would be seen by the population as a sign of government weakness. *Svod postanovlenii I–X s"ezdov upolnomochennykh ob"edinennykh dvorianskikh obshchestv, 1906–14* (Petrograd, 1915), p. 38.
89. RGIA, f. 560, op. 26, d. 600, ll. 53–7.
90. "Ob"iasnitel'naia zapiska k proektu o neprikosvennosti lichnosti", RGIA, f. 1276, op. 3, d. 1, l. 36.
91. See *PSZ*, vol. XXV/I, no. 26962, pp. 837–40, vol. XXVI/I, no. 27815, pp. 481–3, no. 27480, pp. 207–10 and no. 27479, pp. 201–6. For discussion of two areas, see G. R. Swain, "Freedom of association and the trade unions, 1906–1914" and C. Ferenczi, "Freedom of the press under the old regime, 1905–1914" both in Crisp & Edmondson, *Civil rights,* pp. 171–214.
92. "Po voprosu o zakonoproektakh, podlezhashchikh vneseniiu v Gosudarstvennuiu Dumu", Osobyi zhurnal soveta ministrov, 12 January 1907. RGIA, f. 1276, op. 20, d. 7, l. 135.
93. "Materialy po peresmotru rabochego zakonodatel'stva. Ob"iasnitel'naia zapiska". RGIA, f. 1405, op. 543, d. 1389, l. 149.
94. "Po proektam zakonopolozhenii: ob obezpechenii rabochikh na sluchai bolezni, o strakhovanii ikh ot neschastlivykh sluchaev, o prisutstviiakh po delam strakhovaniia rabochikh i o sovete po tem zhe delam", Osobyi zhurnal soveta ministrov, 17 and 19 June, 1908. RGIA, f. 1405, op. 543, d. 1390, ll. 139–46.
95. "Po voprosu o vvedenii v Rossiiskoi Imperii vseobshchego nachal'nogo obrazovaniia", Osobyi zhurnal soveta ministrov, 26 and 30 January 1907. RGIA, f. 1276, op. 20, d. 7, ll. 236–46.
96. See G. E. Snow, "The Kokovtsov commission: an abortive attempt at labour reform in Russia in 1905", *Slavic Review* 31, 1972, pp. 780–96.
97. Interview published in *Volga,* 1 September 1909 and reprinted in E. V[erpakhovskaia], *Gosudarstvennaia deiatel'nost' P. A. Stolypina,* vol. 1 (St Petersburg, 1909), p. 8.
98. D. Atkinson, "The statistics on the Russian land commune, 1905–1917", *Slavic Review* 32, 1973, pp. 777–83.
99. *PSZ,* vol. XXVII, no. 29240.
100. V. Miakotin, "Sovremennaia 'detsentralizatsiia'", *Russkoe Bogatstvo* 4, 1908, p. 128.

# Chapter Three

1. See Izgoev, *Stolypin*, pp. 117–23 for a systematic analysis of the government's achievements.
2. *PSZ*, vol. XXX/I, no. 33743, pp. 746–53.
3. Atkinson, "The statistics on the Russian land commune", pp. 777–83; V. P. Danilov, "Ob istoricheskikh sud'bakh krest'ianskoi obshchiny v Rossii" in *Ezhegodnik po istorii agrarnoi istorii: problemy istorii russkoi obshchiny* (Vologda, 1976), pp. 104–6.
4. A. Ia. Avrekh, "Agrarnyi vopros v tret'ei Dume", *Istoricheskie zapiski* 62, 1958, pp. 26–83 gives details of the different parties' positions.
5. *Trudy I-ogo s"ezda upolnomochennykh dvorianskikh obshchestv, 21–28 mai 1906* (St Petersburg, 1906), pp. 105–8.
6. *Svod postanovlenii I–X s"ezdov upolnomochennykh ob"edinennykh dvorianskikh obshchestv*, p. 5.
7. *Gosudarstvennyi Sovet. Stenograficheskie otchety* (hereafter GSSO), session V, cols 1153–55; Sidel'nikov, *Agrarnaia politika*, pp. 137–43 sets out details of the State Council debates.
8. Hosking, *The Russian constitutional experiment*, p. 72.
9. "Protokoly postoiannogo soveta ob"edinennogo dvorianstva", 27 February 1907. GARF, f. 434, op. 1, d. 76, l. 90.
10. *Trudy III-ogo s"ezda upolnomochennykh dvorianskikh obshchestv* (St Petersburg, 1907), p. 13.
11. P. Koropachinskii, *Reforma mestnogo samoupravleniia po rabotam soveta po delam mestnogo khoziaistva*, (Ufa, 1908), p. 2.
12. Speech to the opening session of the council, 11 March 1908. RGIA, f. 1288, op. 1, d. 29, l. 3.
13. "Doklad komissii po razsmotreniiu zakonoproektov o reforme mestnogo upravleniia", RGIA, f. 1288, op. 1, d. 26, ll. 2–38.
14. *Trudy V-ogo s"ezda upolnomochennykh dvorianskikh obshchestv* (St Petersburg, 1909), p. 103.
15. RGIA, f. 1288, op. 1, d. 29, l. 4.
16. RGIA, f. 1288, op. 1, d. 8, l. 2.
17. *Zhurnaly zasedanii tret'ego ocherednogo s"ezda predstavitelei promyshlennosti i torgovli, 27–31 mart 1908* (St Petersburg, 1908), p. 24.
18. *Trudy IV-ogo s"ezda upolnomochennykh dvorianskikh obshchestv, 9–16 mart 1908* (St Petersburg, 1909), pp. 158–64.
19. GSSO, vol. 7, cols 1756–60.
20. The laws setting up the Duma and the State Council required that in the case of disagreement between the two institutions, a bill should be sent to a conciliatory commission and should then be ratified again by the Duma as a whole.
21. A. Ia. Avrekh, *Stolypin i tret'ia Duma* (Moscow, 1968), pp. 197–8.
22. "Peterburgskoe obshchestvo zavodchikov i fabrikantov. Komissiia po obsuzhdeniiu . . . zakonoproektov po rabochemu voprosu pod predse-

datel'stvom M. A. Ostrova. Otchet . . . o rabotakh komissii", RGIA, f. 150, op. 1, d. 591, l. 9.
23. *Ibid.*, l. 8.
24. *Ibid.*, ll. 74–5.
25. A. N. Ropp, *Chto sdelala tret'ia Gosudarstvennaia Duma dlia narodnogo obrazovaniia?* (St Petersburg, 1912), pp. 46 and 109.
26. Kokovtsov to the Duma, GDSO, III Duma, session 4, vol. 2, col. 511.
27. See *Trudy VI-ogo s"ezda upolnomochennykh dvorianskikh obshchestv, 14–20 mart 1910* (St Petersburg, 1911), p. 458 and Ropp, *Chto sdelala,* p. 237.
28. RGIA, f. 796, op. 188, d. 7620, l. 125.
29. N. F. Platonov, "Pravoslavnaia tserkov' v bor'be s revoliutsionnym dvizheniem v Rossii (1900–1917)", *Ezhegodnik Muzeia Istorii Religii i Ateizma* 4, Moscow–Leningrad, 1960, p. 167.
30. This is best exemplified in a report by Izvol'skii to Nicholas II in 1908 in which the chief procurator noted the danger of an antagonism being established between the spiritual and temporal powers. St Petersburg, Russkaia Natsional'naia Biblioteka, Rukopisnyi otdel' (hereafter RNB, RO), f. 443, d. 852, l. 12.
31. Waldron, "Religious reform after 1905", pp. 133–4.
32. J. H. M. Geekie, *The Church and politics in Russia, 1905–1917: a study of the political behaviour of the Russian Orthodox clergy in the reign of Nicholas II* (PhD thesis, University of East Anglia, 1976), pp. 188–90.
33. GDSO, III Duma, session 2, vol. 4, col. 1762.
34. Stolypin to S. M. Luk'ianov, chief procurator of the Holy Synod, 10 October 1909, RGIA, f. 796, op. 188, d. 7620, ll. 306–10.
35. GSSO, vol. 5, cols 2795–814.
36. Szeftel, *The Russian constitution of 23 April, 1906,* p. 300.
37. *Obzor deiatel'nosti Gosudarstvennoi Dumy tret'ego sozyva, 1907–1912 gg.* (St Petersburg, 1912), vol. 1, p. 172.
38. RGIA, f. 1278, op. 3., d. 171, l. 63.
39. *Ibid.*, l. 73.
40. S. I. Shidlovskii, *Vospominaniia* (Berlin, 1923), vol. 1, p. 113.
41. An exception was the agrarian bill which, after its introduction into the Third Duma, took only three months to gain the approval of the commission examining it. This bill had previously been introduced in the Second Duma and it had been partially examined there, while it also commanded a measure of support amongst different political parties.
42. This was done during the debate on the agrarian bill, but deputies were able to avoid the restriction by making speeches under an article of the Duma's rules that allowed them to speak "to explain their voting". S. I. Shidlovskii, *Vospominaniia* (Berlin, 1923), vol. 1, p. 113.
43. Stolypin to Khomiakov, 17 October 1908. RGIA, f. 1278, op. 3, d. 171, l. 41.

44. *Ibid.*, l. 73. 8 November 1908.
45. *Ibid.*, l. 1.
46. *Ibid.*, l. 87.
47. The weakening of Octobrist unity accelerated after the spring of 1909 when Ia. G. Gololobov, a party adherent acting as rapporteur for an interpellation on trade unions, mounted a vigorous attack on Octobrist policy. See A. S. Viziagin, *Gololobovskii intsident: stranichka iz istorii politicheskikh partii v Rossii* (Khar'kov, 1909), pp. 9–71.
48. Diakin, *Samoderzhavie*, p. 124.
49. PRO, FO 418/38, p. 203.
50. Ascher, *Authority restored*, vol 2 of *The revolution of 1905*, p. 90.
51. Report of conversation between P. Kh. von Schvanebakh and Nicolson, 5 February 1907. PRO, FO 371/321, p. 248.
52. GDSO, III Duma, session 3, vol. 3, cols 2521–30.
53. See S. L. Levitsky, "Interpellations according to the Russian constitution of 1906", *Slavic and East European Studies* 1, 1956–7, pp. 220–31.
54. Under Octobrist pressure, the Third Duma established a committee to deal with defence matters and this body succeeded in establishing good relations with the ministry of war but, in the wake of the Russo-Japanese War, it launched severe attacks on the perceived incompetence of the naval ministry. A. Ia. Avrekh, "Stolypinskii bonapartizm i voprosy voennoi politiki v III Dume", *Voprosy Istorii* (1956, no. 11), pp. 17–33 and A. I. Zvengitsev, "The Duma and imperial defence", *Russian Review* 1, 1912, pp. 49–63.
55. The discussion over the naval ministry's budget in 1908, however, soured relations between government and Duma when Guchkov, the Octobrist leader, attacked the competence of the council of imperial defence headed by Grand Duke Nikolai Nikolaievich. See Hosking, *Russian constitutional experiment*, pp. 77–9.
56. Diakin, "Chrezvychaino-ukaznoe zakonodatel'stvo", p. 270.
57. During the western *zemstvo* crisis, however, Stolypin argued that the government had a duty to implement a measure that had been rejected by the legislature if it was supported by the people whom it would affect.
58. The diligence with which the commission dealing with the Old Believer bill went about its work – interviewing interested parties and asking them for their comments on the government's proposals – is not untypical of the commissions.

## Chapter Four

1. Quoted in B. V. Anan'ich & R. S. Ganelin, "Nicholas II", in *The emperors and empresses of Russia*, D. J. Raleigh (ed.) (Armonk, NY, 1996), p. 394.

2. Grand Duke Aleksandr Mikhailovich, *Kniga vospominanii* (Paris, 1933), vol. 2, p. 178.
3. "Perepiska N. A. Romanova i P. A. Stolypina", p. 105.
4. Quoted in Verner, *Crisis*, p. 238.
5. "Perepiska Nikolaia II i Marii Fedorovny", *Krasnyi Arkhiv* 22, 1927, p. 167.
6. GARF, f. 601, op. 1, d. 1125, l. 2, 14 August 1906.
7. *Ibid.*, ll. 14 & 16.
8. GARF, f. 1467, op. 1. d. 787, l. 45, 22 March 1909.
9. GARF, f. 601, op. 1. d. 1125, ll. 40–1. The care Nicholas took in composing this letter is demonstrated by the existence of a draft in pencil in *ibid.*, l. 42. The final letter is printed in "Perepiska N. A. Romanova i P. A. Stolypina", p. 120.
10. GARF, f. 601, op. 1, d. 1352, l. 5, 30 December 1907. "Iz perepiski P. A. Stolypina", *Krasnyi Arkhiv* 30, 1928, p. 3.
11. Polivanov, *Iz dnevnikov*, p. 70.
12. RGIA, f. 1662, op. 1, d. 325, l. 1. The report of this meeting is hand-written in pencil on paper headed "Chairman of the Council of Ministers".
13. GARF, f. 601, op. 1, d. 1125, l. 53. 9 March 1911.
14. Shidlovskii, *Vospominaniia*, vol. 1, p. 194.
15. GARF, f. 601, op. 1, d. 1352, ll. 12–13. "Iz perepiski", *Krasnyi Arkhiv* 30, 1928, p. 86.
16. Krivoshein, *A. V. Krivoshein*, p. 113. See also Kryzhanovskii, *Vospominaniia*, p. 213.
17. Rawson, *Russian rightists*, p. 143.
18. See, for example, the testimony of A. I. Pruselkov in A. Chernovskii (ed.), *Soiuz russkogo naroda: po materialam chrezvychainoi sledstvennoi komissii vremennogo pravitel'stva* (Moscow–Leningrad, 1929), p. 52.
19. GARF, f. 601, op. 1, d. 1125, l. 62.
20. See Verner, *Crisis*, pp. 228–31.
21. B. Pares (ed.), *Letters of the tsaritsa to the tsar* (London, 1923), p. 452.
22. A. P. Izvol'skii, *The memoirs of Alexander Iswolsky* (London, n.d.), p. 289.
23. GARF, f. 595, d. 45, l. 6.
24. Lieven, *Nicholas II*, pp. 119–21.
25. In his 1917 testimony to the Provisional Government commission investigating the final years of tsarism, Shcheglovitov ascribed such views to Stolypin himself, suggesting that Stolypin "saw limited significance in judicial matters, and if he believed a measure was necessary, then would see no obstacles to its implementation", Shchegolev (ed.), *Padenie tsarskogo rezhima*, vol. 2, p. 439.
26. Quoted in T. Polvinen, *Imperial borderland: Bobrikov and the attempted Russification of Finland 1898–1904* (London, 1995), p. 226.

27. Bok, *Vospominaniia*, p. 263.
28. This was especially true of his comments on the workers' insurance bills, for he had been chairman of a commission to examine the possibility of such reforms in 1903.
29. See, for example, his contribution to the debate on provincial reform when he was concerned that it would be difficult to find suitable candidates for the job of governor and that the duties of the post were insufficiently well defined. Osobyi zhurnal soveta ministrov, 20 and 27 January 1907. RGIA, f. 1405, op. 543, d. 910, l. 64.
30. Stolypin's reply, in which he asked Kokovtsov to remain in the government, is in RGIA, f. 966, op. 2, d. 14, ll. 2–3. This disagreement, as well as others during the summer of 1907, is reported in A. V. Bogdanovich, *Dnevnik. Tri poslednikh samoderzhtsa* (Moscow–Leningrad, 1924), pp. 396 and 424.
31. Bok, *Vospominaniia* p. 148.
32. RGIA, f. 1276, op. 3, d. 18, ll. 79–82. 22 January 1907.
33. Shchegolev (ed.), *Padenie tsarskogo rezhima*, vol. 7, pp. 90–1.
34. Stolypin's daughter testifies to Kurlov's lack of sympathy towards her father. Bok, *Vospominaniia*, p. 242.
35. D. K. Rowney, "Organizational change and social adaptation: the prerevolutionary ministry of internal affairs", in *Russian officialdom: the bureaucratization of Russian society from the seventeenth to the twentieth century*, W. M. Pintner & D. K. Rowney (eds) (London, 1980), p. 299 provides figures to show that although there was a decrease in the number of landowning high civil servants, in 1911 seven out of the ten highest positions in the ministry of internal affairs were held by landowners and 20 per cent of the next highest group were also landowners.
36. P. A. Zaionchkovskii, *Pravitel'stvennyi apparat samoderzhavnoi Rossii v XIX veke* (Moscow, 1978), pp. 214–15.
37. "Gubernskaia reforma", note by I. Ia. Gurliand. RGIA, f. 1629, op. 1, d. 25, ll. 51–8.
38. *Ibid.*, l. 58. He mentioned weakening of the governor's power, a feeling that there was no need for large-scale reform and the undesirability of making such a large break with the past as the chief reasons for their opposition.
39. "Doklad komissii po proektu polozheniia ob uezdnom upravlenii", RGIA, f. 1288, op. 1, d. 1-1908, l. 1.
40. Kryzhanovskii, *Vospominaniia*, pp. 138–41; Shchegolev (ed.), *Padenie tsarskogo rezhima*, vol. 2, pp. 376–8.
41. Chernovskii (ed.), *Soiuz russkogo naroda*, p. 43.
42. *Ibid.*, pp. 77–8.
43. F. S. Zuckerman, *The tsarist secret police in Russian society, 1880–1917* (London, 1996), p. 177.
44. A. Levin, *The reactionary tradition in the election campaign to the Third Duma* (Oklahoma State University Publications 59, no. 16,

Social Studies series no. 8, 1962), analyzes the different groups and their support. Nicholas II had also shown himself to be sympathetic to the Union of the Russian People. A telegram from the tsar to the Union in June 1907 expressed his feelings: "May the Union of the Russian People be to me a trustworthy support and serve for all and at all times as an example of law and order." PRO, FO 371/318, p. 394.

45. Nicholas II to Mariia Fedorovna, 15 December 1905. E. J. Bing (ed.), *The letters of Tsar Nicholas and Empress Marie* (London, 1937), p. 203.

46. The United Nobility wanted to see the franchise restricted and made representations to the government on this point. See *Svod postanovlenii I–X s"ezdov upolnomochennykh ob"edinennykh dvorianskikh obshchestv*, pp. 42–3.

47. Rawson, *Russian rightists*, p. 110.

48. This plan was devised by N. N. Kutler, the head of the government's agriculture department, and is fully described in Sidel'nikov, *Agrarnaia politika*, pp. 59–61.

49. RGIA, f. 1276, op. 2, d. 2, ll. 1–3.

50. G. A. Hosking & R. T. Manning, "What was the United Nobility?", in *The politics of rural Russia, 1905–1914*, L. H. Haimson (ed.) (Bloomington, Indiana, & London, 1979), pp. 152–4.

51. *Trudy II-ogo s"ezda upolnomochennykh dvorianskikh obshchestv* (St Petersburg, 1907), p. 5.

52. *Ibid*, p. 51.

53. *Trudy V-ogo s"ezda upolnomochennykh dvorianskikh obshchestv*, p. 103.

54. RGIA, f. 1288, op. 1, d. 3-1908, ll. 90 & 96.

55. RGIA, f. 796, op. 205, d. 698, ll. 45–6. I am grateful to Dr Simon Dixon for drawing my attention to this source.

56. See J. Meyendorff, "Russian bishops and church reform in 1905", in *Russian orthodoxy under the old regime*, R. L. Nichols & T. G. Stavrou (eds) (Minneapolis, Minnesota, 1978), pp. 170–82 and G. L. Freeze, *The parish clergy in nineteenth-century Russia: crisis, reform, counter-reform* (Princeton, 1983), pp. 468–9.

57. Waldron, "Religious reform after 1905", pp. 127–8.

58. RGIA, f. 796, op. 188, d. 7620, ll. 75–6.

59. RGIA, f. 796, op. 188, d. 7620, ll. 74–81.

60. Quoted in G. L. Freeze, "Subversive piety: religion and the political crisis in late imperial Russia", *Journal of Modern History* 68, 1996, p. 337.

61. RGIA, f. 797, op. 79, d. 549, l. 1. See Rawson, *Russian rightists*, pp. 92–3 for background on the Pochaev monastery.

62. RGIA, f. 797, op. 79, d. 408, ll. 45–7 & 53.

63. RGIA, f. 796, op. 188, d. 7620, ll. 295–9.

64. RNB, RO, f. 443, d. 852, ll. 9–14.

NOTES

65. G. L. Freeze, "Subversive piety", pp. 317–24 gives details of the tsar's participation in religious rituals.
66. Diakin, *Samoderzhavie*, p. 98.
67. GDSO, III Duma, session 2, vol. 4, col. 790.
68. See S. Dixon, "The Church's social role in St Petersburg, 1880–1914", in *Church, nation and state in Russia and Ukraine*, G. Hosking (ed.) (Basingstoke, 1991), pp. 167–92.

## Chapter Five

1. GARF, f. 601, op. 1, d. 912, ll. 1–7.
2. *Ibid.*, l. 19.
3. "Rasporiazhenie otnositel'no proizvodstva vyborov novogo sostava chlenov v Gosudarstvennuiu Dumu" in E. V[erpakhovskaia] (ed.), *Predsedatel' soveta ministrov Petr Arkad'evich Stolypin* (Moscow, 1909), pp. 23–5.
4. See Kryzhanovskii, *Vospominaniia*, pp. 100–4.
5. Such papers had been printed by political parties with votes already placed against the names of their candidates.
6. GARF, f. 601, op. 1, d. 912, l. 21.
7. Kryzhanovskii, *Vospominaniia*, pp. 107–14 sets out the process of preparation of the 3 June 1907 electoral law in some detail.
8. R. Edelman, "The election to the Third Duma: the roots of the Nationalist party", in *The politics of rural Russia*, Haimson (ed.), p. 95.
9. Report of interview between Stolypin and Mackenzie Wallace, 13 June 1907. PRO, FO 418/38, p. 203.
10. See Shipov, *Vospominaniia*, pp. 459–80; also report of interview between Nicolson and Stolypin, 12 July 1906. PRO, FO 371/126, p. 551.
11. Report of meeting between Stolypin and Nicolson, 11 July 1906. PRO, FO 371/127, p. 234.
12. E. Vishnevski, *Liberal'naia oppozitsiia v Rossii nakanune pervoi mirovoi voiny* (Moscow, 1994), pp. 17–21.
13. Interview with A. I. Guchkov in *Novoe vremia*, 29 August 1906.
14. "Zapiska o reformakh, kotorye dolzhno provesti pravitel'stvo", GARF, f. 555, op. 1, d. 17, ll. 1–3.
15. *Novoe vremia*, 29 August 1906.
16. Report of interview between Stolypin and correspondent of *Strana*, 17 August 1906. PRO, FO 418/34, p. 17.
17. PRO, FO 371/127, p. 234.
18. J. F. Hutchinson. *The Octobrists in Russian politics, 1905–1917* (PhD thesis, University of London, 1966), pp. 43–4.
19. Quoted in Diakin, *Samoderzhavie*, p. 119.
20. "Protokoly zasedanii biuro fraktsii 17 oktiabria Gosudarstvennoi Dumy", 4 January 1908. GARF, f. 115, op. 1, d. 20, l. 7.

21. RGIA, f. 869, op. 1, d. 1286, ll. 62–3.
22. For a detailed account of the incident, see Hosking, *Russian constitutional experiment*, pp. 87–91.
23. Viziagin, *Gololobovskii intsident*, pp. 64–5.
24. GARF, f. 102 (1909), op. 265, d. 395, l. 30.
25. GARF, f. 115, op. 1, d. 6, ll. 45–7.
26. GARF, f. 115, op. 1, d. 19, l. 118.
27. Stolypin to Guchkov, 4 March 1910. GARF, f. 555, op. 1, d. 1112, l. 3.
28. Stolypin's strategy was clear to his opponents. Count A. A. Bobrinskii, the chairman of the United Nobility, noted in October 1910 that "Stolypin's game is understood. This lord is getting his own nominees – mediocre people who are obedient to him – appointed everywhere." "Dnevnik A. A. Bobrinskogo", *Krasnyi Arkhiv* 26, 1928, p. 137.
29. B.-C. Pinchuk, *The Octobrists in the Third Duma, 1907–1912* (Seattle, Washington, 1974), p. 106.
30. GDSO, III Duma, session 3, vol. 3, col. 451.
31. R. McNaughton & R. Manning, "Political trends in the zemstvos, 1907–1914", in *The politics of rural Russia*, Haimson (ed.), p. 195.
32. R. Edelman, *Gentry politics on the eve of the Russian revolution: the Nationalist party 1907–1917* (New Brunswick, New Jersey, 1980), pp. 70–1.
33. A. D. Shecket, *The Russian Imperial State Council: bureaucratic and soslovie interests versus reform* (PhD thesis, Columbia University, 1984), pp. 182–5.
34. Kryzhanovskii, *Vospominaniia* pp. 102–3.
35. Bogdanovich, *Dnevnik*, p. 409.
36. An example of this is Stolypin's instructions to Gurliand on how to treat the withdrawal of the religious bills in *Rossiia*. RGIA, f. 1662, op. 1, d. 79, l. 1.
37. Shchegolev (ed.), *Padenie tsarskogo rezhima*, vol. 5, p. 404.
38. This was noted by Izgoev, *Stolypin*, p. 26.
39. Shchegolev (ed.) *Padenie tsarskogo rezhima*, vol. 5, pp. 412–13.
40. *Ibid.*, pp. 409–10.
41. *Ibid.*, pp. 411–12.
42. *Ibid.*, vol. 6, p. 201.
43. *Ibid.*, p. 179.
44. *Ibid.*, p. 182 and vol. 5, p. 408.
45. Chernovskii (ed.), *Soiuz russkogo naroda*, p. 32.
46. The fourth congress of the Union of the Russian People, held in May 1907, had passed resolutions criticizing Stolypin and the Duma for making liberal concessions and calling for the appointment of a dictator. PRO, FO 371/323, p. 492.
47. It was Purishkevich who, at the conclusion of the Duma debate on the Finnish bill, greeted the announcement of its approval by the chamber with a shout of "Finis Finlandiae".
48. D. M. McDonald, "A lever without a fulcrum: domestic factors and

Russian foreign policy, 1905–1914", in *Imperial Russian foreign policy*, H. Ragsdale (ed.) (Cambridge, 1993), p. 284.

49. RGIA, f. 821, op. 10, d. 40, l. 101. 18 November 1909.

50. See Polvinen, *Imperial borderland* for a clear outline of Bobrikov's policy.

51. GDSO, Third Duma, session 1, vol. 2, col. 2941.

52. "Zhurnal komissii dlia vyrabotki proekta o poriadke izdaniia kasaiush-chikhsia Finliandii zakonov obshchegosudarstvennogo znacheniia", pp. 1–14. Helsinki, Kansallisarkisto (hereafter KA), KKK, 1910. II.18/1 (Fb 550).

53. KA, KKK, 1908. II.4/47 (Fb 418).

54. "Po proektu pravil o poriadke izdaniia kasaiushchikhsia Finliandii zakonov i postanovlenii obshchegosudarstvennogo znacheniia", Osobyi zhurnal soveta ministrov, 22 February 1910. KA, KKK, 1910. II.18/1 (Fb 550).

55. See Chmielewski, *The Polish question in the Russian State Duma* for details of the various anti-Polish measures that reached the Duma.

56. This was mentioned both in the government declaration in *Pravitel'stvennyi vestnik* in August 1906 and in Stolypin's speech to the Third Duma in November 1907.

57. RGIA, f. 1278, op. 2, d. 1171, ll. 3–49.

58. This had been the attitude adopted by Witte to the project when it had been mooted in the first years of the century. T. R. Weeks, *Nation and state in late imperial Russia: nationalism and Russification on the western frontier, 1863–1914* (DeKalb, Illinois, 1996), pp. 140–1.

59. "Po proektu MVD o vydeleniii ... s obrazovaniem ... osoboi Kholmskoi gubernii", Osobyi zhurnal soveta ministrov, 13 January 1909. RGIA, f. 1276, op. 20, d. 30, ll. 38–41.

60. See Weeks, *Nation and state in late imperial Russia*, pp. 172–92 for a full discussion of the process of creating the province of Kholm.

61. GSSO, vol. 6, cols 1781–95; GDSO, III Duma, session 4, vol. 3, cols 2855–61.

62. Guchkov to Stolypin, 12 March 1911. GARF, f. 555, op. 1, d. 693, ll. 1–2.

63. See Stolypin to Nicholas II, 1 May 1911. GARF, f. 601. op. 1, d. 1352, ll. 12–13, for Stolypin's attempt to dissuade the tsar from this course of action.

64. Stolypin to Krivoshein, 19 June 1911. RGIA, f. 1571, op. 1, d. 324, l. 23. There was no suggestion that it was ill-health that forced Stolypin to remain on his estate, merely that he found it preferable to St Petersburg.

65. Kokovtsov, *Out of my past*, p. 271.

66. See Avrekh, *Stolypin i tret'ia Duma*, pp. 367–406 for a detailed account of the circumstances surrounding the murder.

67. Izgoev, *Stolypin*, p. 103.

68. His establishment of an information bureau for *zemstvo* members was a part of this policy.

# Chapter Six

1. Shipov, *Vospominaniia* p. 511.
2. PRO, FO 371/127, p. 506.
3. Quoted in Izgoev, *Stolypin*, p. 15.
4. Quoted in J. Bradley, "Russia's parliament of public opinion: association, assembly, and the autocracy, 1906–1914", in *Reform in modern Russian history: progress or cycle?*, T. Taranovski (ed.) (Cambridge, 1995), p. 235.

# Bibliography

## Archival sources

Helsinki, Kansallisarkisto (KA)

KKK Kenraalikuvernoorinkanslia

London, Public Record Office (PRO)

FO 371   British diplomatic correspondence
FO 418

Moscow, Gosudarstvennyi Arkhiv Rossiiskoi Federatsii (GARF)

*fond*  102  Department politsii
        115  Soiuz 17-ogo oktiabria
        434  Postoiannyi sovet ob"edinennykh dvorianskikh obshchestv
        555  A. I. Guchkov
        595  D. N. Trepov
        601  Nikolai II
       1467  Chrezvychainaia sledstvennaia komissiia vremennogo pravi-
             tel'stva

St Petersburg, Russkaia Natsional'naia Biblioteka, Rukopisnyi otdel' (RNB,
RO)

*fond*   443  P. P. Izvol'skii

St Petersburg, Rossiiskii Gosudarstvennyi Istoricheskii Arkhiv (RGIA)

*fond* 150 Peterburgskoe obshchestvo zavodchikov i fabrikantov
560 Ministerstvo Finansov, Obshchaia kantseliariia
796 Sviateishii sinod, Kantseliariia
797 Ober-Prokuror sinoda, Kantseliariia
821 Ministerstvo Vnutrennykh Del, Department dukhovnykh del inostrannykh ispovedanii
869 Iu. N. Miliutin
966 V. N. Kokovtsov
1276 Sovet Ministrov
1278 Gosudarstvennaia Duma
1288 Ministerstvo Vnutrennykh Del, Glavnoe upravlenie po delam mestnogo khoziaistva
1405 Ministerstvo Iustitsii
1571 A. V. Krivoshein
1629 I. Ia. Gurliand
1662 P. A. Stolypin

# Published sources

*Agrarnoe dvizhenie v Rossii v 1905–1906 gg.* (St Petersburg, 1908).

Agursky, M. Caught in a cross-fire: the Russian church between Holy Synod and radical right (1905–1908). *Orientalia Christiana Periodica* 50, 1984, pp. 163-96.

Akhun, M. Istochniki dlia izucheniia istorii gosudarstvennykh uchrezhdenii tsarskoi Rossii. *Arkhivnoe Delo* 49, 1991, pp. 77–91.

Amburger, E. *Geschichte der Behordenorganisation Russlands von Peter dem Grossen bis 1917* (Leiden, 1966).

Anan'ich, B. V. *et al. Krizis samoderzhaviia v Rossii 1895–1917* (Leningrad, 1984).

Ascher, A. *The revolution of 1905* [2 vols] (Stanford, Calif., 1988 & 1992).

Atkinson, D. *The end of the Russian land commune 1905–1930* (Stanford, Calif., 1983).

—The statistics on the Russian land commune, 1905–1917. *Slavic Review* 32, 1973, pp. 777–83.

Avrekh, A. Ia. Agrarnyi vopros v tret'ei Dume. *Istoricheskie Zapiski* 62, 1958, pp. 26–83.

—*P. A. Stolypin i sud'by reform v Rossii* (Moscow, 1991).

—*Raspad tret'eiiun'skoi sistemy* (Moscow, 1985).

—*Stolypin i tret'ia Duma* (Moscow, 1968).

—Stolypinskii bonapartizm i voprosy voennoi politiki v III Dume. *Voprosy Istorii* (1956, no. 11), pp. 17–33.

—Tret'ia Duma i nachalo krizisa tret'eiiun'skoi sistemy. *Istoricheskie Zapiski* 53, 1955, pp. 50–109.

—*Tsarizm i tret'eiiun'skaia sistema* (Moscow, 1968).

Balmuth, D. *Censorship in Russia, 1865–1905* (Washington DC, 1979).

Becker, S. *Nobility and privilege in late imperial Russia* (DeKalb, Illinois, 1985).

Berlin, P. A. *Russkaia burzhuaziia v staroe i novoe vremia* (Moscow, 1922).

Bestuzhev, I. V. *Bor'ba po voprosam vneshnei politiki Rossii, 1906–1910* (Moscow, 1964).

Bing, E. J. (ed.). *The letters of Tsar Nicholas and Empress Marie* (London, 1937).

Blinov, I. *Gubernatory* (St Petersburg, 1905).

Blobaum, R. E. *Rewolucja: Russian Poland, 1904–1907* (Ithaca, New York, 1995).

Bobrinskii, A. A. Dnevnik A. A. Bobrinskogo. *Krasnyi Arkhiv* 26, 1928, pp. 127–50.

Bogdanovich, A. V. *Dnevnik. Tri poslednikh samoderzhtsa* (Moscow–Leningrad, 1924).

Bok, M. P. *Vospominaniia o moem otse P. A. Stolypine* (New York, 1953).

Bokhanov, A. I. *Krupnaia burzhuaziia Rossii* (Moscow, 1992).

Borodin, A. P. Usilenie pozitsii ob"edinennogo dvorianstva v Gosudarstvennom Sovete v 1907–1914 godakh. *Voprosy Istorii* (1977, no. 2), pp. 56–66.

Borodkin, M. *Finland: its place in the Russian state* (St Petersburg, 1911).

Brancovan, C. E. Grand Duke Nikolay Mikhailovich on the ministerial and parliamentary crisis of March–April 1911. *Oxford Slavonic Papers*, New Series 6, 1973, pp. 66–81.

Buchanan, G. W. *My mission to Russia and other memories* (London, 1923).

Burmistrova, T. Iu. & V. S. Gusakova. *Natsional'nyi vopros v programmakh i taktike politicheskikh partii Rossii, 1905–1917 gg.* (Moscow, 1976).

Buryshkin, P. A. *Moskva kupecheskaia* (New York, 1954).

Bushnell, J. *Mutiny amid repression: Russian soldiers in the revolution of 1905–1906* (Bloomington, Indiana, 1985).

Chermenskii, E. D. *Burzhuaziia i tsarizm v revoliutsii 1905–7gg.* (Moscow, 1939).

Chernovskii, A. (ed). *Soiuz russkogo naroda: po materialam chrezvychainoi sledstvennoi komissii vremennogo pravitel'stva* (Moscow–Leningrad, 1929).

Chernukha, V. G. *Vnutrennaia politika tsarizma s serediny 50-kh do nachala 80-kh gg. XIX v.* (Leningrad, 1978).

Chmielewski, E. *The Polish question in the Russian State Duma* (Knoxville, Tennessee, 1970).

—Stolypin and the Russian ministerial crisis of 1909. *California Slavic Studies* 4, 1967, pp. 1–38.

—Stolypin's last crisis. *California Slavic Studies* 3, 1968, pp. 95–126.

Clowes, E. W., S. D. Kassow, J. L. West (eds). *Between tsar and people: educated society and the quest for public identity in late imperial Russia* (Princeton, New Jersey, 1991).

Conroy, M. S. *Peter Arkad'evich Stolypin: practical politics in late tsarist Russia* (Boulder, Colorado, 1976).

—Stolypin's attitude towards local self-government. *Slavonic and East European Review* **44**, 1968, pp. 446–61.

Crisp, O. & L. Edmondson (eds). *Civil rights in imperial Russia* (Oxford, 1989).

Curtiss, J. S. *Church and state in Russia, 1900–17: the last years of the empire* (New York, 1940).

Czap, P. Peasant-class courts and peasant customary justice in Russia, 1861–1912. *Journal of Social History* **1**, 1967, pp. 149–78.

Diakin, V. S. Chrezvychaino-ukaznoe zakonodatel'stvo v Rossii (1906–14). *Vspomogatel'nye Istoricheskie Distsipliny* **7**, Leningrad, 1976, pp. 240–71.

—*Samoderzhavie, burzhuaziia i dvorianstvo v 1907–11 gg.* (Leningrad, 1978).

—Stolypin i dvorianstvo. In *Problemy krest'ianskogo zemlevladeniia i vnutrennei politiki*, N.E. Nosov (ed.) (Leningrad, 1972), pp. 231–73.

—Zemstvo i samoderzhavie v tret'eiiun'skoi monarkhii. In *Voprosy istorii Rossii XIX–nachala XX veka* (Leningrad, 1983).

Dubrovskii, S. M. *Stolypinskaia zemel'naia reforma: iz istorii sel'skogo khoziaistva i krest'ianstva Rossii v nachale XX veka* (Moscow, 1963).

Edelman, R. *Gentry politics on the eve of the Russian revolution: the Nationalist party, 1907–1917* (New Brunswick, New Jersey, 1980).

Eklof, B. *Russian peasant schools: officialdom, village culture and popular pedagogy, 1861–1914* (Berkeley, Calif., 1986).

Eklof, B & S. P. Frank (eds). *The world of the Russian peasant: post-emancipation culture and society* (Boston, Mass., 1990).

Elistratov, A. I. *Gosudarstvennoe pravo* (Moscow, 1912).

Emmons, T. *The formation of political parties and the first national elections in Russia* (Cambridge, Mass., 1983).

—*The Russian landed gentry and the peasant emancipation of 1861* (Cambridge, 1968).

Emmons, T. & W. S. Vucinich (eds). *The zemstvo in Russia: an experiment in local self-government* (Cambridge, 1982).

Eropkin, A. *Chto delala i chto sdelala tret'ia Gosudarstvennaia Duma* (St Petersburg, 1912).

Eroshkin, N. P. *Istoriia gosudarstvennykh uchrezhdenii dorevoliutsionnoi Rossii* (Moscow, 1968).

Ershov, M. D. *Doklad po proektam 'Polozhenii o volostnom i poselkovom upravleniiakh' sostavlennyi po porucheniiu Soveta Obshchezemskogo S''ezda 1907 g.* (Moscow, 1907).

Freeze, G. L. Handmaiden of the state? The Church in imperial Russia reconsidered. *Journal of Ecclesiastical History* **36**, 1985, pp. 82-102.

—*The parish clergy in nineteenth-century Russia: crisis, reform, counter-reform* (Princeton, New Jersey, 1983).

—Subversive piety: religion and the political crisis in late imperial Russia.

*Journal of Modern History* 68, 1996, pp. 308–50.

Fuller, W. *Civil–military conflict in imperial Russia, 1881–1914* (Princeton, New Jersey, 1985).

Galai, S. *The liberation movement in Russia, 1900–1905* (Cambridge, 1973).

Ganelin, R. Sh. *Rossiiskoe samoderzhavie v 1905 godu: reformy i revoliutsiia* (St Petersburg, 1991).

—Tsarizm posle nachala pervoi russkoi revoliutsii (akty 18 fevralia 1905 g.). In *Voprosy istorii Rossii XIX–nachala XX veka* (Leningrad, 1983).

Ukaz 18 fevralia 1905 g. o petitsiiakh i pravitel'stvennaia politika. *Vspomogatel'nye Istoricheskie Distsipliny* 15, 1983, pp. 170–85.

Geekie, J. H. M. *The Church and politics in Russia, 1905–1917: a study of the political behaviour of the Russian Orthodox clergy in the reign of Nicholas II* (PhD thesis, University of East Anglia, 1976).

Geifman, A. *Thou shalt kill: revolutionary terrorism in Russia, 1894–1917* (Princeton, New Jersey, 1993).

Gerle, V. *Znachenie tret'ei dumy v istorii Rossii* (St Petersburg, 1912).

Gorfein, G. M. Osnovnye istochniki po istorii vysshikh i tsentral'nykh uchrezhdenii XIX–nachala XX vv. In *Nekotorye voprosy izucheniia istoricheskikh dokumentov XIX–nachala XX vv.* (Leningrad, 1967), pp. 73–110.

*Gosudarstvennaia Duma. Stenograficheskie otchety* [22 vols] (St Petersburg, 1906–12).

*Gosudarstvennyi Sovet. Stenograficheskie otchety* [5 vols] (St Petersburg, 1906–11).

Gribovskii, V. M. *Gosudarstvennoe ustroistvo i upravlenie rossiiskoi imperii* (Odessa, 1912).

Gurko, V. I. *Features and figures of the past: government and opinion in the reign of Nicholas II* (Stanford, Calif., 1939).

Gushka, A. O. *Predstavitel'nye organizatsii torgovo-promyshlennogo klassa v Rossii* (St Petersburg, 1912).

Haimson, L. H. (ed.). *The politics of rural Russia, 1905–1914* (Bloomington, Indiana, & London, 1979).

—The problem of social stability in urban Russia, 1905–1917. *Slavic Review* 23, 1964, pp. 619–42, & 24, 1965, pp. 1–22.

Heilbronner, H. Piotr Khristianovich von Schwanebach and the dissolution of the first two Dumas. *Canadian Slavonic Papers* 9, 1969, pp. 31–55.

Hennessy, R. *The agrarian question in Russia, 1905–07* (Geissen, 1977).

Hosking, G. A. P. A. Stolypin and the Octobrist party. *Slavonic and East European Review* 47, 1969, pp. 137–60.

—*The Russian constitutional experiment: government and Duma 1907–14* (Cambridge, 1973).

Hutchinson, J. F. The Octobrists and the future of imperial Russia as a great power. *Slavonic and East European Review* 50, 1972, pp. 220–37.

Iasevich-Borodaevskaia, V. I. *Bor'ba za veru* (St Petersburg, 1912).

Iashunskii, I. Voprosy Dumskogo nakaza. *Pravo*, 11.4.1908 and 11.5.1908.
Ioffe, M. S. *Vazhneishie zakonodatel'nye akty, 1908–12* (St Petersburg, 1913).
Iordanskii, N. K. Gorodskoe samoupravlenie i obshchestvennaia bezopasnost'. *Obrazovanie* 4, 1905, pp. 16–27.
Iurskii, G. *Pravye v tret'ei Gosudarstvennoi Dume* (Kharkov, 1912).
Iz perepiski P. A. Stolypina s Nikolaem Romanovym. *Krasnyi Arkhiv*, 30, 1928, pp. 80–88.
Izgoev, A. S. *P. A. Stolypin: ocherk zhizni i deiatel'nosti* (Moscow, 1912).
—Russkoe obshchestvo i revoliutsiia (Moscow, 1910).
Judge, E. H. *Plehve: repression and reform in imperial Russia, 1902–1904* (Syracuse, New York, 1983).
Jussila, O. Nationalism and revolution. Political dividing lines in the Grand Duchy of Finland during the last years of Russian rule. *Scandinavian Journal of History* 2, 1977, pp. 289–309.
K istorii agrarnoi reformy Stolypina. *Krasnyi Arkhiv* 17, 1926, pp. 83–7.
Karpov, N. *Agrarnaia politika Stolypina* (Leningrad, 1925).
Klibanov, A. I. *Istoriia religioznogo sektantstva v Rossii* (Moscow, 1965).
Kochakov, B. M. Russkii zakonodatel'nyi dokument XIX–XX vv. *Vspomogatel'nye Istoricheskie Distsipliny*, Moscow–Leningrad, 1937, pp. 319 –71.
Kokovtsov, V. N. *Out of my past* (Stanford, Calif., 1935).
Korelin, A. P. *Dvorianstvo v poreformennoi Rossii, 1861–1904* (Moscow, 1979).
—Rossiiskoe dvorianstvo i ego soslovnaia organizatsiia, 1861–1904 gg. *Istoriia SSSR* (1971, no. 5), pp. 56–81.
Korf, S. A. Predvoditel' dvorianstva, kak organ soslovnogo i zemskogo samoupravleniia. *Zhurnal Ministerstva Iustitsii* 3, 1902, pp. 93–116.
Korkunov, N. M. *Russkoe gosudarstvennoe pravo* [2 vols] (St Petersburg, 1909).
Koroleva, N. G. *Pervaia rossiiskaia revoliutsiia i tsarizm: sovet ministrov v 1905–1907 gg.* (Moscow, 1982).
—Sovet ministrov v Rossii v 1907–1914gg. *Istoricheskie zapiski* 110, 1984, pp. 105–25.
Koropachinskii, P. *Reforma mestnogo samoupravleniia po rabotam soveta po delam mestnogo khoziaistva* (Ufa, 1908).
—*Reforma mestnogo upravleniia, zemskie guzhevye dorogi i drugie zakonoproekty po rabotam 2-oi i 3-ei sessii soveta po delam mestnogo khoziaistva* (Ufa, 1910).
Koshko, I. F. *Vospominaniia gubernatora* (Petrograd, 1916).
Kovalevskii, M. M. *Chem Rossiia obiazana Soiuzu Ob"edinennogo Dvorianstva* (St Petersburg, 1914).
—p. A. Stolypin i ob"edinennoe dvorianstvo. *Vestnik Evropy* (1913, no. 10), pp. 406–23.
Krasil'nikov, N. D. *Petr Arkad'evich Stolypin i ego deiatel'nost' v pervoi, vtoroi, i tret'ei Gosudarstvennoi Dume* (St Petersburg, 1912).

*Kratkie zhurnaly zasedanii obshchezemskogo s"ezda v Moskve, 25.7–8.8.1907* (Poltava, 1907).

Krechetov, P. I. *Petr Arkad'evich Stolypin* (Riga, 1910).

Krivoshein, K. A. *A. V. Krivoshein (1857–1921)* (Paris, 1973).

Kryzhanovskii, S. E. *Vospominaniia* (Berlin, 1925).

Laverychev, V. Ia. *Po tu storonu barrikad: iz istorii bor'by moskovskoi burzhuazii s revoliutsiei* (Moscow, 1967).

Lazarevskii, N. I. *Lektsii po russkomu gosudarstvennomu pravu*, vol. 2 (St Petersburg, 1910).

—(ed.). *Zakonodatel'nye akty perekhodnogo vremeni, 1904–1908 gg.* (St Petersburg, 1909).

Leikina-Svirskaia, V. R. *Russkaia intelligentsia v 1900–1917 godakh* (Moscow, 1981).

Levin, A. Peter Arkad'evich Stolypin: a political appraisal. *Journal of Modern History* 37, 1965, pp. 445–63.

—Russian bureaucratic opinion in the wake of the 1905 revolution. *Jahrbücher für Geschichte Osteuropas* 11, 1963, pp. 1–12.

—*The reactionary tradition in the election campaign to the Third Duma* (Oklahoma State University Publications 59, no. 16, Social Studies Series no. 8, 1962).

—*The Second Duma* (New Haven, Connecticut, 1940).

—*The Third Duma: election and profile* (Hamden, Connecticut, 1973).

Levitsky, S. L. Interpellations according to the Russian constitution of 1906. *Slavic and East European Studies* 1, 1956–57, pp. 220–31.

Lieven, D. *Nicholas II: emperor of all the Russias* (London, 1993).

—*Russia's rulers under the old regime* (New Haven, Connecticut, 1989).

Macey, D. A. J. Gorbachev and Stolypin: Soviet agrarian reform in historical perspective. In *Perestroika in the countryside: agricultural reform in the Gorbachev era*, W. Moskoff (ed.) (Armonk, New York, 1990).

—*Government and peasant in Russia, 1861–1906: the prehistory of the Stolypin reforms* (DeKalb, Illinois, 1987).

Magaziner, Ia. M. *Chrezvychaino-ukaznoe pravo v Rossii* (St Petersburg, 1911).

Maklakov, V. A. *Vlast' i obshchestvennost' na zakate staroi Rossii* (Paris, 1930).

Manning, R. T. *The crisis of the old order in Russia: gentry and government* (Princeton, New Jersey, 1982).

Margolis, Iu. D. (ed.). *Novoe o revoliutsii 1905–1907 gg. v Rossii* (Leningrad, 1989).

Martov, L., P. Maslov, A. Potresov (eds). *Obshchestvennoe dvizhenie v Rossii v nachale XX-ogo veka* [4 vols] (St Petersburg, 1909–12).

McDonald, D. M. A lever without a fulcrum: domestic factors and Russian foreign policy, 1905–1914. In *Imperial Russian foreign policy*, H. Ragsdale (ed.) (Cambridge, 1993), pp. 268–311.

—*United government and foreign policy in Russia, 1900–1914* (Cambridge, Mass., 1992).

McKean, R. B. (ed.). *New perspectives in modern Russian history* (Basingstoke, 1992).

—*St Petersburg between the revolutions: workers and revolutionaries June 1907–February 1917* (New Haven, Connecticut, 1990).

Mehlinger, H. D. & J. M. Thompson, *Count Witte and the tsarist government in the 1905 revolution* (Bloomington, Indiana, 1972).

Miakotin, V. Sovremennaia 'detsentralizatsiia'. *Russkoe Bogatstvo* 4, 1908, pp. 121–38.

Miliukov, P. N. *Political memoirs, 1905–1917* (Ann Arbor, Michigan, 1967).

Milovidov, V. F. *Staroobriadchestvo v proshlom i nastoiashchem* (Moscow, 1969).

Mosse, W. E. Aspects of tsarist bureaucracy: recruitment to the State Council 1855–1914. *Slavonic and East European Review* 57, 1979, pp. 240–54.

—Stolypin's villages. *Slavonic and East European Review* 43, 1964–5, pp. 257–74.

Murav'ev, B. N. *Melkaia edinitsa samoupravleniia v russkom zakonodatel'stve* (Novgorod, 1912).

Naumov, A. N. *Iz utselevshikh vospominanii, 1868–1917* (New York, 1955).

Nichols, R. L. & T. G. Stavrou, (eds). *Russian orthodoxy under the old regime* (Minneapolis, Minnesota, 1978).

Nikitin, A. Reforma volostnogo samoupravleniia. In *Okolo Dumy. Sbornik statei* (Moscow, 1907), pp. 13–22.

Novikov, A. *Zapiski zemskogo nachal'nika* (St Petersburg, 1899).

*Obzor deiatel'nosti Gosudarstvennoi Dumy tret'ego sozyva, 1907–1912 gg.* (St Petersburg, 1912).

*Obzor deiatel'nosti Vserossiiskogo Natsional'nogo Soiuza za 1910 god* (St Petersburg, 1911).

*Obzor trudov vysochaishe utverzhdennyi, pod predsedatel'stvom statssekretaria Kakhanova osoboi komissii* (St Petersburg, 1908).

Ol'denburg, S. S. *Tsarstvovanie imperatora Nikolaia II* (Munich, 1938–49).

Ostrovskii, I. V. *P. A. Stolypin i ego vremia* (Moscow, 1992).

Owen, L. A. *The Russian peasant movement, 1906–1917* (London, 1937).

Pazhitnov, K. A. *Gorodskoe i zemskoe samoupravlenie* (St Petersburg, 1913).

Perepiska N. A. Romanova i P. A. Stolypina. *Krasnyi Arkhiv* 5, 1924, pp. 102–28.

Pinchuk, B.-C. *The Octobrists in the Third Duma, 1907–1912* (Seattle, Washington, 1974).

Pintner, W. M. & D. K. Rowney, (eds). *Russian officialdom: the bureaucratization of Russian society from the seventeenth to the twentieth century* (London, 1980).

Pipes, R. *Struve: liberal on the right, 1904–1944* (Cambridge, Mass., 1980).

Platonov, N. F. Pravoslavnaia tserkov' v bor'be s revoliutsionnym dvizheniem v Rossii (1900–17). *Ezhegodnik Muzeia Istorii Religii i Ateizma* 4,

Moscow–Leningrad, 1960, pp. 103–209.

Polezhaev, P. *Za shest' let (1906–12)* (St Petersburg, 1912).

*Polnoe sobranie zakonov Rossiiskoi imperii* (St Petersburg, 1885–1916).

*Promyshlennost' i torgovlia v zakonodatel'nykh uchrezhdeniiakh, 1907–12* (St Petersburg, 1912).

Rawson, D. C. *Russian rightists and the revolution of 1905* (Cambridge, 1995).

Rieber, A. J. *Merchants and entrepreneurs in imperial Russia* (Chapel Hill, North Carolina, 1982).

Rigberg, B. The efficacy of tsarist censorship operations, 1894–1917. *Jahrbücher für Geschichte Osteuropas* 14, 1966, pp. 327–46.

Robbins, R. G. *The tsar's viceroys: Russian provincial governors in the last years of the empire* (Ithaca, New York, 1987).

Robinson, G. T. *Rural Russia under the old regime* (New York, 1932).

Rogger, H. *Jewish policies and right-wing politics in imperial Russia* (Berkeley, Calif., 1986).

—Russian ministers and the Jewish question, 1881–1917. *California Slavic Studies* 8, 1975, pp. 15–76.

Ropp, A. N. *Chto sdelala tret'ia Gosudarstvennaia Duma dlia narodnogo obrazovaniia?* (St Petersburg, 1912).

Russobtovskii, M. *Istoricheskoe osveshchenie finliandskogo voprosa* (St Petersburg, 1912).

Rybas, S. & L. Tarakanova. *Reformator: zhizn' i smert' Stolypina* (Moscow, 1991).

Sazonov, S. D. *Vospominaniia* (Paris, 1927).

Seletskii, V. N. Obrazovanie partii Progressistov. *Vestnik Moskovskogo Universiteta, Istoriia* (1970, no. 5), pp. 32–48.

Shanin, T. *The roots of otherness: Russia's turn of century* [2 vols] (London, 1985 & 1986).

Shatsilo, K. F. *Russkii liberalizm nakanune revoliutsii 1905–1907 gg.* (Moscow, 1985).

Shchegolev, P. E. (ed.). *Padenie tsarskogo rezhima* [7 vols] (Leningrad, 1924–7).

Shelokhaev, V. V. *Kadety – glavnaia partiia liberal'noi burzhuazii v bor'be s revoliutsiei 1905–1907 gg.* (Moscow, 1983).

Shidlovskii, S. I. *Vospominaniia* (Berlin, 1923).

Shipov, D. N. *Vospominaniia i dumy o perezhitom* (Moscow, 1918).

Shvarts, A. N. *Moia perepiska so Stolypinym* (Moscow, 1994).

Sidel'nikov, S. M. *Agrarnaia politika samoderzhaviia v period imperializma* (Moscow, 1980).

—*Agrarnaia politika Stolypina* (Moscow, 1973).

—*Obrazovanie i deiatel'nost' pervoi Gosudarstvennoi Dumy* (Moscow, 1962).

Simonova, M. S. *Krizis agrarnoi politiki tsarizma nakanune pervoi russkoi revoliutsii* (Moscow, 1987).

Skripitsyn, V. A. *Bogatyr' mysli, slova i dela* (St Petersburg, 1911).

213

Snow, G. E. The Kokovtsov commission: an abortive attempt at labour reform in Russia in 1905. *Slavic Review* 31, 1972, pp. 780–96.

Solov'ev, Iu. B. *Samoderzhavie i dvorianstvo v 1902–1907 gg.* (Leningrad, 1981).

—*Samoderzhavie i dvorianstvo v 1907–1914 gg.* (Leningrad, 1990).

*Sovet ministrov Rossiiskoi imperii 1905–1906 gg. Dokumenty i materialy* (Leningrad, 1990).

Spirin, L. M. *Krushenie pomeshchich'ikh i burzhuaznykh partii v Rossii (nachalo XX v.–1920 g.)* (Moscow, 1977).

Starr, S. F. *Decentralization and self-government in Russia, 1830–70* (Princeton, New Jersey, 1972).

Startsev, V. I. *Russkaia burzhuaziia i samoderzhavie v 1905–1917 (Bor'ba vokrug "otvetstvennogo" ministerstva i "pravitel'stva doveriia")* (Leningrad, 1977).

Stavrou, T. G. (ed.). *Russia under the last tsar* (Minneapolis, Minnesota, 1969).

Stepanskii, A. D. Politicheskie gruppirovki v Gosudarstvennom Sovete v 1906–07 gg. *Istoriia SSSR* (1965, no. 4), pp. 49–64.

Sternheimer, S. Administering development and developing administration: organizational conflict in tsarist bureaucracy, 1906–1914. *Canadian–American Slavic Studies* 9, 1975, pp. 277–301.

Stolypin, P. A. & A. V. Krivoshein, *Poezdka v Sibir' i Povolzh'e* (St Petersburg, 1911).

Strakhovskii, I. M. *Gubernskoe ustroistvo* (St Petersburg, 1913).

Strakhovsky, L. I. The statesmanship of Peter Stolypin: a reappraisal. *Slavonic and East European Review* 37, 1958–9, pp. 348–70.

*Svod postanovlenii I–X s"ezdov upolnomochennykh ob"edinennykh dvorianskikh obshchestv, 1906–14* (Petrograd, 1915).

Szeftel, M. The legislative reform of August 6, 1905. *Commission Internationale pour l'Histoire des Assemblées d'États* 34, 1968, pp. 137–83.

—The reform of the electoral law to the State Duma on June 3, 1907. *Commission Internationale pour l'Histoire des Assemblées d'États* 38, 1970, pp. 319–67.

—The representatives and their powers in the Russian legislative chambers, 1906–17. *Commission Internationale pour l'Histoire des Assemblées d'États* 27, 1965, pp. 219–57.

—*The Russian constitution of 23 April, 1906: political institutions of the Duma monarchy* (Brussels, 1976).

Taranovski, T. (ed.). *Reform in modern Russian history: progress or cycle?* (Cambridge, 1995).

Thaden, E. C. (ed.). *Russification in the Baltic provinces and Finland, 1855–1914* (Princeton, New Jersey, 1981).

Tokmakoff, G. B. P. A. Stolypin and the Second Duma. *Slavonic and East European Review* 50, 1972, pp. 49–62.

—*P.A. Stolypin and the Third Duma: an appraisal of the three major issues* (Washington DC, 1981).

—Stolypin's agrarian reform: an appraisal. *Russian Review* 30, 1971, pp. 124–38.

Treadgold, D. W. *The great Siberian migration* (Princeton, New Jersey, 1957).

—Was Stolypin in favour of kulaks? *Slavic Review* 14, 1955, pp. 1–14.

*Trudy mestnykh komitetov o nuzhdakh sel'skokhoziaistvennoi promyshlennosti*, vol. 11 (St Petersburg, 1903).

*Trudy pervogo s"ezda upolnomochennykh dvorianskikh obshchestv* (St Petersburg, 1906) [similar titles for congresses up to the sixth in 1910].

*Trudy sed'mogo vserossiiskogo s"ezda staroobriadtsev i vtorogo chrezvychainogo s"ezda staroobriadtsev* (Nizhnii-Novgorod, 1906) [similar titles for congresses up to the eleventh in 1911].

Tverskoi, P. A. K istoricheskim materialam o pokoinom P. A. Stolypine. *Vestnik Evropy* (1912, no. 4), pp. 183–201.

Urusov, S. D. *Memoirs of a Russian governor* (London, 1908).

Verner, A. M. *The crisis of Russian autocracy: Nicholas II and the 1905 revolution* (Princeton, New Jersey, 1990).

V[erpakhovskaia], E. (ed.). *Gosudarstvennaia deiatel'nost' P. A. Stolypina* (St Petersburg, 1909–11).

—*Predsedatel' Soveta Ministrov Petr Arkad'evich Stolypin* (St Petersburg, 1909).

Veselovskii, B. B. *Istoriia zemstva* (St Petersburg, 1909–11).

Veselovskii, B. B., V. I. Pichet, V. M. Friche, (eds). *Agrarnyi vopros v Sovete Ministrov (1906g.)* (Leningrad, 1924).

Vishnevski, E. *Liberal'naia oppozitsiia v Rossii nakanune pervoi mirovoi voiny* (Moscow, 1994).

Viziagin, A. S. *Gololobovskii intsident: stranichka iz istorii politicheskikh partii v Rossii* (Khar'kov, 1909).

Volobuev, P. V. (ed.). *1905 god – nachalo revoliutsionnykh potriasenii v Rossii XX veka* (Moscow, 1996).

Vredenskii, A. *Deistvuiushchiie zakonopolozheniia kasatel'no staroobriadtsev i sektantov* (Odessa, 1912).

*Vsepoddanneishii otchet Ober-Prokurora sviateishego sinoda po vedomstve Pravoslavnogo ispovedaniia za 1905–7* (St Petersburg, 1910).

*Vsepoddanneishii otchet Saratovskogo gubernatora P. Stolypina za 1904 god. Krasnyi Arkhiv* 17, 1926, pp. 83–7.

Wade, R. A. & S. J. Seregny (eds). *Politics and society in provincial Russia: Saratov, 1590–1917* (Columbus, Ohio, 1989).

Waldron, P. Religious reform after 1905: Old Believers and the Orthodox Church. *Oxford Slavonic Papers*, New Series 20, 1987, pp. 110–39.

—States of emergency: autocracy and extraordinary legislation, 1881–1917. *Revolutionary Russia* 8, 1995, pp. 1–25.

—Stolypin and Finland. *Slavonic and East European Review* 63, 1985, pp. 41–55.

Wallace, D. M. *Russia on the eve of war and revolution* (New York, 1961).

Wcislo, F. W. *Reforming rural Russia: state, local society and national politics 1855–1914* (Princeton, New Jersey, 1990).

Weeks, T. R. *Nation and state in late imperial Russia: nationalism and Russification on the western frontier, 1863–1914* (DeKalb, Illinois, 1996).

Weissman, N. B. *Reform in tsarist Russia: the state bureaucracy and local government, 1900–1914* (New Brunswick, New Jersey, 1981).

—Regular police in tsarist Russia, 1900–1914. *Russian Review* 20, 1985, pp. 45–68.

Whelan, H. W. *Alexander III and the State Council: bureaucracy and counter-reform in late imperial Russia* (New Brunswick, New Jersey, 1982).

Witte, S. Iu. *Vospominaniia* (Berlin, 1922).

Yaney, G. L. The concept of the Stolypin land reform. *Slavic Review* 23, 1964, pp. 275–93.

—Some aspects of the imperial Russian government on the eve of the First World War. *Slavonic and East European Review* 43, 1964–5, pp. 68–90.

—*The systematization of Russian government, 1711–1905* (Urbana, Illinois, 1973).

—*The urge to mobilize: agrarian reform in Russia, 1861–1930* (Urbana, Illinois, 1982).

Zaionchkovskii, P. A. *Pravitel'stvennyi apparat samoderzhavnoi Rossii v XIX veke* (Moscow, 1978).

—*Rossiiskoe samoderzhavie v kontse XIX stoletiia* (Moscow, 1970).

Zen'kovskii A. V. *Pravda o Stolypine* (New York, 1956).

*Zhurnaly i postanovleniia vserossiiskogo s"ezda zemskikh deiatelei 10–15.6.1907* (Moscow, 1907).

*Zhurnaly zasedanii tret'ego ocherednogo s"ezda predstavitelei promyshlennosti i torgovli, 27–31 mart 1908* (St Petersburg, 1908).

Zvengitsev, A. I. The Duma and imperial defence. *Russian Review* 1, 1912, pp. 49–63.

Zyrianov, P. N. Tret'ia Duma i vopros o reforme mestnogo suda i volostnogo upravleniia. *Istoriia SSSR* (1969, no. 6), pp. 45–62.

# *Index*